The Present Truth and the LGBTQ+ Movement

Understanding the Dangers of Affirmation, while Acting Redemptively.

Nelson Mercado

ISBN 979-8-89345-559-5 (paperback)
ISBN 979-8-89345-560-1 (digital)

Copyright © 2024 by Nelson Mercado

All rights reserved. No part of this publication may be reproduced, distributed, or transmitted in any form or by any means, including photocopying, recording, or other electronic or mechanical methods without the prior written permission of the publisher. For permission requests, solicit the publisher via the address below.

Christian Faith Publishing
832 Park Avenue
Meadville, PA 16335
www.christianfaithpublishing.com

Printed in the United States of America

INTRODUCTION

IT IS POSSIBLE THAT WHEN you picked up this book or heard of its title, you were a bit puzzled. *The Present Truth and the LGBTQ+ Movement?* What does one have to do with the other? The concept of Present Truth is not foreign to any Seventh-day Adventist, or at least it shouldn't be. Seventh-day Adventists believe that God raised them as a last-day prophetic movement to prepare the world to meet Jesus at His Second Coming. Part of that preparation involves the understanding and proclamation of the Present Truth.

What is the Present Truth? In my book *The Present Truth and the Three Angels' Messages*, I define it as the following:

> [It is] a message that applies to the present. It is the truth for the time we are living in. As the name of the denomination suggests, Seventh-day Adventists believe in the soon coming of Jesus, and, therefore, they believe they are living in the time of the end. The present truth is God's last message to the world: a message of preparation to meet Jesus.[1]

The Present Truth message is found in Revelation 14:6–12, which is commonly known as "The Three Angels' Messages." A careful study of these messages of Revelation 14 will reveal that much of what we believe as Seventh-day Adventists is found in the messages of these three angels.

For the sake of review and to help those who may not have read *The Present Truth and the Three Angels' Messages*, I will list the

---

[1] Nelson Mercado, *The Present Truth and the Three Angels' Messages* (Nampa, ID: Pacific Press, 2021), 9.

doctrines (as taught and believed by Seventh-day Adventists) found in each of the messages.

The Message of the First Angel

> Then I saw another angel flying in the midst of heaven, having the everlasting gospel to preach to those who dwell on the earth—to every nation, tribe, tongue, and people—saying with a loud voice, "Fear God and give glory to Him, for the hour of His judgment has come; and worship Him who made heaven and earth, the sea and springs of water." (Revelation 14:6–7)

Doctrines or teachings covered

1. *The Everlasting Gospel.* Most Christians are not used to hearing about the "Everlasting Gospel" but simply "the gospel." What is the Gospel? You may find several definitions, but here is a good one:

   > The gospel is good news—the good news of what God has done in Jesus Christ. The Bible depicts human beings, all human beings everywhere, as in revolt against God, and therefore under his judgment. But although God stands over against us in judgment because of our sin, quite amazingly he stands over against us in love, because he is that kind of God—and the gospel is the good news of what God, in love, has done in Jesus Christ, especially in Jesus's cross and resurrection, to deal with our sin and to reconcile us to himself. Christ bore our sin on the cross. He bore the penalty, turned aside God's judgment, God's wrath, from us, and cancelled sin. The

brokenness of our lives he restores; the shattered relationships he rebuilds in the context of the church; the new life that we human beings find in Christ is granted out of the sheer grace of God. It is received by faith as we repent of our sins and turn to Jesus. We confess him as Lord and bow to him joyfully. The gospel is good news—the good news of what God has done in Jesus Christ.[2]

While this is a wonderful description of the gospel, I believe it is incomplete. In fact, my view is that most Christians believe in what I call an "incomplete gospel." You see, for most Christians, as we can see above, the gospel is about what God has done through Christ. The word *done* implies something already completed, something that took place in the past; and while the death and resurrection of Jesus took place in the past and while it is foundational, it is not the entirety of the gospel. This is where the doctrine of the sanctuary comes in. In the sanctuary service, there were three great acts depicted:

- The death of the sacrifice
- The ministry of the priest and the transfer of sin to the sanctuary
- The removal of sins from the sanctuary[3]

Thus, the gospel not only includes what God, through Jesus, did in the past but also includes what Jesus is doing for us now and what He will do after the one thousand years of Revelation 20, all of which are still in the future.

2. *The one thousand years (the millennium).* Why is the doctrine of the millennium under the heading of the first

---

[2] "What Is the Gospel?" *The Gospel Coalition*, accessed August 24, 2023, https://www.thegospelcoalition.org/what-is-the-gospel.

[3] Mercado, 18.

angel's message? Because, as explained above, part of the gospel message includes what Jesus will still do in the future, specifically the removal of sin from the sanctuary. As I explain in *The Present Truth and the Three Angels' Messages*, in the sanctuary service, the removal of sin took place at the end of the services connected with the Day of Atonement. Commenting on this, Ellen White said,

> As the priest, in removing the sins from the sanctuary, confessed them upon the head of the scapegoat, so Christ will place all these sins upon Satan, the originator and instigator of sin. The scapegoat, bearing the sins of Israel, was sent away "unto a land not inhabited" (Leviticus 16:22); so Satan, bearing the guilt of all the sins which he has caused God's people to commit, will be for a thousand years confined to the earth, which will then be desolate, without inhabitant, and he will at last suffer the full penalty of sin in the fires that shall destroy all the wicked.[4]

3. *The Second Coming of Jesus.* The doctrine of the Second Coming is pivotal to Adventism. After all, that is what *Adventist* means. Obviously, if we addressed the one thousand years of Revelation 20, we must also address the event that takes place before or that inaugurates it. This includes not only the certainty of Jesus's soon return but also the manner of His coming.

4. *The Judgment.* "Fear God and give glory to Him, for the hour of *His judgment has come*; and worship Him who made heaven and earth, the sea and springs of water" (Revelation 14:7, emphasis supplied). Part of the Present Truth consists

---

[4] Ellen G. White, *The Great Controversy between Christ and Satan* (Nampa, ID: Pacific Press®, 2005), 485–486.

in the fact that an investigative judgment started in 1844 at the end of the 2,300-year prophecy of Daniel 8:14.

5. *Creation, the Law, and the Sabbath.* "Fear God and give glory to Him, for the hour of His judgment has come; and *worship Him who made heaven and earth, the sea and springs of water*" (Revelation 14:7, emphasis supplied). The idea of worship is tied to the fact that God is our Creator. That is, the reason we are to worship God is that He has created us. In a time when science contradicts creationism, this doctrine is very important (we will touch on this doctrine later when we discuss the implications of the LGBTQ+ movement). The Bible, of course, talks about the memorial of creation, that is, the Sabbath. However, one cannot talk about the Sabbath without discussing the importance of keeping the law as a love response to the gift of salvation manifested in Jesus (see John 14:15).

The Message of the Second Angel

And another angel followed, saying, "Babylon is fallen, is fallen, that great city, because she has made all nations drink of the wine of the wrath of her fornication" (Revelation 14:8). In the book of Revelation, Babylon is a religious-political system that defies God, confuses the world, and oppresses God's people; therefore, it is the enemy of both God and His people. In Revelation 17:4, Babylon is described as an impure woman arrayed in purple and scarlet, and adorned with gold and precious stones and pearls, having in her hand a golden cup full of abominations and the filthiness of her fornication.

A woman in Bible prophecy is a symbol of a church (Isaiah 54:5–6, Jeremiah 3:20, Amos 5:2, 2 Corinthians 11:2, and Ephesians 5:25). In this case (Revelation 17), she is the opposite of the pure and chaste woman of Revelation 12. Now history and scripture show that the early church referred to Rome as Babylon. So does history provide us with a religious-political power that, in turn, is also a church and has its base in Rome? Yes, the Roman Catholic Church.

Babylon (papal Rome) is judged because of her fornications, "because she has made all nations drink of the wine of the wrath of *her fornication*." "In scripture, fornication is a figure of the illicit connection between the church and the world... The church should be married to her Lord, but when she seeks the support of the state, she leaves her lawful spouse."[5] The problem with Babylon is that she has made all nations drink the wine of the wrath of her fornication. "This 'wine of her fornication' represents the false teachings that deceive the whole world; therefore, it must represent something the vast majority of the world believes—something contrary to the teaching of God's word."[6] Thus, these fornications are the unbiblical doctrines that most Christians are following. This leads to the doctrines under the heading of the second angel's message.

Doctrines or teachings covered

1. *The nature of man (the false teaching of the immortality of the soul)*. This includes not only what the Bible says happens at death, but the concepts of eternity and hell.
2. *The change of the Sabbath from the seventh day of the week to the first.*

The Message of the Third Angel

Then a third angel followed them, saying with a loud voice, "If anyone worships the beast and his image, and receives his mark on his forehead or on his hand, he himself shall also drink of the wine of the wrath of God, which is poured

---

[5] Nichol, *Seventh-day Adventist Bible Commentary*, 7:831.
[6] Kenneth Cox, *Revelation Pure and Simple* (West Frankfurt, IL: 3ABN Books, 2012), 183.

out full strength into the cup of His indignation. He shall be tormented with fire and brimstone in the presence of the holy angels and in the presence of the Lamb. And the smoke of their torment ascends forever and ever; and they have no rest day or night, who worship the beast and his image, and whoever receives the mark of his name." (Revelation 14:9–11)

Doctrines or teachings covered

1. *Identification of the beast of Revelation 13*
2. *The United States in Bible Prophecy*
3. *The Mark of the Beast*

While the doctrines or teachings mentioned above are not the bulk of the beliefs of the Seventh-day Adventist Church, and while we could probably think of others that may fall under the messages of these angels (perhaps in a future book), they do represent the end-time message that we must be proclaiming to every tribe, tongue, and people. But I know what you are thinking: What does this have to do with the LGBTQ+ movement? Should we be proclaiming to the world that the LGBTQ+ ideology is part of God's end-time message that will prepare the world to meet Jesus? Well, not exactly. It is the belief of this author and the premise of this book that the LGBTQ+ ideology and the push from activists for the church to affirm its lifestyle is a danger to the Three Angels' Messages. That is, the acceptance of this ideology will hinder our proclamation, not only weakening the message but damaging our credibility.

The genesis of this book took place this past year while I was at the KY-TN Camp meeting. While talking to a fellow Seventh-day Adventist about my book *The Present Truth and the Three Angels' Messages*, the gentleman was honest with me and said, "I wish that as we talk about the Present Truth, we addressed some of the more relevant issues that we are facing today, specifically, the transgender ideology. How do I talk to my kids about this when they come home from school asking questions?"

This is indeed a contemporary and relevant issue, which is why, after much prayer and meditation, I have decided to write about this, not because I am an expert in the field but because, as mentioned above, I believe the push to accept or to affirm the LGBTQ+ ideology is a hindrance the proclamation of the Present Truth. That being said, believe it or not, there are people visiting our churches or perhaps even church members who are dealing with issues of gender dysphoria and consider themselves members, if you will, of the LGBTQ+ movement. Recently, we have heard stories through the media about Seventh-day Adventist pastors who have come out as supporting the LGBTQ+ ideology or who identify as members of this movement. In some cases, they have published videos proclaiming that they do not support the church's stance, as they say, against LGBTQ+ ideology.

In her book *The Bible and LGBTQ Adventists*, Alicia Johnston says,

> The church's challenge is not of LGBTQ people who are not Adventists showing up in our churches on Saturday mornings and asking to become members. I'm sure this happens occasionally, but it's not the church's primary challenge. It's not about a challenge from the outside with secular LGBTQ people. LGBTQ people are already in our churches, silently observing, asking if they are wanted. We face the primary challenge of gay, bisexual, and transgender people growing up inside our churches and schools.[7]

I will refer to this book many times in the next few chapters because not only is it well written but it is a book that paints a picture of a reality in our churches and, while I disagree with her find-

---

[7] Alicia Johnston, *The Bible and LGBTQ Adventists* (Affirmative Collection, 2022), 4.

ings and beliefs on the issue, it is a great source for conversation. And conversation is, indeed, what we must be doing as Seventh-day Adventists. Talking about this does not mean that all of a sudden we are subscribing to an affirming theology; but we cannot ignore this, sweeping it under the rug, as it were, hoping it goes away. If we know anything about the end of time, it is that the morality of the world will go downhill quickly.

> According to a recent Gallup poll, 54% of Americans say the state of moral values in the country is "poor"—a record number. Some 83% say they believe morals are in decline. They aren't alone: Survey data from a study published this week in Nature suggest that people in more than 60 nations share a general sense that people are less moral now than they used to be. The study, based on more than 12 million surveys administered to people around the world between 1949 and 2021, argues that people have felt this way for at least 70 years.[8]

Some people believe that moral decline is an illusion,[9] but could it be that people's definition of what is right or wrong has changed? The apostle Paul certainly seemed to be talking about a time like this:

> But know this, that in the last days perilous times will come: For men will be lovers of themselves, lovers of money, boasters, proud, blasphemers, disobedient to parents, unthankful, unholy, unloving, unforgiving, slanderers, without self-control, brutal, despisers of good,

---

[8] Christie Wilcox, "People Everywhere Believe Society's Morals Are in Decline," *Science.org* (June 2023), accessed August 28, 2023, https://www.science.org/content/article/people-everywhere-believe-society-s-morals-are-decline.

[9] Daniel T. Gilbert, "The Illusion of Moral Decline," *Nature* (June 2023), accessed August 28, 2023, https://www.nature.com/articles/s41586-023-06137-x.

> traitors, headstrong, haughty, lovers of pleasure rather than lovers of God, having a form of godliness but denying its power. And from such people turn away! For of this sort are those who creep into households and make captives of gullible women loaded down with sins, led away by various lusts, always learning and never able to come to the knowledge of the truth. (2 Timothy 3:1–7)

Thus, it seems clear that we cannot expect morality in the world to improve before the Second Coming of Jesus. In fact, what we see is that history tends to repeat itself. In Isaiah 5, the prophet speaks to Judah, although his message certainly could have been applied to Israel as well. God's message for His people through Isaiah presents Him as a caretaker Who fenced His vineyard in order to protect it (v. 2). But God's people turned their backs on God, and God speaks to them about their impending judgment. There are series of "woes" in Isaiah 5, but one seems to describe our world today, "Woe to those who call evil good, and good evil; Who put darkness for light, and light for darkness; Who put bitter for sweet, and sweet for bitter" (v. 20)! In *Testimonies for the Church*, vol. 2, Ellen White said it this way:

> I have been shown that we live amid the perils of the last days. Because iniquity abounds, the love of many waxes cold. The word "many" refers to the professed followers of Christ… A terrible picture of the condition of the world has been presented before me. Immorality abounds everywhere. Licentiousness is the special sin of this age. Never did vice lift its deformed head with such boldness as now. The people seem to be benumbed, and the lovers of virtue and true goodness are nearly discouraged by its boldness, strength, and prevalence. The iniquity which abounds is not merely confined to the unbeliever and the scoffer. Would that this were the case,

but it is not. Many men and women who profess the religion of Christ are guilty. Even some who profess to be looking for His appearing are no more prepared for that event than Satan himself. They are not cleansing themselves from all pollution. They have so long served their lust that it is natural for their thoughts to be impure and their imaginations corrupt. It is as impossible to cause their minds to dwell upon pure and holy things as it would be to turn the course of Niagara and send its waters pouring up the falls.[10]

As it will be made clear throughout this book, I believe that the LGBTQ+ issue is one of morality and sin. However, what we are hearing from society is that "right is wrong and wrong is right. Sure, this may have been a tabu before, but times have changed, and society has improved." While it should not surprise us that this is what society at large is saying, it is sad when we are hearing the same thing in Christian churches today. It is even sadder that we are hearing it in the Adventist Church as well.

As a Seventh-day Adventist pastor but, more importantly, as a member of this prophetic movement, I believe that the church should not compromise on this issue because, as we will see, it will damage our witness and credibility, and it will also weaken our message. However, I will admit that I am taking a balanced approach to this issue. Being balanced is not always popular. This was revealed clearly to me during the years 2020–2021. It was in those years that our country faced the COVID-19 crisis as well as issues surrounding social justice. As a pastor, I have learned the hard way that I cannot please everybody, and these issues were more complex as a pastor of a multicultural church. I decided not to be extreme to the right or

---

[10] Ellen G. White, "Moral Pollution," *Testimonies for the Church, vol 2*, accessed August 25, 2023, https://egwwritings.org/read?panels=p120.1513(120.1514)&index=0 346.

left on these issues. This led many on the right and left to become defensive and, in some cases, leave the church.

I imagine this will be the result as I write this book. Why? Well, as it may be obvious, those pushing for acceptance of the LGBTQ+ lifestyle will not agree with me that this issue is a moral one. On the other hand, I do believe that as a church, we need to minister to those struggling with gender dysphoria and that consider themselves gay, bisexual, transgender, or queer. For that to happen, they must become part of our church. We must not be afraid to talk about this and to have conversations with visitors and members of those groups. Unfortunately, many saints in our church believe that the LGBTQ+ issue is not "a sin" but "the sin." They treat this sin as more serious than other sins and do not even want LGBTQ+ people in our churches. To try to minister to them would be seen as a compromise. They will not be happy about this book either.

Recently, I saw a post on social media that describes the challenge of pastoring, the author is unknown.

> Pastoring is weird. I've poured my heart and soul into people who now act like I don't exist. I have done hours of counseling and deliverance with people who later deleted me. I've publicly honored people who chose to slander me and act like I was a villain. And then there were people I rarely have conversations with that honor and respect me to the highest degree. Some leaders have washed my feet while others have thrown dirt on my name.
>
> Pastoring is weird. I'm too much for some, yet too little for others. The same preaching that convicts one person angers another. The same sermon that was boring to one was massively impactful to another. Praised for being so loving and grateful yet slandered for being too loving and grateful in certain situations.

THE PRESENT TRUTH AND THE LGBTQ+ MOVEMENT

Pastoring is weird. We're accused of just wanting money, yet we're also expected to live in humble poverty like a lonely shepherd. If you have nice things, then you're greedy and materialistic. If you don't have nice things, then you must be in rebellion since God isn't blessing you. People are always asking us for our personal time, money, and resources. Yet when we set healthy boundaries to care for our mental health and our families, we are considered selfish.

Pastoring is weird. Everything you say and do can and will be used against you by anyone disgruntled, annoyed, petty, or even just bored. Every mistake is broadcasted as proof that you are unqualified, yet victories seem less talked about because they're expected. Your personal life, hobbies, interests, friendships, relationships, ministry alignments, and family are under a constant microscope and being monitored by people searching for faults and failures.

Pastoring is weird. You give everything you have and somehow still feel like you didn't give enough. You never meet certain people's expectations. You didn't do enough according to someone's opinion. And there's always someone confident they could do a better job, yet all they do is criticize from the sidelines.

Pastoring is weird. You try your best to protect the sheep from wolves and somehow in the process you end up accused of being a wolf yourself. Sometimes other shepherds who don't even know you spread lies about you and your flock.

Pastoring is weird… And yet there's so much fulfillment in precious moments. The feeling you get when someone gives their life to Christ is beautiful. When you marry a couple whom you met at your church, bring restoration to a broken family, or dedicate a child that mom and dad prayed hard for, it makes everything else worth it. When you're asked for by name to be with someone in their last moments. When you're the first person they seek when they need hope. When the healing comes. When the deliverance comes. When the breakthrough comes. When someone who thought they had no purpose gets discipled and preaches their first sermon. When the glory of the Lord fills the room, and the congregation goes wild without restraint in His presence. Nothing compares to this.

Pastoring is weird. It's challenging, heartbreaking, and can be discouraging, but it's also fulfilling, inspiring, and awesomely life changing I get to do this. Pastoring is not for the faint of heart. It can be brutal, but it can also be beautiful. Pastoring is weird, but I guess I'm weird too.

Writing can be weird as well, especially when the topic is as sensitive and controversial as this one is. So what does LGBTQ+ stand for? The letters stand for *L*esbian, *G*ay, *B*isexual, *T*ransgender, *Q*ueer. The "+" is to include the many other variations in gender that have been found today. In fact, as I write this, Facebook has seventy-two different genders that you can choose from your page, but others say that there are as many as eighty-one types of genders and gender identities.[11]

Clearly, the issue of people being gay or lesbian is not a new one. In fact, even being bisexual is not a new phenomenon. However, transgender ideology is one that, although some will argue has been around for some time, seems to be "the" issue today. We hear about

---

[11] Chris Drew, "81 Types of Genders and Gender Identities," *HelpfulProfessor.com* (July 2023), accessed August 25, 2023, https://helpfulprofessor.com/types-of-genders-list.

it consistently on the news and social media, and it is a political hot button, at least in the United States. Thus, what is in most people's minds today is this transgender ideology. But we cannot address transgender ideology without referring to those who are lesbian, gay, bisexual, queer, etc. because the arguments given by its defenders are the same. Furthermore, those who believe that the Bible justifies the transgender lifestyle also believe it justifies all the other ones. Thus, there is going to be an overlap as we address these issues. However,

> One might have thought that this current era of transgender acceptance would benefit all members of LGBTQ, but many lesbians insist that it hasn't been the case. In the last decade, lesbians have seen the disappearance of their bars, their publications, women's-only colleges, and single-sex bathrooms and locker rooms. Convicted rapists who suddenly "identify" as women are housed in women's prisons, and natal males demand access to battered women's shelters... In the mid-90's lesbians were thriving in America and lesbian culture was enjoying a heyday. Now...lesbians have "gone underground."[12]

It sounds like some women who identify as lesbian have a problem with what the transgender movement has become. Still, since the issues are pretty much the same, we must cover it all together, which is why the book is titled *The Present Truth and the LGBTQ+ Movement* and not *The Present Truth and the Transgender Movement*, as I originally intended.

It is the belief of this author that God is the God of transformation. As such, throughout the book, you will find several stories of transformation from former members of the LGBTQ+ community. I do this in the hope that anyone reading this book who is struggling

---

[12] Abigail Shrier, *Irreversible Damage: The Transgender Craze Seducing Our Daughters* (Washington, DC: Regnery Publishing, 2020), 150-151.

with gender or sexual orientation confusion or who knows of anybody who is may find hope.

As you read this book, you may feel uncomfortable, but it is important that this issue is addressed honestly and boldly. The apostle Paul said it this way, "And have no fellowship with the unfruitful works of darkness, but rather *expose them*" (Ephesians 5:11, emphasis supplied). Satan is working overtime as we get closer to the coming of Christ, and, as we have already said, now right is wrong, and wrong is right. Why is this the case? Because Satan's strategy is to convince people that either some issues are not that important or that not everything is black or white, that there are some gray areas. He is even using the Bible to justify sin. This should not surprise us because Paul told young Timothy,

> I charge you therefore before God and the Lord Jesus Christ, who will judge the living and the dead at His appearing and His kingdom: Preach the word! Be ready in season and out of season. Convince, rebuke, exhort, with all longsuffering and teaching. For the time will come when *they will not endure sound doctrine*, but *according to their own desires*, because they have *itching ears*, they will heap up for themselves teachers; and they *will turn their ears away from the truth*, and be turned aside to fables. But you be watchful in all things, endure afflictions, do the work of an evangelist, fulfill your ministry. (2 Timothy 4:1–4, emphasis supplied)

How was Timothy to expose truth from error? He was to "preach the word!" This is what we must do. True, in some cases, people will misinterpret us, some may get offended, some will feel uncomfortable, and some people may stand up and leave the church. Some people will be convicted; others will get angry. One may think this is boring, but it will massively impact somebody else. I may be praised for being so loving, yet somebody else will slander me for being too loving on this issue. But with all the love in our hearts, as Jesus did, we must preach the word and stand for the truth even when it may not be politically correct. We must "stand for the right though the heavens fall."[13] Let's do it together. Please pray that the Holy Spirit will give you clarity and conviction as you read the rest of this book.

---

[13] Ellen G. White. "True and Honest Men," *Education 57*, accessed August 28, 2023, https://egwwritings.org/read?panels=p29.242&index=0.

CHAPTER 1

Jim Venice
I'm a Brand-New Man[1]

I WAS BORN AND RAISED in the St. Louis metropolitan area. Both of my parents were just sixteen and newly married when I was born. They married to escape the turmoil of their sin-filled homes, thinking that things would be better on their own. Their relationship was doomed from the beginning, being so young and both without even a high school education. My father turned to alcohol to deal with the pressures of his young life and family.

After the birth of my second brother, just three years later, my parents' marriage came to an unexpected end. My father ended up in prison for several years because of a crime that he had committed. Alcohol and sin had taken my daddy away, and my mother was left to raise three baby boys on her own. She worked hard, determined to feed and clothe us boys. Sometimes, she'd work two and three jobs at a time, just to be able to provide for her babies. I remember being left with very young female sitters. While I was just a toddler, on two separate occasions, the sitters molested me. I never told my mother until years later.

My daddy was gone. I knew that he had done something very wrong, but my three-year-old mind didn't understand fully why. I did not have a daddy to hold me when I cried, no one to teach me how to play catch or throw a ball, to fight and roughhouse with, or even to use the restroom like boys do. I don't remember a time when

---

[1] Jim Venice, "I'm a Brand-New Man," *Restored Hope Network*, accessed October 9, 2023, https://www.restoredhopenetwork.org/im-a-brand-new-man. Used with permission.

I got to be bounced on my daddy's lap, to be held and kissed, or to be told, "I love you," by my dad. All that I knew was that my daddy did something very bad and that I didn't want to be anything like him. All of this happened at a time when most boys were saying, "I want to grow up and be just like my daddy."

Instead, my mother was my hero, the only one I could depend on for whatever I needed. She had to be both mother and father to her boys. I became "a mama's boy" and somewhat of a "sissy." I was never affirmed in my masculinity. I didn't want to be mean, rough, and tough; and I didn't know anything about sports. There came a time when I remember watching the other boys and wishing that I could be more like them. I felt different, alienated, and separated from them. I envied the other boys. I was the one who always played with the girls, their dollhouses, hopscotch, and jump rope. When I was forced to play team sports games, I was always one of the last ones picked.

Then came puberty; I was so ashamed and embarrassed of my changing body. I did not want this to happen. Most boys are excited when they start becoming a man, when they get that first whisker or that first hair on their chest. Not me—I did not want to be a man. The girls I had played with were now becoming attracted to young men. They had crushes on them and talked about their great looks or how cute they were. Where did this leave me? I became more alienated from the guys. The envy that I felt toward the other boys gradually turned into an attraction toward their masculinity. I didn't understand why this was happening to me. I became attracted to my own sex. I began fantasizing about what it would be like to be one of those "cute" guys.

My fantasies turned to lust, and I began to have a problem with masturbation. I needed help desperately.

When I was twelve, I was invited into the church's youth group and became involved in their Bible Quiz program. Jesus became my Lord, I was baptized in the Holy Spirit, and I loved the Lord with all of my heart. My family quit going to church with me. I was determined to serve the Lord. Various people from the church saw that I got back and forth to church. I went to three weeks of church camp every summer. I became involved in many other church activities. Every time the church doors were opened, I was there, usually in the front pew. I became very close to the Lord and even had a very special anointing in my life. His presence was so real and so strong. I felt a calling to some kind of ministry, not of preaching but of teaching, encouraging, and healing. This ministry never had a chance to develop because of my secret struggle.

All through junior and senior high school, my best friends were always girls. My alienation from my masculine identity continued to deepen. I would never play sports, not only because I never learned to play but I felt inferior. I had a very poor self-image and even stuttered. I became a loner. The church was my escape from my world. I never became close enough to anyone to share my private sexual struggles. I was embarrassed and ashamed. I kept it all to myself for all of those years; I never told a soul. I knew what the Bible said about homosexuality and perversion, but I still had my secret problem with fantasizing and masturbation; it became "my thorn in the flesh" to keep me humble and continually on my knees asking for God's forgiveness. I even fasted frequently, praying for deliverance. Because of my lack of athletic and social ability, I chose to excel in academics. I was an honor student at school. My Bible Quiz Team won the national finals in 1981, 1982, 1984, and 1986. In 1986, I was the number 1 National Bible Quizzer of the year. I won several scholarships in high school. I was still very close to the Lord with a humble heart.

After high school, I became very frustrated with God and tired of waiting for Him to "fix" me. I had what I thought was a bright idea and decided to "help God out." I had learned in 1 Corinthians 7:9 that the apostle Paul said that "if any of you burn with lust," then you should get married so that at least we could have a "God-sanctioned" sexual outlet. I decided to take Apostle Paul up on his advice, and I also decided that getting married to a woman was going to be how God was going to "fix" me. I decided that I was going to marry my best friend Debbie, whom I had met when we were just thirteen and fourteen at church camp. It was going to be a huge leap of faith for me. She would never need to know, and I would never have to tell her anything about my struggles because getting married was going to fix everything for me.

Getting married did *not* fix me at all! My attractions toward men did not go away—if anything, they intensified. I loved my wife dearly, but shamefully, I wanted men more than I wanted my wife. After five years of marriage, I was introduced to homosexual activity. In my desperation to make sense of my life, I bought into the concept that I must have a gay gene and was born gay. I opened up to my wife for the first time, and I decided that we should separate. In the middle of all of this, we found out that we were going to have a child. Becoming a father did *not* make those feelings go away either. We finally did divorce.

I became very promiscuous and drank a lot to numb the pain and confusion of my life. I then entered my first long-term gay relationship; it lasted three years, and my second almost three years. During that time, I became very angry and bitter with God and with the church. I even grew to hate God. I could not reconcile His Word, which was hidden deep in my heart with the reality of what was going on in my life. "God, *You* did this to me, and I hope that I hurt You!"

To make this already long story shorter, in November 1996, I found myself in church for the first time in about seven years. It felt good to be in God's house and to feel His love softening my hardened heart. I told God that after everything that I had been through, nobody wanted to be changed more than I did. I had always wanted God to take those feelings away. God's love continued to overwhelm my now-broken and softening heart. I found myself kneeling at an old-fashioned altar, crying out to God to fix me, change me, heal me, take it all away. Before I knew it, I had told God that I was so very sorry for all that I had done and the mess that I had made of my life. I then asked Him to forgive me, and to my surprise, I instantly felt clean on the inside for the first time in years. I had forgotten what it had felt like. It felt so good to have my slate wiped clean. My sins were forgiven and cast as far as the east is from the west (Psalm 103:12). It dawned on me that I had never felt *love* like I was feeling at that moment in the arms of another man and never wanted it to end, even if it meant giving up my homosexuality. I thought that maybe it would be a matter of "going back into the closet" and becoming a gay celibate man. There were no divine transformations or glory cloud experiences, but when I got done praying, I knew that I didn't want to go back to my homosexual life. I knew that it would be a walk of faith, obedience, and self-denial.

I then found a local "sexual redemption ministry" where I learned that I had believed a lie—that I was not born gay and that there are *no* gay genes and *no* scientific evidence that homosexuality was biological. I learned that God had *not* been responsible for this cruel joke on me. I also learned that I was *not* alone—that there were countless thousands and undocumented millions of people like myself who were having encounters with God or Jesus where He was calling them out of homosexuality or lesbianism. (*Unfortunately,* you will *not* hear any of this on the five o'clock news!) I then started to learn that there were legitimate God-given unmet needs in my life that I was trying to satisfy in an illegitimate way. Just like it says in an old country song, I was basically "looking for love in all the wrong places." Inside every little boy, there is a legitimate hunger for masculinity that God intends for us to satisfy by having healthy gender-affirming relationships with our same-gender parents and same-gender peer group. If we don't get that hunger satisfied before the onset of puberty, then that hunger becomes intertwined with our emerging sexuality. This then leads to trying to satisfy this hunger for same-gender affirmation by having sexual relations with someone of the same sex. *It does not work!* And it *never* will—having sex with someone of the same gender will *never* satisfy the deeper unmet need for same-gender affirmation. It always leaves us desperately hungry for more and never satisfied. I also learned that there was a way to reverse the effects of what I experienced. The most ironic thing was that I did, indeed, desperately need men to help me satisfy this hunger for masculinity. I needed to have healthy *non*sexual gender-affirming relationships with *men*! This revelation started my journey out of homosexuality. It was not a quick fix but rather a long process. I did not get this way overnight, and it was not going to go away overnight either.

Our son was six when my wife and I remarried. Six months later, we were expecting our daughter. My wife was willing to walk out my healing journey with me. We both became involved with that local ministry for several years, eventually becoming involved in leadership. Then in 2002, God called us back to the Saint Louis area to start our own local "sexual redemption ministry" while I continued my own healing journey. Today, I can tell you that I am no longer a homosexual and am no longer interested in having sex with men. I am an ordained minister, and my wife and I allow God to use what He has brought us through to help countless others. (We estimate well over a thousand individuals have come through our offices, and we have had the opportunity to speak to countless thousands in small and large churches and other gatherings during the first ten years of full-time ministry.) I'm not at all proud of my past, but I am very proud of our Lord and what He has done in my life.

I'M A BRAND-NEW MAN!

The Transgender Ideology
History, Causation, Implications, Risks, and Challenges

When I was a child, one of my favorite movies was *The Wizard of Oz*. One of the iconic phrases of the movie is "Toto, I have a feeling we're not in Kansas anymore!" Today, people often repeat this phrase when they want to comment on the fact that things have changed in our world. Well, "ain't that the truth!"

"The world is changing fast. And not just politics, technology, and communication, but our whole culture, morality, and attitudes. Christians living in Western culture enjoyed the benefits of being in a world which largely shared our assumptions about what is fundamentally right and wrong." We can no longer assume that this is the case. In two short generations, we have moved to a widespread adoption of liberal values, many of which are in conflict with the teaching of the Bible. Increasingly, believers are finding themselves to be the misunderstood minority, and feeling at odds with where the world seems to be heading.[2]

Transgender ideology is at the forefront of our time. "In less than two decades 'transgender' has gone from a term representing individuals and little used outside of specialist communities, to signifying a powerful political ideology driving significant social change."[3] Yet, if we are honest, most people outside of the LGBTQ+ community are not familiar with what it means to be "transgender." This is especially true in the church. I will be the first to admit that before I started doing the research for this book, my knowledge of LGBTQ+ people was based on assumptions that I have been hearing all my life. When I was a school-age boy, we would poke fun at individuals whom we suspected of being "gay." Calling someone "gay" was meant as an insult, "those were fight words." Perhaps this is the reason so many boys and girls didn't "come out" even if they felt they were struggling with sexual identity. Today, all that has changed. In fact, some years ago, I remember talking to a family member who told me that his daughter was a lesbian and that he had changed his mind on this issue. "Things have changed," he told me. Indeed, they have, and that change is a positive one. Nobody should be demeaned, excluded, or treated badly for the sole reason of being lesbian, gay, bisexual, queer, or transgender.

One of the best-known passages in scripture is John 3:16, "For God so loved *the world* that He gave His only begotten Son, that whoever believes in Him should not perish but have everlasting life" (emphasis supplied). John does not say "for God so loved 'heterosexuals'"; he says "the world." The apostle John also states, "He who does not love does not know God, for God is love" (1 John 4:8). And "A new commandment I give to you, that you love one another; as I have loved you, that you also love one another. By this all will know that you are My disciples, if you have love for one another." This means that we ought to love the LGBTQ+ community as well, even

---

[2] Vaughan Roberts, *Transgender* (India, The Good Book Company, 2021), 7.
[3] Joanne Williams, *The Corrosive Impact of Transgender Ideology* (London: Civitas, 2020), vii.

when we may not fully understand them or agree with them. In fact, I would say that true love is tested by our ability and desire to love those whom we disagree with. We will talk more about love later. This being said,

> Hardly a week goes by, it seems, without there being some kind of transgender story in the news—and the stories will keep on coming. There has been transitioning of Bruce, now Caitlin, Jenner, the former decathlon world record holder. Then we've had debates over the rights and wrongs of which public bathrooms to use, which prison transgender people should be sent to, whether transgender people can serve in the military, what to put on passports. How should Christians respond to all this—not just in the media and wider culture but, closer to home, in our communities, families and churches? How should we relate to someone who is transitioning gender or has already transitioned? And what if the sense of not fitting with the sex of one's birth is a deeply personal one for us? How should we respond?[4]

As I said in my introduction, we need to have a conversation about this. Yet, if we are going to have a conversation with those belonging to the LGBTQ+ community, we need to be familiar with what this is about. We cannot come to the table with assumptions. We must educate ourselves about the issues, and most of all, we need to be willing to listen. Now I do know that some, especially some Christians, are very skeptical about the sources out there that are explaining the "science" behind the LGBTQ+ ideology. After doing much research, I can see why. However, at the very least, you would have some knowledge because if all you have are assumptions, the

---

[4] Roberts, 13–14.

conversation will end before it starts. This is partly the purpose of this book.

However, when we come to an issue that is sensitive and yet as divisive and controversial as this one is, we must have the right foundation. That is, we must have the proper worldview through which we see what is happening around us. It goes without saying that Christians must have a biblical worldview. Why should the Christian see the world through a biblical lens? In the introduction of her book *The Great Controversy*, Ellen White writes,

> Through the illumination of the Holy Spirit, the scenes of the long-continued conflict between good and evil have been opened to the writer of these pages. From time to time I have been permitted to behold the working, in different ages, of *the great controversy between Christ, the Prince of life, the Author of our salvation, and Satan, the prince of evil, the author of sin, the first transgressor of God's holy law.* Satan's enmity against Christ has been manifested against His followers. The same hatred of the principles of God's law, the same policy of deception, by which error is made to appear as truth, by which human laws are substituted for the law of God, and men are led to worship the creature rather than the Creator, may be traced in all the history of the past. Satan's efforts to misrepresent the character of God, to cause men to cherish a false conception of the Creator, and thus to regard Him with fear and hate rather than with love; his endeavors to set aside the divine law, leading the people to think themselves free from its requirements; and his persecution of those who dare to resist his deceptions, have been steadfastly pursued in all ages. They may be traced in the history of patriarchs, prophets, and apostles, of martyrs and

reformers. In the great final conflict, Satan will employ the same policy, manifest the same spirit, and work for the same end as in all preceding ages. That which has been, will be, except that the coming struggle will be marked with a terrible intensity such as the world has never witnessed. Satan's deceptions will be more subtle, his assaults more determined. If it were possible, he would lead astray the elect. Mark 13:22, R.V. As the Spirit of God has opened to my mind the great truths of His word, and the scenes of the past and the future, I have been bidden to make known to others that which has thus been revealed—to trace *the history of the controversy* in past ages, and especially so to present it as to shed a light on the fast-approaching struggle of the future.[5] (emphasis supplied)

Clearly, we are in the midst of war, a controversy between good and evil, between the God, Who created heaven and earth and the one who lies, cheats, and confuses. Thus, the Bible should be the lens through which we see everything. "If we don't know the biblical perspective on an issue, we're in trouble. If we do know it, we have all the intellectual fortification we could possibly need to wade into the brokenness of our fallen realm."[6] Unfortunately, what I have found in my research is that much of what the "experts" say on LGBTQ+ ideology comes from a secular worldview. The Bible is completely ignored—after all, "what does the Bible know about science and psychology?" Others try to make it appear they have a biblical perspec-

---

[5] Ellen G. White, *The Great Controversy between Christ and Satan* (Nampa, ID: Pacific Press®, 2005), x-xi.

[6] Owen Strachan, "Transition or Transformation: A Moral-Theological Exploration of Christianity and Gender Dysphoria," in *Understanding Gender Identities*, ed. James K. Beilby and Paul Rhodes Eddy (Grand Rapids, MI: Baker Academic, 2019), 73.

tive, but as we shall see later, they see only what they want to see and interpret the Bible according to their own desires.

So what are we talking about here?

What in the World Is Being a Transgender?

Let us start by presenting some key terms as defined by Mark Yarhouse, a professor and doctor of psychology; Dr. Arthur P. Rech; and Mrs. Jean May Rech, endowed chair in Psychology and director of the Sexual and Gender Identity Institute at Wheaton College.

- Biological sex: As male or female (typically with reference to chromosomes, gonads, sex hormones, and internal reproductive anatomy and external genitalia).
- Primary sex characteristics: Features that are directly part of the reproductive system, such as testes, penis, and scrotum in males, and ovaries, uterus, and vagina in females.
- Secondary sex characteristics: Have no direct reproductive functions, for example, facial hair in males, and enlarged breasts in females.
- Gender: The psychological, social and cultural aspects of being male and female.
- Gender identity: How you experience yourself (or think of yourself) as male or female, including how masculine or feminine a person feels.
- Gender role: Adoptions of cultural expectations for maleness and femaleness.
- Gender dysphoria: The experience of distress associated with the incongruence wherein one's psychological and emotional gender identity does not match one's biological sex.

- Transgender: An umbrella term for *the many ways* in which people might experience and/or present and express (or love our) their gender identities, differently from people whose sense of gender identity is congruent with their biological sex. (emphasis supplied)
- Cisgender: A word to contrast with transgender and to signify that one's psychological and emotional experience of gender identity is congruent with one's biological sex.
- Intersex: A term to describe conditions (e.g., congenital adrenal hyperplasia) in which a person is born with sex characteristics or anatomy that do not allow clear identification as male or female. The cause of an intersex condition can be chromosomal, gonadal, or genital.[7]

Notice that, according to the definition, there are many ways in which being transgender can be manifested or experienced. For the "conservative" Christian, these definitions make no sense. In fact, some may see them as terms used to justify this "sinful" behavior. From a biblical perspective, this may be true. Yet it is important that we are familiar with these terms if we are going to have a conversation with those in the LGBTQ+ community, some of whom, as I mentioned in the introduction, are worshiping in our churches every Sabbath.

I acknowledge that this issue seems very complicated. Thus, we need a lot of patience if we are going to completely understand this issue and the church members who are struggling with "gender dysphoria." Please do not dismiss this as unimportant. As a church,

---

[7] Mark A. Yarhouse, *Understanding Gender Dysphoria: Navigating Transgender Issues in a Changing Culture* (Downers Grove, IL: IVP Academic, 2015), 17, 20, 21.

we need to spend some time with this because it is not going away simply because we may want to ignore it.

The History of Transgenderism

While for most of us it seems like it is only more recently where we have been hearing about being transgender, this has been going on for some time. In fact, some believe it has been going on for centuries. In the book *Before We Were Trans*, Kit Heyam shares stories of people across the globe, from antiquity to the present, whose experiences of gender defy binary categories. For the sake of understanding, the term *nonbinary* is used to describe people who feel their gender cannot be defined within the margins of gender binary. Instead, they understand their gender in a way that goes beyond simply identifying as either a man or woman.[8] The term *binary* would mean the opposite, that is, a person who defines gender as either male or female. Heyam says,

> It's history that shows us that—notwithstanding the outraged claims of anti-trans commentators today—what constitutes a man, a woman, or gender itself has continually been defined, contested, and redefined. It's the history of people who've troubled the relationship between our bodies and how we live; people who've taken creative, critical approaches to gender binaries; people who approach gender disruptively or messily. Before our current moment, before we were trans, these people showed us that gender was ours to play with, ours to challenge, ours to change.[9]

---

[8] "Non-binary inclusion, *LGBT Foundation*, accessed August 28, 2023, https://lgbt.foundation/who-we-help/trans-people/non-binary.

[9] Kit Heyam, *Before We Were Trans: A New History of Gender* (New York: Seal Press, 2022), 28.

To prove her thesis, Heyam shares stories from Renaissance Venice to seventeenth-century Angola, from Edo Japan to early America. If you think this is strange, in her book *The Bible and the Transgender Experience*, author Linda Tatro Herzer explains that gender-variant individuals existed even in Bible times.[10] More on this later. There are several theories out there as to how and when beliefs about gender led to our current transgender fiasco.

If you are fan of old Hollywood movies, the name Christine Jorgensen may ring a bell. Mark Yarhouse shares his story. Christine was born as George William Jorgesen. He says,

> Growing up in New York, George Jr. often felt that he had some kind of sexual and emotional disorder. In search of answers, he would investigate possible explanations by scouring books and articles at the New York Academy of medicine library. His fear was he was homosexual; after all, he was sexually attracted to men. However, that did not appear to explain everything. George Jr. Eventually experimented with the female hormone estradiol, and he learned during this time about a possible intervention taking place in Sweden that extended his experiments into a more meaningful and satisfying resolution. He went overseas and eventually found Dr. Christian Hamburger, an endocrinologist who was willing to provide him with hormonal replacement therapy. George Jr. would later have his testicles and penis removed; he also had vaginal plastic surgery. In 1952, George Jr. Change his name to *Christine* Jorgesen out of respect for Dr. Christian hamburger... This course of events would make headlines. Indeed, *the New*

---

[10] Linda Tatro Herzer, *The Bible and the Transgender Experience: How Scripture Supports Gender Variance* (Cleveland, OH: The Pilgrim Press, 2016), 82–94.

York Daily News banner headline read in all capital letters: Ex-GI becomes blonde beauty: Operations transforms Bronx youth.[11]

While Jorgensen was the first transsexual person to gain widespread recognition in America, others preceded her in this journey, both in the US and beyond. Certain medical advances were necessary before sex reassignment surgery (SRS) could become truly viable, including anesthesia, hormone therapy, and plastic surgery. Genital reconstruction surgery initially grew as a response to children with intersex conditions and victims of accidents and war injuries. But medical advances were not the only necessary condition for SRS to arise. Technological captivity had to be paired with a hospitable theory of sexuality. And just such a theory was in the air in the late nineteenth and early twentieth centuries: the theory of the universal constitutional bisexuality of humanity (i.e., the idea that human sexual differentiation is nonbinary in nature). The germ of this idea can be traced back to Charles Darwin, who set the stage for a new genderless human nature, and it can be found running through the thought of many of the early leading sexologists (e.g., Magnus Hirschfeld, Havelock Ellis, Sigmund Freud, and James Kiernan). This idea leads to the conclusion that the male and female sexes do not conform to a strict binary but instead reflect something of a continuum. Within this intellectual atmosphere, the idea that a man could become a woman, or vice versa, seemed increasingly plausible.[12]

I find it interesting that the authors mention Charles Darwin as the "germ" of this idea. Darwin, of course, wrote *On the Origin of Species by Means of Natural Selection*, which is considered the foundation of evolutionary biology. In explaining Genesis 1–2 and the fact that God created humanity as male and female (more on this later), Voddie Baucham says that the Genesis account is under attack in our day. It has been under attack by those who argue against creation,

---

[11] Yarhouse, 13–14.
[12] James K. Beilby and Paul Rhodes Eddy, *Understanding Transgender Identities* (Grand Rapids, MI: Baker Academic, 2019), 3–4.

that is, by those who argue for evolution. Inherently, when you argue that man evolved, you are saying that Genesis is a lie. If man evolved, then that means that man was not created. If man was not created, then Genesis is a lie.[13] I do not think this is a coincidence, as many who argue for what I will call "affirmation theology" (the belief that Christians should not only support the LGBTQ+ community but approve of their lifestyle, not only with regards to same-sex marriage and/or sexual relations with a member of the same sex but also with transgender identity as normal and even God ordained) do not accept the Genesis account as it is written. We will see this in a later chapter.

The culture change as to how people feel toward members of the LGBTQ+ community and the reason for same-sex attraction may be in part due to changes in psychology. More recently, we have seen the issue of "transgender ideology" come to the forefront of the media, politics, and even Christianity. There are reasons for this.

In the professional literature, the *Diagnostic and Statistical Manual of Mental Disorders*, fifth edition (DSM-5) reflected a shift away from "gender identity disorder" toward the use of the phrase "gender dysphoria" to reduce stigma. Actually, several steps in the new nomenclature were intended to reduce stigma. The first is the shift from an emphasis on identity as the disorder to the emphasis on the dysphoria or distress associated with the gender incongruence for many people who report it… Our culture has in some ways moved past afternoon television shows that capitalize on "shock and awe" in their presentations, where you might see producers orchestrate dramatic a confrontation between a male-to-female transgender person who once dated a woman and is now surprising her with her true sense of self. These colorful presentations in the media were once an expression of almost gawking at the phenomenon, but they did not represent the kind of cultural sea change that would soon follow.[14]

---

[13] Voddie Baucham, "Man and Woman by God's Design," *YouTube* (January 2023), accessed July 26, 2023, https://youtu.be/TrSr8l2u5-w?si=RUTYUbBhfBSGOfzu.

[14] Yarhouse, 14–15.

Who can forget the many talk shows in the 1990s, like the *Jerry Springer Show*, for example, where they had members of the LGBTQ+ community, specifically "transexuals" being made fools of or making fools of themselves. That will not happen today, as it is no longer politically correct, which, incidentally, is the apparent reason for the change in the DSM-5 as mentioned above, which took place in 2013. But there is more to the story of how we arrived here. When we talk about how the world and some Christians think about sexuality today, an important name to remember is Alfred C. Kinsey.

One of the most influential Americans of the twentieth century, Alfred Charles Kinsey conducted landmark studies of male and female sexual behavior that helped usher in the "sexual revolution" of the 1960s and 1970s... In January 1948, Kinsey and his collaborators published *Sexual Behavior in the Human Male*. It made the best-seller list within three weeks, despite its 804 pages, generally dry scientific style, and ponderous weight of statistics, tables, and graphs. By mid-March, it had sold two hundred thousand copies. The book, based on over five thousand sexual histories, provided a series of revelations about the prevalence of masturbation, adulterous sexual activity, and homosexuality... Kinsey's next major project was *Sexual Behavior in the Human Female*, published in 1953. Based on almost six thousand sexual histories, this book contained many revelations about such matters as women's masturbatory practices, premarital sexuality, and orgasmic experiences. As before, Kinsey documented an enormous gap between social attitudes and actual practices.[15]

Aldred Kinsey is hailed as a hero by many in the LGBTQ+ community, and in fact, they defend him. Jamie Paul, writing for Queer Majority, writes, "Kinsey's contributions have reshaped the way we think and talk about human sexuality, regardless of anything his most fervent haters might say."[16] However, I am reminded of a

---

[15] Theodore M. Brown and Elizabeth Fee, "Alfred C. Kinsey: A Pioneer of Sex Research," *National Library of Medicine* (June 2003), accessed August 29, 2023, https://www.ncbi.nlm.nih.gov/pmc/articles/PMC1447862.

[16] Jamie Paul, "The Culture Wars Come from Sex Research," *QueerMajority.com*, accessed August 29, 2023, https://www.queermajority.com/essays-all/the-culture-wars-come-for-sex-research.

phrase I heard some years ago regarding the COVID-19 fiasco that describes the problem we face many times relating to important issues such as this one. "The problem with the media is not what they tell you but what they don't." The so-called experts in science and psychology do not always tell us the whole story, and the whole story is both shocking and disturbing, so please be advised.

In the book *Kinsey, Sex and Fraud*, Dr. Judith Reisman writes,

> What Kinsey claimed about "statistically common behavior" in the United States population of the 1940s surprised most, shocked many and delighted a number of others. It was assumed that his "scientific" research among a sample of several thousand men and women could be extrapolated to the U.S. population as a whole to provide an accurate picture of national sexual behavior. Kinsey's findings were thus nothing short of stunning, but the most stunning finding of all went almost unnoticed, except, it appears, by the FBI. Even before the 1948 appearance of the Male Report, magazine and newspaper articles proclaimed that a scientific study would reveal that:
>
> - 85% of males in the U.S. have intercourse prior to marriage.
> - Nearly 70% have sex with prostitutes.
> - Between 30% and 45% of husbands have extramarital intercourse.
> - 37% of all males have homosexual experiences between adolescence and old age.

Writing in Harper's, Albert Deutsch exclaimed, "The Kinsey survey explodes traditional concepts of what is normal and abnormal, natural and unnatural in sex behavior."

The *Female Report* in 1953 was almost anticlimactic by comparison. However, despite Kinsey's protestations that his books were presenting facts without moral interpretations, the "facts" of the *Female Report* continued the process begun in the male volume—"a persistent hammering at Judeo-Christian legal and moral codes," according to Albert Hobbs in the *American Journal of Psychiatry*. Stressed in the *Female Report* were data showing that premarital sexual intercourse was beneficial for women. This practice would help them adjust emotionally, sexually, and socially. Avoidance of premarital intercourse was said to be a potential cause of damaging inhibitions that could persist for years after marriage. However, the most profoundly shocking findings of both Kinsey Reports were almost totally ignored. These were Kinsey's conclusions on childhood sexuality. Kinsey's "scientific" "research" purported to prove that children were sexual beings, even from infancy, and that they could, and should, have pleasurable and beneficial sexual interaction with adult "partners" who could lead them into the proper techniques of fulfilling sexual activity. The damage done to children from sexual relations with adults—what the public thought was molestation—was almost always, in Kinsey's view, the result of overreaction and hysteria by parents, schoolteachers, police, etc. But one aspect of Kinsey's research was completely missed by everyone. That was the criminal childhood sexuality experimentation, which formed the basis of Kinsey's conclusions on childhood sexual potential. *The results of these experiments are the basis for beliefs on childhood sexuality held and taught by academic sexologists today*[17] (emphasis supplied).

One of the reasons Kinsey's book is so controversial is the research that was conducted to justify his findings. Chapter 5 included within it the details of sexual experiments involving between 317 and 1,746 male children aged five months to fourteen years old. These experiments involved "manual and oral stimulation" of the children's genitals by adults. In a detailed table entitled "Examples of Multiple

---

[17] Dr. Judith A. Reisman and Edward W. Eichel, *Kinsey, Sex and Fraud: The Indoctrination of a People*, ed. Dr. J. Gordon Muir and Dr. John H. Court (Lafayette, LA: Huntington House Publishers, 1990), 2–3.

Orgasms in Pre-Adolescent Males" (table 34), Kinsey detailed the time taken by the babies and children to achieve "multiple orgasms." The timings were made with a stopwatch. The data shown in this table (which is one of several similar tables) makes plain that babies, toddlers, preadolescents, and early teenagers were "stimulated" by one or more adults for periods of between seventy seconds and twenty-four hours in order to measure their capacity of "multiple orgasms." In one instance alone, Kinsey records an eleven-month-old baby as achieving eleven "orgasms" within one hour.[18]

Paul Gebhard was a close colleague of Kinsey and a participant in the research done for his book. In the documentary cited above, Gebhard comments on the experiments that were conducted and says, "It was illegal, and we knew it was illegal. But it's very important for people to study childhood sexuality. In other cultures, anthropologists can sometimes do this. But in our culture, because of our insistence that children are non-sexual the study of childhood sexuality was essentially impossible."[19] So the modern landscape in terms of what we think about sexuality is rooted in the work of Kinsey. When we hear the rhetoric about being born either gay, lesbian, bisexual, or transgender, that is all from Kinsey. This is perhaps the reason this transgender ideology is being pushed so much by the powers that be in our education system. We are being told that we need to listen to young children regarding their sexuality. It is ironic that we do not necessarily take our kids' word on most things they say and/or believe, because, after all, they are just kids. "They don't know any better." But regarding their sexuality, they know better than anybody else. Where does this come from? You got it, Alfred Kinsey!

While a secular person may not care about the source of their beliefs regarding LGBTQ+ ideology, we Christians should, and we should not ignore this. Something so disturbing and evil does not come from God, nor is it approved by Him.

---

[18] Tim Tate, "Secret History: Kinsey's Paedophiles," *Yorkshire Television* (August 1998), accessed August 29, 2023, https://youtu.be/UVC-1d5ib50?si=UomcX-dGV5xNC6m7-.

[19] Ibid.

Another name that is important to mention in connection with the modern view of sexuality is John Money. This is a name mentioned in almost every source that addresses LGBTQ+ ideology. Although he was a contemporary of Kinsey, he is not as well known. Dr. John Money was internationally known for his work in psycho-endocrinology and developmental sexology. He defined the concepts of gender role and identity. Dr. Money's gifts to the Kinsey Institute include his archives, which comprise the John Money Collection, and funds to establish the Scholars of Sexology Fellowship to support graduate students and young scholars.[20] You will notice that he is connected to Alfred Kinsey; that should tell you all you need to know. "Like Kensey, he believed that sex between adults and children could be beneficial. He was a proponent of so-called adult child love and even incest. He also believed that gender was a social construct."[21]

In his academic work, Money argued in favor of the increasingly mainstream idea that gender was a societal construct, malleable from an early age; and fortunately for him, into his life came Bruce Reimer. Bruce Peter Reimer was born on August 22, 1965, in Winnipeg, Ontario, to Janet and Ron Reimer. At six months of age, both Reimer and his identical twin, Brian, were diagnosed with phimosis, a condition in which the foreskin of the penis cannot retract, inhibiting regular urination. On April 27, 1966, Reimer underwent circumcision, a common procedure in which a physician surgically removes the foreskin of the penis. Usually, physicians performing circumcisions use a scalpel or other sharp instrument to remove the foreskin. However, Reimer's physician used the unconventional technique of cauterization, or burning to cause tissue death. Reimer's circumcision failed. Reimer's brother did not undergo circumcision, and his phimosis healed naturally. While the true extent of Reimer's penile damage was unclear, the overwhelming majority of biographers and journalists maintained that it was either totally severed or otherwise damaged beyond the possibility of function. In 1967,

---

[20] "John Money, Ph.D.," *Kinsey Institute Indiana University*, accessed August 29, 2023, https://kinseyinstitute.org/collections/archival/john-money.php.
[21] Voddie Baucham, "Man and Woman by God's Design," *YouTube* (January 2023).

Reimer's parents sought the help of John Money, a psychologist and sexologist who worked at the Johns Hopkins Hospital in Baltimore, Maryland.

Following their consultation with Money, Reimer's parents decided to raise Reimer as a girl. Physicians at the Johns Hopkins Hospital removed Reimer's testes and damaged penis and constructed a vestigial vulvae and a vaginal canal in their place. The physicians also opened a small hole in Reimer's lower abdomen for urination. Following his gender reassignment surgery, Reimer was given the first name Brenda, and his parents raised him as a girl. He received estrogen during adolescence to promote the development of breasts. Throughout his childhood, Reimer was not informed about his male biology.

Throughout his childhood, Reimer received annual checkups from Money. His twin brother was also part of Money's research on sexual development and gender in children. As identical twins growing up in the same family, the Reimer brothers were what Money considered ideal case subjects for a psychology study on gender. Reimer was the first documented case of sex reassignment of a child born developmentally normal, while Reimer's brother was a control subject who shared Reimer's genetic makeup, intrauterine space, and household.

During the twins' psychiatric visits with Money, and as part of his research, Reimer and his twin brother were directed to inspect one another's genitals and engage in behavior resembling sexual intercourse. Reimer claimed that much of Money's treatment involved the forced reenactment of sexual positions and motions with his brother. In some exercises, the brothers rehearsed missionary positions with thrusting motions, which Money justified as the rehearsal of healthy childhood sexual exploration. In his *Rolling Stone* interview, Reimer recalled that at least once, Money photographed those exercises. Money also made the brothers inspect one another's pubic areas. Reimer stated that Money observed those exercises both alone and with as many as six colleagues. Reimer recounted anger and verbal abuse from Money if he or his brother resisted orders, in contrast to the calm and scientific demeanor Money presented to their parents.

Reimer and his brother underwent Money's treatments at preschool and grade-school age. Money described Reimer's transition as successful and claimed that Reimer's girlish behavior stood in stark contrast to his brother's boyishness. Money reported on Reimer's case as the John/Joan case, leaving out Reimer's real name. For over a decade, Reimer and his brother unknowingly provided data that, according to biographers and the Intersex Society of North America, was used to reinforce Money's theories on gender fluidity and provided justification for thousands of sex reassignment surgeries for children with abnormal genitals.

Contrary to Money's notes, Reimer reports that as a child, he experienced severe gender dysphoria, a condition in which someone experiences distress as a result of their assigned gender. Reimer reported that he did not identify as a girl and resented Money's visits for treatment. At the age of thirteen, Reimer threatened to commit suicide if his parents took him to Money on the next annual visit. Bullied by peers in school for his masculine traits, Reimer claimed that despite receiving female hormones, wearing dresses, and having his interests directed toward typically female norms, he always felt that he was a boy. In 1980, at the age of fifteen, Reimer's father told him the truth about his birth and the subsequent procedures. Following that revelation, Reimer assumed a male identity, taking the first name David. By age twenty-one, Reimer had received testosterone therapy and surgeries to remove his breasts and reconstruct a penis. He married Jane Fontaine, a single mother of three, on September 22, 1990.

In adulthood, Reimer reported that he suffered psychological trauma due to Money's experiments, which Money had used to justify sex reassignment surgery for children with intersex or damaged genitals since the 1970s. In the mid-1990s, Reimer met Milton Diamond, a psychologist at the University of Hawaii, in Honolulu, Hawaii, and academic rival of Money. Reimer participated in a follow-up study conducted by Diamond, in which Diamond cataloged the failures of Reimer's transition.

In 1997, Reimer began speaking publicly about his experiences, beginning with his participation in Diamond's study. Reimer's first interview appeared in the December 1997 issue of *Rolling Stone* magazine. In interviews and a later book about his experience, Reimer described his interactions with Money as torturous and abusive. Accordingly, Reimer claimed he developed a lifelong distrust of hospitals and medical professionals.

With those reports, Reimer caused a multifaceted controversy over Money's methods, honesty in data reporting, and the general ethics of sex reassignment surgeries on infants and children. Reimer's description of his childhood conflicted with the scientific consensus about sex reassignment at the time. According to NOVA, Money led scientists to believe that the John/Joan case demonstrated an unreservedly successful sex transition. Reimer's parents later blamed Money's methods and alleged surreptitiousness for the psychological illnesses of their sons, although the notes of a former graduate student in Money's lab indicated that Reimer's parents dishonestly represented the transition's success to Money and his coworkers. Reimer was further alleged by supporters of Money to have incorrectly recalled the details of his treatment. In Reimer's case, Money publicly dismissed his criticism as antifeminist and anti-trans bias but, according to his colleagues, was personally ashamed of the failure.

In his early twenties, Reimer attempted to commit suicide twice. According to Reimer, his adult family life was strained by marital problems and employment difficulties. Reimer's brother, who suffered from depression and schizophrenia, died from an antidepressant drug overdose in July 2002. On May 2, 2004, Reimer's wife told him that she wanted a divorce. Two days later, at the age of thirty-eight, Reimer committed suicide by firearm.[22]

---

[22] Phil Gaetano, "David Reimer and John Money Gender Reassignment Controversy: The John/Joan Case," *The Embryo Project Encyclopedia* (November 2017), accessed August 29, 2023, https://embryo.asu.edu/pages/david-reimer-and-john-money-gender-reassignment-controversy-johnjoan-case#:~:text=In%20his%20academic%20work%2C%20Money,and%20recommended%20sexual%20reassignment%20surgery.

You may wonder why I am sharing this story with you. Because some use this story to reach improper conclusions. Alice Johnston asks,

> Why did David (David is the name chosen by Reimer after he transitioned back to a male) experience the psychological difficulties he did? Why do intersex babies who are surgically altered as infants often grow up to struggle with the results of that choice? It must be because a person's sense of gender isn't driven by their genitals or socialization. Gender doesn't come from life circumstances, personal desire or choice. Instead, a person's sense of gender is natural, enduring, and interchangeable.[23]

Reimer's experience shows without a shadow of a doubt that gender is based on biological sex. It is based on how God created us and not on our feelings (more on this later), and gender does not change simply because one feels like it or has transitioned to the sex opposite to one's biology. John Money was interested in Reimer's case because he wanted to prove his theory, and he failed.

Alfred C. Kinsey and John Money—the research and beliefs of these men are at best questionable, if not disturbing and evil. This is where modern thinking on sexuality comes from, the entire industry, the entire gender ideology, all these clinics, hospitals, and gender education, the flags, the whole movement, which has become a civil rights movement in and of itself, is entirely based on a concept that was never proved.[24]

---

[23] Alicia Johnston, *The Bible and LGBTQ Adventists* (Affirmative Collective, 2022), 67.
[24] Baucham.

The reality is that the rise of the transgender movement was just a matter of time. In 2014, Katy Steinmetz, writing for *Time* magazine, wrote,

> Almost one year after the Supreme Court ruled that Americans were free to marry the person they loved, no matter their sex, another civil rights movement is poised to challenge long-held cultural norms and beliefs. Transgender people—those who identify with a gender other than the sex they were "assigned at birth," to use the preferred phrase among trans activists—are emerging from the margins to fight for an equal place in society.[25]

So much has changed since she wrote this article in 2014. At the time, she thought the transgender revolution was far from where it wanted to be; perhaps that is not the case anymore.

The Cause of Transgenderism

Everybody wants to know what causes a person to believe that they were born in the wrong sex. There are certainly many theories, and, for the sake of educating ourselves, we will review some of them. But the reality is, we simply don't know. But don't take my word for it.

> When all of the research and the different perspectives are taken into account, it seems that many scholars today are concluding that the specific causal mechanism of transgender experience are exceedingly complex, are probably multidi-

---

[25] Katy Steinmetz, "The Transgender Tipping Point," *Time* (May 2014), accessed September 19, 2023, https://time.com/135480/transgender-tipping-point.

mensional, and, at this point in time, are simply something that we cannot be certain about.[26]

These are simply personal experiences and feelings a person has. They cannot be empirically verified. Thus, one must just take their word for it.

The DSM-5, which is the standard classification of mental disorders used by mental health professionals in the United States, estimates that between 0.005 percent and 0.014 percent of adult males and between 0.002 percent and 0.0003 percent of adult females experience gender dysphoria.[27] It is important to point out that it is gender dysphoria that leads a person to become transgender. In other words, transgender implies action, that is, a person struggling with gender dysphoria will decide to become a male or a female based on their beliefs and/or feelings about the gender in which they were born, or, to use the modern lingo, the sex assigned at birth. As you may imagine, the numbers change depending on whom you ask. For example, the Pew Research Center estimates that about 5 percent of young adults in the US say their gender is different from their sex.[28] This does not necessarily mean that they have transitioned. Reuters estimates that nearly 1.64 million people over the age of thirteen in the United States identify themselves as transgender, based on an analysis of newly expanded federal health surveys. The study estimates that about 0.5 percent of all US adults, some 1.3 million people, and about 1.4 percent, or 300,000, of youth aged between thirteen and seventeen identify as transgender, having a different gender identity than the sex they were assigned at birth.[29]

---

[26] Beilby and Rhodes, *Understanding Transgender Identities*, 33.
[27] Ibid., 19.
[28] Anna Brown, *About 5% of Young Adults in the US Say Their Gender Is Different from Their Sex Assigned at Birth* (June 2022), accessed August 29, 2023, https://www.pewresearch.org/short-reads/2022/06/07/about-5-of-young-adults-in-the-u-s-say-their-gender-is-different-from-their-sex-assigned-at-birth.
[29] Jonathan Allen, "New Study Estimates 1.6 Million in US. Identify as Transgender," *Reuters* (June 2022), accessed August 29, 2023, https://www.reuters.com/world/us/new-study-estimates-16-million-us-identify-transgender-2022-06-10.

It is easy to assume that these numbers will increase as being transgender becomes more popular (more on this later). As mentioned above, the issues surrounding the cause of gender dysphoria and transgenderism are complex. Mark Yarhouse asks, "Can any one theory really speak to the complex and diverse presentations in our culture today? No."[30] That being said, although some of this may be a bit technical, here are a few theories.

Brain-sex theory

This is the most popular theory. The idea here is that there are parts of our brains that are different in both males and females.

Since the brain is the organ determining or scripting male or female behaviors, the term "brain sex" is shorthand to reflect on how an individual thinks and organizes the world, whether in stereotypical male or female ways. It is certainly true that the brain is the most used sexual organ of the body and the term "brain sex" reflects its male or female disposition. It directs the individual to think and act more like a stereotypical male or more like a female.[31]

Proponents of this theory say that

> As sexual differentiation of the genitals takes place much earlier in the development (i.e., in the first two months of pregnancy) than sexual differentiation of the brain, which starts in the second half of pregnancy and becomes over upon reaching adulthood, these two processes may be influenced independently of each other. It is then possible that a discrepancy may exist between prenatal and genital differentiation and brain differentiation such that the external geni-

---

[30] Yarhouse, 65.
[31] Dean Kotula, "A Conversation with Dr. Milton Diamond" (2002), accessed August 29, 2023, http://hawaii.edu/PCSS/biblio/articles/2000to2004/2002-conversation-html.

tals develop for example as male while the brain develops as female.[32]

So if this is true, that then explains why a person may be born, say, with male genitalia but think he is a female because the brain, in regard to gender, developed later.

Psychological theory

Those who argue for psychological reasons for gender dysphoria and transgenderism say that it can develop in a child as a result of an overly enmeshed relationship with the parent of the opposite sex and/or a distant relationship with the parent of the same sex. In some cases, it may occur when a parent wishes that their baby boy had been a girl (or vice versa) or when a mother takes revenge on her son for being masculine. Others have proposed a link between gender dysphoria and childhood sexual abuse. Those subscribing to this theory advocate for a psychological approach to treatment as opposed to hormones and/or sex reassignment surgery (SRS). Unfortunately, those who hold to psychopathologies to explain gender dysphoria and transgenderism are often stigmatized and are thought of as transphobic.[33]

What is sex reassignment surgery (SRS), also known as gender-affirming surgery? Sex reassignment surgery refers to procedures that help people transition to their self-identified gender… Gender-affirming surgery gives transgender people a body that aligns with their gender. It may involve procedures on the face, chest, or genitalia. Common transgender surgery options include the following:

- Facial reconstructive surgery to make facial features more masculine or feminine

---

[32] Yarhouse, 67.
[33] James K. Beilby and Paul Rhodes Eddy, 23–25.

- Chest or "top" surgery to remove breast tissue for a more masculine appearance or enhance breast size and shape for a more feminine appearance
- Genital or "bottom" surgery to transform and reconstruct the genitalia

Not everyone who is transgender or nonbinary chooses to have surgery. Depending on your age and preferences, you may choose any of the following:

- Hormone therapy to increase masculine or feminine characteristics, such as your amount of body hair or vocal tone
- Puberty blockers to prevent you from going through puberty
- Voice therapy to adjust your voice or tone or help with communication skills, such as introducing yourself with your pronouns

Those who advocate for SRS cite research that shows that transgender individuals who choose gender-affirming surgery experience long-term mental health benefits. In one study, a person's odds of needing mental health treatment declined by 8% each year after the gender-affirming procedure.[34] Yet not everyone agrees that SRS should be the standard treatment for gender dysphoria. For example, Dr. Paul McHugh says,

> For forty years as the University Distinguished Service Professor of Psychiatry at Johns Hopkins Medical School—twenty-six of which were also spent as Psychiatrist in Chief of Johns Hopkins Hospital—I've been studying

---

[34] "Gender Affirmation (Confirmation) or Sex Reassignment Surgery," *Cleveland Clinic*, accessed September 6, 2023, https://my.clevelandclinic.org/health/treatments/21526-gender-affirmation-confirmation-or-sex-reassignment-surgery#:~:text=What%20are%20the%20benefits%20of,after%20the%20gender%2Daffirming%20procedure.

people who claim to be transgender. Over that time, I've watched the phenomenon change and expand in remarkable ways... The idea that one's sex is a feeling, not a fact, has permeated our culture and is leaving casualties in its wake. *Gender dysphoria should be treated with psychotherapy, not surgery.*[35] (emphasis supplied)

Dr. Ryan T. Anderson says it this way:

> The medical evidence suggests that sex reassignment does not adequately address the psychosocial difficulties faced by people who identify as transgender. Even when the procedures are successful technically and cosmetically, and even in cultures that are relatively "trans-friendly," transitioners still face poor outcomes.[36]

It is not popular to say things like this in our culture today. Some are targeted as bigots and transphobes. Dr. Anderson's book *When Harry Became Sally: Responding to the Transgender Moment* was removed from Amazon simply because he suggested that there are medical reasons for gender dysphoria and transgenderism. We are living in a very interesting time!

---

[35] Paul McHugh, "Transgenderism: A Pathogenic Meme," *Public Discourse: The Journal of the Witherspoon Institute* (June 2015), accessed September 6, 2023, https://www.thepublicdiscourse.com/2015/06/15145.

[36] Ryan T. Anderson, Ph.D., "Sex Reassignment Doesn't Work. Here Is the Evidence," *The Heritage Foundation* (May 2018), accessed September 6, 2023, https://www.heritage.org/gender/commentary/sex-reassignment-doesnt-work-here-the-evidence.

Blanchard's theory

Ray M. Blanchard is an American-Canadian sexologist, best known for his research studies on pedophilia, sexual orientation, and gender identity.

Blanchard proposed a two-part typology of male-to-female transsexuals based on sexual orientation. The first type, referred to as "androphilic" (or homosexual) transsexuals, includes all transsexual men who experience androphilia—i.e., a sexual attraction toward men. According to the typology, this group of transsexuals is a subgroup of gay men who typically come out as transsexual quite early in life and who are primarily motivated toward transitioning by their attraction to the idea of heterosexual men being attracted to them as a woman. The second type, termed "autogynephilic," is composed of heterosexual men who commonly come out later in life and whose primary motivation toward transitioning is that they are sexually aroused by the image of themselves as a woman. In his view, autogynephilia is a type of paraphilia (i.e., an unusual pattern of sexual arousal involving atypical behaviors, objects of desire, etc.). According to typology, there are additional differences between these two groups. Specifically, the claim is that, compared to the androphilic/homosexual type, autogynephilic transsexuals are less feminine as children, are likelier to have a history of engaging in erotic cross-dressing, have a more difficult time passing as women, and have a greater likelihood of postoperative dissatisfaction or regret.[37]

Blanchard's theory has been criticized by the LGBTQ+ community.

> Common criticisms include (1) it does not fit the actual reported experiences of many transsexuals; (2) it's binary typologies to restrictive; (3) it confuses gender identity with sexual orientation; (it does not account for the sexual experiences of female to male transsexuals; (5)

---

[37] James K. Beilby and Paul Rhodes Eddy, 32–33.

> it is scientifically unfalsifiable; (6) it is socially and politically damaging in that *it pathologizes much of the transgender community;* and (7) the language used is often insensitive and arrogant.[38] (emphasis supplied)

For the sake of clarity, "gender identity" is defined as how you experience yourself (or think of yourself) as male or female, including how masculine or feminine a person feels. "Sexual orientation" is defined as an inherent or immutable enduring emotional, romantic, or sexual attraction to other people.[39] So an individual's sexual orientation is independent of their gender identity. Notice from the above criticisms to Blanchard's theory, the LGBTQ+ community, for the most part, is not interested in finding a reason for their feelings and/or struggles, that is, finding a pathology, because in their minds what they are experiencing is natural and, for those who believe in God, it is God ordained.

We could spend a lot more time on theories of causation, but it really would not get us anywhere because even the so-called experts tell us this:

> When all the research and the differing perspectives are taken into account, it seems that many scholars today are concluding that the specific causal mechanisms of transgender experience are exceedingly complex, are probably multidimensional, and, at this point in time, are simply *something that we cannot be certain about.*[40] (emphasis supplied)

---

[38] Ibid, 33.
[39] "Sexual Orientation and Gender Identity Definitions," *The Human Rights Campaign*, accessed September 6, 2023, https://www.hrc.org/resources/sexual-orientation-and-gender-identity-terminology-and-definitions.
[40] James K. Beilby and Paul Rhodes Eddy, 33.

How Did We Get Here?

While it could be argued that people struggling with sexual identity issues is not a new thing, the reality is that, at the very least, the transgender ideology is at the forefront in the mainstream media, social media, and politics. "We look out on the horizon around this and realize that our culture has been radically changed. In this case, the storm is a vast moral revolution, and that revolution is not even close to its conclusion."[41] So how did we get here? And why? Over the years, I have noticed that Satan uses an interesting strategy to arrive at his goal. I call it "baby steps." I am reminded of God's first command to His new creation, "And the Lord God commanded the man, saying, "Of every tree of the garden you may freely eat; but of the tree of the knowledge of good and evil you shall not eat, for in the day that you eat of it you shall surely die" (Genesis 2:16–17). Chapter 3 quickly jumps to the conversation between Eve and the Serpent, so by that time, she was by the tree. However, in my experience, that is not how sin works. We just do not wake up one day and say, "You know, I am going to rob a bank today," or "I am going to have an affair today." Sin starts in the mind. We start to think about it, walking closer and closer to the proverbial line.

So I imagine Eve getting up one day and, from afar looking at the tree, thinking, "Hmm, I wonder why God told us not to eat of the tree. It looks okay from here." A few days later, she walks a bit closer to the tree and comments to Adam, "Say, honey, the fruit in that tree looks very good. There doesn't seem to be anything wrong with it. Are you sure God told us not to eat from it?" As the days went by, she walked closer and closer to the tree until "Now the serpent was more cunning than any beast of the field which the Lord God had made. And he said to the woman, 'Has God indeed said, "You shall not eat of every tree of the garden"'" (Genesis 3:1)? And the rest is history!

---

[41] R. Albert Mohler Jr., *We Cannot Be Silent: Speaking Truth to a Culture Redefining Sex, Marriage, and the Very Meaning of Right and Wrong* (Nashville, TN: Nelson Books, 2015), xiii.

THE PRESENT TRUTH AND THE LGBTQ+ MOVEMENT

How did we get here? Baby steps! Little changes, barely unnoticeable until wham! LGBTQ+ ideology is accepted and affirmed; and those who disagree are labeled as bigots, homophobes, intolerants, harmful, or at least, uninformed and antiquated.

Every Christian church—and every Christian—will face huge decisions in the wake of this moral storm. When marriage is redefined, an entire universe of laws, customs, rules, and expectations changes as well. Words such as *husband* and *wife*, *mother* and *father*, at one time the common vocabulary in every society, are now battlegrounds of moral conflict… Some argue that Christians need to revise our sexual morality and the definition of marriage to avoid costly and controversial confrontations with the culture at large.[42]

Friend, "I don't think we are in Kansas anymore!" A historic decision was reached by the US Supreme Court on June 26, 2015:

> In a long-sought victory for the gay rights movement, the Supreme Court ruled by a 5-to-4 vote on Friday that the Constitution guarantees a right to same-sex marriage. "No longer may this liberty be denied," Justice Anthony M. Kennedy wrote for the majority in the historic decision. "No union is more profound than marriage, for it embodies the highest ideals of love, fidelity, devotion, sacrifice and family. In forming a marital union, two people become something greater than once they were." Marriage is a "keystone of our social order," Justice Kennedy said, adding that the plaintiffs in the case were seeking "equal dignity in the eyes of the law." The decision, which was the culmination of decades of litigation and activism, set off jubilation and tearful embraces across the country, the first same-sex marriages in several states, and resistance—or at least stalling—in others. It came against the

---

[42] Ibid., xiv.

backdrop of fast-moving changes in public opinion, with polls indicating that *most Americans now approve of the unions.*[43] (emphasis supplied)

Over the last fifty years, American Christians have watched as our society has fashioned a brave new order for itself. Feminism and the sexual revolution have transformed the American home. Many men have lost any sense of responsibility for their family. They're tuned out, passive, and self-focused. Many women feel great tension between their career and home. They are told by secular lifestyle magazines to pursue the perfect "work-life" balance, but it's hard to find. Increasingly, the sexes are in competition. These troubling developments represent phase 1 of the transformation of men and women.

Phase 2 is the spread of the homosexual movement. Led by celebrities in the 1980s, the homosexual movement gained momentum from the feminist push and the sexual revolution. It sought to mainstream homosexual behavior. Men and women, it assumed, were not different in any meaningful way. The moral constraints of the biblical worldview had already been cast off. Romantic love was not subject to any shape or design. It was just a feeling. As such, it had no duties, no covenantal dimensions, and no enduring commitment. If it persists, great. If the feeling of love dies out, then the relationship dies with it.

In phase 1, gender roles were recast. In phase 2, romantic love was recast. In phase 3, the body itself is recast. "Transgender" ideology is grounded in the idea that the body isn't an essential part of our being (a view known as essentialism). Our "gender identity" is fluid, a social construct that can change. We may well be a man trapped in a woman's body, for example, our identity does not match our body.

---

[43] Adam Liptak, "Supreme Court Ruling Makes Same-Sex Marriage a Right Nationwide," *The New York Times* (June 2015), accessed September 7, 2023, https://www.nytimes.com/2015/06/27/us/supreme-court-same-sex-marriage.html.

In such instances, many transgender people opt for reconstructive surgery, so their identity fits with their body.[44]

As we can see, everything we hold dear today is being redefined. Many would see this as societal progress, but as mentioned before, as Christians seeing the world through a biblical lens, we know that morality will not improve as the world moves toward the Second Coming of Jesus, but it will worsen. Today, we are all witnesses to this reality. In his book *We Cannot Be Silent*, R. Albert Mohler Jr. exposes some of the steps taken by society that have gotten us to this place.

We're facing a complete transformation of the way human beings relate to one another in the most intimate context of life. We are facing nothing less than a comprehensive redefinition of life, love, liberty, and the very meaning of right and wrong. This massive revolution is taking place across the entire cultural landscape, affecting virtually every dimension of life and demanding total acceptance of its claims and affirmation of its aims.[45]

The truth is that we are amid both a sexual revolution (nothing new) and secularization.

> Secularization is not about rejecting all religion. In fact, even hyper-secularized Americans often consider themselves to be religious or spiritual... The implications of this worldview shift are massive... It is surely the case in large stretches of the advanced West today, many sophisticated people do not believe that the churches have any authority whatsoever to dictate constraints on individual freedom.[46]

---

[44] Dr. Owen Strachan, "Transgender Identity: Wishing Away God's Design," *Answers Magazine*, July 2016, 3–4.
[45] Mohler, 1–2.
[46] Ibid., 5.

How did we get here? Baby steps!

> The idea of a sexual revolution can be traced back to the nineteenth century when intellectuals in Europe began to push against the inherited sexual morality that had come into western civilization through the Christian tradition. Fueled with a desire to redefine love and sex for a new age, these individuals argue that Christian sexual morality was inherently repressive, and that true liberty could only come to human beings if the sexual morality derived from the Bible was overthrown and subverted… By the middle of the 1970s, most of the legal groundwork for the sexual revolution had been accomplished in the United States. Virtually all that remained was the normalization of homosexuality. The Supreme Court struck down all criminal laws prohibiting consensual same sex behavior in the 2003 case *Lawrence v. Texas*. Then in 2013, it struck down the federal government's definition of marriage as exclusively the union of a man and a woman in *United Stares v. Windsor*. Thus, by the year 2013, very little remained of the correspondence between American law and the moral convictions that had shaped the society just a century before.[47]

In her book *The Corrosive Impact of Transgender Ideology*, author Joanna Williams says,

> Beliefs about sex and gender have changed over time. Throughout most of human history there has been no concept of gender: it was

---
[47] Ibid., 9, 12.

assumed that sex determined everything about a person. Men, considered physically strong, intelligent and stoical, were best suited to manual work or roles in the public sphere; women, meanwhile, were apparently physically weaker but more caring and nurturing, best suited to domestic roles. These perceived differences shaped legal rights and social expectations. From the late eighteenth century onwards, thinkers such as Mary Wollstonecraft began to question whether women were naturally inferior to men or whether society, most notably through differences in upbringing and education, made males and females intellectually, emotionally and even physically different from one another. This view was developed by Simone De Beauvoir who wrote in The Second Sex (1949) that, "One is not born, but rather becomes, a woman." De Beauvoir's argument was not that people were born sex-less but that the meaning given to sex, in particular to being female, is created within a particular social context. People are born male or female but the values and qualities attached to being a man or a woman are determined by the dominant culture of an era.[48]

And here we are in the last quarter of the year 2023 when LGBTQ+ ideology is seen as normal and deserving of legal protection. Now let me qualify this statement. While I do not agree with same-sex marriage (although my opinion on this does not matter, what matters is what scripture teaches), there is something to be said about same-sex couples who have lived together for many years and have cared for one another as a husband (male) and wife (female)

---

[48] Joanna Willims, *The Corrosive Impact of Transgender Ideology* (London: Civitas, 2020), 3.

would have done. There are issues involving life insurance benefits, taxes, rights to property, or privacy in which a doctor can advise about medical issues and decisions, etc. These issues should be taken into consideration when it comes to persons of the same sex living as husband and wife. In my opinion, these are political matters that should be handled as such by those whom we have voted into office, and it is beyond the scope of this book. I am sure there are ways the issues mentioned above could be handled without necessarily making same-sex marriage legal. But we are beyond that now.

Some may ask, why are we making such a big deal about this? People's lifestyle choices are their business and nobody else's. I fully agree with that. However, the problem is that it is not just affecting the adults who are making those choices. These issues are also affecting our children.

By the 1990s, the most respected mainstream academic institutions in America featured academic departments that were devoted entirely to the study and promotion of the strangest and most exotic theories of human sexuality—and often their practice as well. Many of these academics and intellectuals argued that all morality was merely socially constructed and was generally put in place by repressive authorities in order to preserve their power. Thus, the impulse toward liberation that was recognized as driving the dynamic toward democracy in much of the world was extended to morality with the explicit argument that those who were identified as "sexual minorities" must be liberated as part of the project of democracy and liberty. And of course, *these new ideologies ultimately trickled down into high schools and even into grade schools. By the time the average American child graduates from a public school in the United States, he has been bombarded with the propaganda of the moral revolutionaries.* In many school systems and districts, parents do not even have an "opt-out" provision to remove their children from these sex education programs[49] (emphasis supplied).

---

[49] Mohler, 13.

Transgender Ideology and Children

As we have already said, today "experts" in psychology and medicine have redefined the concept of gender dysphoria.

Despite increased attention to transgender people, the first two editions of DSM contained no mention of gender identity. It was not until 1980 with the publication of DSM-3 that the diagnosis "transsexualism" first appeared. In 1990, the World Health Organization followed suit and included this diagnosis in ICD-10. With the release of DSM-4 in 1994, "transsexualism" was replaced with "gender identity disorder in adults and adolescents" in an effort to reduce stigma. However, controversy continued with advocates, and some psychiatrists pointing to ways in which this diagnostic category pathologized identity rather than a true disorder. With the publication of DSM-5 in 2013, "gender identity disorder" was eliminated and replaced with "gender dysphoria." This change further focused the diagnosis on the gender identity–related distress that some transgender people experience (and for which they may seek psychiatric, medical, and surgical treatments) rather than on transgender individuals or identities themselves.[50]

Obviously, children and adolescents suffer from gender dysphoria much like adults. I suppose this is to be expected considering we live in a fallen world; after all, sickness and disease also affect children. There is nothing inherently immoral about this. The problem comes when so-called professionals and, sadly, parents make lifelong decisions for children who cannot yet decide for themselves. It is kind of funny when most people acknowledge that children are too immature to make important decisions about life. This is why society does not allow children and early adolescents to drive a car, drink alcohol, vote, serve in the military, etc. This makes sense. After all,

---

[50] "Gender Dysphoria Diagnosis," *American Psychiatric Association*, accessed September 7, 2023, https://www.psychiatry.org/psychiatrists/diversity/education/transgender-and-gender-nonconforming-patients/gender-dysphoria-diagnosis#:~:text=With%20the%20publication%20of%20DSM%E2%80%935%20in%202013%2C%20%E2%80%9Cgender,%2C%20medical%2C%20and%20surgical%20treatments.

"the brain finishes developing and maturing in the mid-to-late 20s. The part of the brain behind the forehead, called the prefrontal cortex, is one of the last parts to mature."[51] However, in today's society, there is an exception to this, that is, a child is too immature to make lifelong decisions, with the exception of which sex they feel like.

> The great majority of young children develop a self-perceived gender identity consonant with their gender assigned at birth, but some, from the age of 3 or 4 years, develop a self-perceived gender identity which is other than that assigned at birth. This sense of another gender identity can be accompanied by a feeling of discomfort or gender dysphoria.[52]

So there it is, young children struggle with gender dysphoria. Could there be a reason for this? One possible culprit is our misconceptions of gender roles.

Unhelpful stereotypes exist around gender that can confuse individuals if they do not fit that stereotype. Being a man, for example, does not entail an automatic love of football, and being a woman does not demand an automatic love for cooking. When society attaches stereotypes to gender and sex, it can easily send the signal that anyone who fails to conform to those stereotypes is somehow failing to epitomize manhood or womanhood. Consider a five-year-old boy who prefers playing with dolls. With a hyper-masculine view, a parent could think that their son is displaying feminine qualities and wonder whether their child is transgender. (Some parents would

---

[51] "The Teen Brain: 7 Things to Know," *National Institute of Mental Health*, accessed September 7, 2023, https://www.nimh.nih.gov/health/publications/the-teen-brain-7-things-to-know#:~:text=Although%20the%20brain%20stops%20growing,the%20last%20parts%20to%20mature.

[52] Phillip Graham, "Transgender Children and Young People: How the Evidence Can Point the Way Forward," *National Library of Medicine*, (April 2023), accessed September 7, 2023, https://www.ncbi.nlm.nih.gov/pmc/articles/PMC10063975.

be fearful about this; others would be very quick to affirm it. But both are adopting a societal basis for their view of what is a "man" or a "woman.") Or consider a seven-year-old girl who would rather play football than watch Disney Princess movies. With a hyper-feminine view, a parent could view their daughter as displaying masculine qualities and may begin to wonder whether their daughter is transgender.[53]

In my research, I have found that proponents of LGBTQ+ ideology are critics of gender roles, yet, at least unconsciously, it is this understanding of gender roles that is causing so many children to enter into the transgender path, and unfortunately, this path does not always end with peaches and cream, as it were. Last year, the *Associated Press* published an article titled "Trans Kids' Treatment Can Start Younger, New Guidelines Say," where it said,

> The World Professional Association for Transgender Health said hormones could be started at age 14, two years earlier than the group's previous advice, and some surgeries done at age 15 or 17, a year or so earlier than previous guidance. *The group acknowledged potential risks but said it is unethical and harmful to withhold early treatment.*[54] (emphasis supplied)

Earlier, I cited a phrase I remembered that explains part of the challenge in our society when it comes to what we hear from the media. "The problem with the media is not what they tell you but what they don't." The media and LGBTQ+ authors and activists only want to talk about what they consider success stories, but they do

---

[53] Andrew T. Walker, *God and the Transgender Debate: What Does the Bible Actually Say About Gender Identity?* (Turkey: The Good Book Company, 2022), 62.
[54] Lindsey Tanner, "Trans Kids' Treatment Can Start Younger, New Guidelines Say," *Associated Press* (June 2022), accessed September 7, 2023, https://apnews.com/article/gender-transition-treatment-guidelines-9dbe54f670a3a0f5f2831c2bf14f9bbb.

not tell you the whole story. Does this remind you of anyone when it comes to "The Great Controversy"?

Chloe Cole is an American activist who opposes gender-affirming care for minors and supports bans on such care following her own detransition. I would like to share with you the transcript of her testimony before Congress.

> My name is Chloe Cole and I am a de-transitioner. Another way to put that would be: I used to believe that I was born in the wrong body and the adults in my life, whom I trusted, affirmed my belief, and this caused me lifelong, irreversible harm. I speak to you today as a victim of one of the biggest medical scandals in the history of the United States of America. I speak to you in the hope that you will have the courage to bring the scandal to an end, and ensure that other vulnerable teenagers, children and young adults don't go through what I went through. At the age of 12, I began to experience what my medical team would later diagnose as gender dysphoria. I was well into an early puberty, and I was very uncomfortable with the changes that were happening to my body. I was intimidated by male attention. And when I told my parents that I felt like a boy, in retrospect, all I meant was that I hated puberty, that I wanted this newfound sexual tension to go away.
>
> I looked up to my brothers a little bit more than I did to my sisters. I came out as transgender in a letter I sent on the dining room table. My parents were immediately concerned. They felt like they needed to get outside help from medical professionals. But this proved to be a mistake. It immediately set our entire family down a path of ideologically motivated deceit and coercion. The

general specialist I was taken to see told my parents that I needed to be put on puberty-blocking drugs right away. They asked my parents a simple question: Would you rather have a dead daughter or a living transgender son? The choice was enough for my parents to let their guard down, and in retrospect, I can't blame them. This is the moment that we all became victims of so-called gender-affirming care. I was fast-tracked onto puberty blockers and then testosterone. The resulting menopausal-like hot flashes made focusing on school impossible. I still get joint pains and weird pops in my back. But they were far worse when I was on the blockers.

A month later, when I was 13, I had my first testosterone injection. It has caused permanent changes in my body: My voice will forever be deeper, my jawline sharper, my nose longer, my bone structure permanently masculinized, my Adam's apple more prominent, my fertility unknown. I look in the mirror sometimes, and I feel like a monster. I had a double mastectomy at 15. They tested my amputated breasts for cancer. That was cancer-free, of course; I was perfectly healthy. There is nothing wrong with my still-developing body, or my breasts other than that, as an insecure teenage girl, I felt awkward about it. After my breasts were taken away from me, the tissue was incinerated—before I was able to legally drive.

I had a huge part of my future womanhood taken from me. I will never be able to breastfeed. I struggle to look at myself in the mirror at times. I still struggle to this day with sexual dysfunction. And I have massive scars across my chest and the skin grafts that they used, that they took of my nipples, are weeping fluid today, and they're grafted into a more masculine positioning, they said. After surgery, my grades in school plummeted. Everything that I went through did nothing to address the underlying mental health issues that I had. And my doctors with their theories on gender that all my problems would go away as soon as I was surgically transformed into something that vaguely resembled a boy—their theories were wrong. The drugs and surgeries changed my body, but they did not and could not change the basic reality that I am, and forever will be, a female.

When my specialists first told my parents they could have a dead daughter or a live transgender son, I wasn't suicidal. I was a happy child who struggled because she was different. However, at 16, after my surgery, I did become suicidal. I'm doing better now, but my parents almost got the dead daughter promised to them by my doctors. My doctor had almost created the very nightmare they said they were trying to avoid.

So, what message do I want to bring to American teenagers and their families? I didn't need to be lied to. I needed compassion. I needed to be loved. I needed to be given therapy that helped me work through my issues, not affirming my delusion that by transforming into a boy, it would solve all my problems. We need to stop telling 12-year-olds that they were born wrong, that they are right to reject their own bodies and feel uncomfortable with their own skin. We need to stop telling children that puberty is an option, that they can choose what kind of puberty they will go through, just like they can choose what clothes to wear or what music to listen to.

Puberty is a rite of passage to adulthood, not a disease to be mitigated. Today, I should be at home

> with my family celebrating my 19th birthday. Instead, I'm making a desperate plea to my elected representatives. Learn the lessons from other medical scandals, like the opioid crisis. Recognize that doctors are human, too, and sometimes they are wrong. My childhood was ruined along with thousands of de-transitioners that I know through our networks. This needs to stop. You alone can stop it. Enough children have already been victimized by this barbaric pseudoscience.[55]

There are clearly psychological reasons for gender confusion. Another example is Dr. Linda Seiler, author of the book *Transformation: A Former Transgender Responds to LGBTQ*. Seiler gives her testimony on a YouTube video titled: *How Jesus Redeemed My Gender Confusion*. In it, she breaks down what she thinks is the source of her gender confusion. Part of the problem is her view of gender roles. She says,

> My parents thought I was just a tomboy, a lot of girls like to grow up and climb trees and not play with barbies and makeup and all of that stuff, which was true of my sister, she wanted to be inside with makeup and Barbies and all that. Nancy's three years older than I am and she was just a normal little girl, but me, I wanted to be outside playing with the boys. Nancy would be imitating mom, putting makeup on and playing with dolls, and I'm outside pretending to mow the lawn like dad or in the mirror pretending to shave. I just desperately wanted to be in that world of man, and I rejected my own mother,

---

[55] Chloe Cole, "Detransitioner Chloe Cole's Full Testimony to Congress Is a 'Final Warning' to Stop Gender Surgery," *The New York Post* (July 2023), accessed September 7, 2023, https://nypost.com/2023/07/28/detransitioner-chloe-coles-full-testimony-to-congress-is-a-final-warning-to-stop-gender-surgery.

despite her best efforts to mother me. She loves me and she did her best, but I rejected her growing up. I looked at her and I thought, "You know what you're emotional, you're weak, you're not strong like dad," and I just thought, "I want nothing to do with the world of woman," and so I rejected her love. I didn't know, *but that left a vacuum in my heart for female love feminine love* that I didn't receive it the way God designed it through my natural mother, so that vacuum in my heart wanted to be filled because God designs it to be filled. We all need a mommy, we all need a daddy, we need that same sex parent to invite us into the world of the sex that God made us and so I needed a mom that would invite me into the world of women so I could be a woman among women, but I also needed a father who would affirm me as distinct from yet cherished by men. We all need that.[56] (emphasis supplied)

In her book, she explains,

> I reacted to painful experiences in my past by becoming jealous of men and viewing women as second-class citizens. In my mind, males were superior to females. As a result, I longed to identify as male and despised my female body. Additionally, because I rejected my own mother (despite her best attempts to nurture me), the emotional deficit in my heart for motherly nurture became sexualized and aimed at females when I hit puberty. My desire to bond sexually with other women was

---

[56] Linda A. Seiler, Ph.D., "How Jesus Redeemed My Gender Confusion," September 18, 2013, 3:16, accessed September 23, 2023 https://www.youtube.com/watch?v=W4WxPhWdU60&t=196s.

a subconscious attempt to complete the formative step of connecting meaningfully with my own gender. I skipped that step during my formative years, so my sexuality became confused.[57]

Jackie Hill Perry, author of the book *Gay Girl, Good God*, shares a similar story in which she explains why she was attracted to females:

> When I was born to a single mother, my mother loved me, my daddy loved me…sometimes. He loved me when he felt like he loved me, when he went down to the altar and got halfway saved and would be present, and then would leave again. *So I grew up having this view of men that told me that men were very inconsistent beings*, that they said things that they did not truly believe. *The first man to ever actually show me affection was through abuse, so I already have this messed up framework that now affection from men is a dangerous thing, something that's not safe, something that isn't built on love. But I also have this framework that women are a loving thing, that women are the present ones, the loyal ones, the loving ones…* Maybe by first grade… I recognized that I was same-sex attracted. It didn't have those words for it because, again, I'm five. But I knew I noticed that the same way in which other girls liked the little boys on the field was the same way that they liked the little girls on the field.[58] (emphasis supplied)

---

[57] Linda A. Seiler, Ph.D., *Transformation: A Former Transgender Responds to LGBTQ* (Grand Rapids, MI: Credo House Publishers, 2023), 47.

[58] Jackie Hill Perry, "Leaving Homosexuality and Finding Forgiveness," April 8, 2022, 3:23, accessed September 23, 2023, https://www.youtube.com/watch?v=8k9ajsiOaD4&t=203s.

I do realize that these are not the testimony of every child, adolescent, and adult who has decided to deal with their gender dysphoria or has been misdiagnosed with having gender dysphoria. However, they are telling testimonies that should make the powers that be think about what they are doing.

My daughter has given me permission to share her own testimony. In 2013, we enrolled her in one of the boarding Seventh-day Adventist Schools. She was fourteen years old. In hindsight, my wife and I should have realized that she was too young and immature to be on her own. But you live and learn. The first couple of months of the school year seemed to go well. She was doing well in her classes, had a job on campus, and was involved in extracurricular and church activities. Everything was going well until we got a very upsetting phone call from the school. As it turned out, my daughter had apparently been involved romantically with another female student. As you may imagine, this was heartbreaking for Mom and Dad, especially with Dad being a pastor.

We had a long conversation with our daughter and the school official, and we decided to disenroll our daughter from the school. Throughout this experience, we never chastised or belittled her, even though we have our biblical beliefs that do not support same-sex sexual relationships. Well, as is often the case, our daughter grew out of this experience and is fine today. In the process of writing this book, I interviewed her about her experience at the boarding school to determine what happened behind the scenes. She said to me,

> I was very lonely and depressed at the time, so going to a boarding school didn't help. I remember that I had a crush on a guy who rejected me. As it turns out, the girl in the room across the hallway (who turned out to be the one she had the same-sex experience with) had the same experience of rejection. She was also dealing with depression. So we had things in common, and we bonded, which led us to misinterpret our feelings. I thought, "This makes sense to me

because I was a 'tomboy.'" At the same time, I was going through puberty, so there were lots of changes."

She said that the feeling of rejection was a key issue in her experience.

Ten years have passed since that experience, but I wonder what would have happened if that took place today. I am thankful that she was in a Seventh-day Adventist Institution at the time (although these days, more and more Adventist teenagers and adolescents are coming out as gender dysphoric or transgender) and that school officials handled the issue properly, that is, calling Mom and Dad. Had this happened today or taken place in a secular school, the results may have been drastically different. Perhaps she would have been sent to the school psychologist who would have said she was a lesbian and would have encouraged the relationship. Considering my daughter labeled herself a "tomboy," they would have said she was a transgender and would have ordered hormone therapy and puberty blockers leading to SRS without calling us and without our permission. If we refused, they may have taken her away from us by social services. Is this a conspiracy theory? Not at all—it has already happened to some parents as far back as 2018.

On Friday, a judge from Hamilton County, Ohio, gave custody of a transgender teen to his grandparents rather than his parents, allowing them to make medical decisions regarding his transition. The parents didn't want the teen, a seventeen-year-old who identified as male, to undergo hormone treatment and refused to call him by his chosen name, triggering suicidal feelings, according to court testimony. The parents wanted custody in order to make medical decisions for the teen and prohibit the treatment that his medical team had recommended.[59]

---

[59] Jen Christensen, "Judge Gives Grandparents Custody of Ohio Transgender Teen," *CNN Health* (February 2018), accessed September 7, 2023, https://www.cnn.com/2018/02/16/health/ohio-transgender-teen-hearing-judge-decision/index.html.

More recently, a bill was proposed in California that should be concerning to every parent.

The California Assembly Judiciary Committee advanced a bill Tuesday aimed at protecting LGBTQ+ youth that encourages parents to affirm their child's gender identity. Assembly Bill 957, also known as the TGI (Transgender, Gender-Diverse, and Intersex) Youth Empowerment Act, was created by Assemblywoman Lori D. Wilson (D-Suisun City). The initial legislation said courts deciding custody cases must consider whether each parent affirmed the child's gender. AB 957 encourages parents who support their TGI children by "making it clear that affirming a child's gender identity is part of the health, safety, and welfare of the child." *It also allows courts to consider a parent's affirmation of their child's gender identity when making decisions about visitation and custody.*

"If you have a child going through that system, a judge has discretion, like they do looking at the totality of circumstances related to the health, safety and welfare of a child, to consider different factors," said Wilson, who's the mother of a trans child. "One of the factors, not the factor, but one of the factors, would be the parent's affirmation of a child's gender identity." The bill will also require courts to "strongly consider" that affirming a child's gender identity is "in the best interest of the child" when one parent doesn't consent to a child's legal name change to conform with the child's gender identity. *It would also classify parents in custody battles as abusive if*

> *they refuse to affirm their child's gender identity.*[60]
> (emphasis supplied)

Commenting in the same bill, Emily Valadez writes,

> According to the state of California, for a parent to be deemed fit to provide for "the health, safety, and welfare" of a child, the parent must "be affirming of a child's gender identity... parents who choose not to recognize the gender their child wishes to go by could lose custody of their child to another parent or the state."[61]

These days, it seems, the "state" knows better and has more rights over children than their parents do. Of course, some will argue that the state should intervene in cases where the parent is abusive to the child, and I would agree with that. The issue here is that the state has now redefined *abuse* to include parents not agreeing with the desire of a child who does not yet possess the maturity to make life-altering decisions. Parents have the civil and God-given responsibility to make decisions for their children, and the state agrees with this, except for gender issues. This is hypocritical and dangerous, especially when, in many cases, the feelings about how children feel about their gender change over time.

The pro-transgender advocates do not want to know that studies show between 70 percent and 80 percent of children who express transgender feelings "spontaneously lose those feelings" over time.

---

[60] Sophie Flay, "CA Bill Aimed at Protecting LGBTQ+ Youth Encourages Parents to Affirm Their Child's Gender Identity," *ABC7 Eyewitness News* (June 2023), accessed September 12, 2023, https://abc7.com/california-proposed-bill-gender-affirming-children/13377700.

[61] Emily Valadez, "Legislated Evil California's Shocking New Law: If You Disagree with Your Child's Gender Identity, You Could Risk Losing Them," *Wealthy Living*, accessed September 12, 2023, https://www.msn.com/en-us/lifestyle/parenting/legislated-evil-california-s-shocking-new-law-if-you-disagree-wigh-your-child-s-gender-identity-you-could-risk-losing-them/ss-AA1gAtmh#image=1.

Also, of those who had sexual reassignment surgery, most said they were "satisfied" with the operation "but their subsequent psycho-social adjustments were no better than those who didn't have the surgery. And so at Hopkins, we stopped doing sex reassignment surgery, since producing 'satisfied' but still troubled patients seemed an inadequate reason for surgically amputating normal organs," said Dr. McHugh, former Johns Hopkins chief of Psychiatry.

He also warned against enabling or encouraging certain subgroups within the transgender community, such as young people "susceptible to suggestion from 'everything is normal' sex education," and schools' "diversity counselors" who, like cult leaders, may "encourage these young people to distance themselves from their families and offer advice on rebutting arguments against having transgender surgery." Dr. McHugh also reported that there were "misguided doctors" who, working with the very young children who seemed to imitate the opposite sex, would administer "puberty-delaying hormones to render later sex-change surgeries less onerous—even though the drugs stunt[ed] the children's growth and risk[ed] causing sterility." Such action comes "close to child abuse," said Dr. McHugh, given that close to 80 percent of those kids would "abandon their confusion and grow naturally into adult life if untreated."

> Sex change is biologically impossible... People who undergo sex reassignment surgery do not change from men to women or vice versa. Rather, they become feminized men or masculinized women. Claiming that this is a civil-rights matter and encouraging surgical intervention is in reality collaborating with and promoting a mental disorder.[62]

---

[62] Lisa Lineuieaver, "Johns Hopkins Psychiatrist: Transgender Is 'Mental Disorder;' Sex Change 'Biologically Impossible,'" *CNS NEWS*, accessed September 12, 2023, https://www.boarddocs.com/vsba/scpsva/Board.nsf/files/B8UR4X6C2467/$file/01-08-19%20Citizen%20Handouts%20(L.%20Lineweaver).pdf.

The Popularity Game

At the risk of aging myself, from childhood through adolescence, my friends were the neighborhood kids. Entertainment consisted of playing ball in the streets and hanging out with my friends at the corner store. As a teenager, I loved to go to school dances, which at the time in the Island of Puerto Rico we called "disco parties." I remember that I longed to be popular as a child and teenager, but I never measured up to my brother and some of the "cool kids." It is not unusual for a teenager to want to be accepted, to be part of the gang, as it were, or to want to be popular. But things have changed. Most children and teenagers today do not even leave their homes, they are glued to their phones and computers, and their lives consist of imaginary or long-distance relationships made through social media. Social media has a great influence on our children and teens. In fact, if we are honest with ourselves, it has an influence on all of us.

Today's adolescents spend far less time in person with friends—up to an hour less per day—than did members of Gen. X. And dear God, they are lonely. They report greater loneliness than any generation on record... To understand how some of the brightest, most capable young women of this era could fall victim to a transgender craze, we should begin by noting that adolescent girls today are in a lot of pain. In America, Britain, and Canada, teenagers are in the midst of what academic psychologist Jonathan Haidt has called a "mental health crisis"—evincing record levels of anxiety and depression.[63]

While the above citation only mentions girls, the same is true with boys; they just do not want to admit it.

In the book *Real Boys: Rescuing Our Sons from the Myths of Boyhood*, author William S. Pollock states,

> Parents and educators must not be fooled by
> a boy's mask. Teenage boys tend to ignore their

---

[63] Abigail Shrier, *Irreversible Damage: The Transgender Craze Seducing Our Daughters* (Washington, DC: Regnery Publishing, 2021), 3.

depression through distractions, such as playing games, getting together with friends, listening to music, or watching television. They are also less likely than girls to voice their concerns or emotions to friends and family. In fact, only 26% of boys in a study admitted to turning to friends for support…although society teaches boys to be stoic and toughened individuals, they aren't "lone rangers" and still need to be told they're good, that they make good friends, and that they're needed and loved. If a boy senses a lack of familial support or sympathy, or if events in his life feel beyond his control, the pain of depression might become unmanageable, leading to serious consequences for the teen's mental—and physical—well-being…[64]

And where do today's teenagers go for acceptance, belonging, and help with their loneliness and depression? You got it, the Internet, social media in particular. In her book *Irreversible Damage*, Abigail Shrier quotes Dr. Lisa Littman, who researched the reason there seemed to be a spike in the number of teenage girls coming out as transgender. She writes,

> In America and across the western world, adolescents were reporting a sudden spike in gender dysphoria—the medical condition associated with the social designation "transgender." Between 2016 and 2017 the number of gender surgeries for natal females in the U.S. quadrupled, with biological women suddenly accounting for—as we have seen—70% of all gender

---

[64] "Depression in Teenage Boys," *All Psychology Careers*, accessed September 7, 2023, https://www.allpsychologycareers.com/mental-health/teenage-depression-in-boys.

surgeries. In 2018, the UK reported a 4,400 percent rise over the previous decade in teenage girls seeking gender treatments. In Canada, Sweden, Finland, and the UK, clinicians and gender therapists began reporting a sudden and dramatic shift in the demographic of those presenting with gender dysphoria-from predominantly preschool age boys to predominantly adolescent girls.[65]

The interesting part of her research was the pattern that emerged.

First, the clear majority (65 percent) of the adolescent girls who had discovered transgender identity in adolescence—"out of the blue"—had done so after a period of *prolonged social media immersion.* Second, the prevalence of transgender identification within some of the girls' friend groups was more than seventy times the expected rate… The atypical nature of this dysphoria—occurring in adolescents with no childhood history of it—nudged Dr. Littman toward a hypothesis everyone else had overlooked: peer contagion. Doctor Littman gave this atypical expression of gender dysphoria a name: "rapid-onset gender dysphoria" ("ROGD").[66] (emphasis supplied)

Helena Kerschner—a twenty-three-year-old detransitioner from Cincinnati, Ohio, who was born a biological female—first felt gender dysphoric at age fourteen. She said that Tumblr sites filled with transgender activist content spurred her transition. "I was going through a period where I was just really isolated at school, so I turned to the Internet," she recalled. In her real life, Kerschner had a falling out with friends at school; online, however, she found a commu-

---

[65] Shrier, 26.
[66] Ibid., 26–27.

nity that welcomed her. "My dysphoria was definitely triggered by this online community. I never thought about my gender or had a problem with being a girl before going on Tumblr." She said she felt political pressure to transition, too. "The community was very social justice-y. There was a lot of negativity around being a cis, heterosexual, white girl, and I took those messages really, really personally."[67]

With the popularity of social media, the term "transgender influencer" has become mainstream. An influencer, as the word suggests, is "one who exerts influence: a person who inspires or guides the actions of others."[68] Thus, a "transgender influencer" is someone who inspires or guides others into becoming transgender. You only have to go into YouTube and type "Am I a transgender" or "How to become a transgender," and you will see a plethora of videos on recognizing the signs, hormone treatment, SRS, and even about how to talk to your parents about coming out and lying if necessary. Some of these influencers have become famous—who can forget the fiasco involving Dylan Mulvaney and the infamous beer commercial?

The influence of social media on our children and teens and a powerful reason parents should be involved in their children's lives. Many progressive parents may say that our children need their privacy and parents should not interfere, but considering what is out there and the times that we are living in, parents need to be alert. This is the way the apostle Paul said it,

> Put on the whole armor of God, that you may be able to stand against the wiles of the devil. For *we do not wrestle against flesh and blood, but against principalities, against powers, against the rulers of the darkness of this age, against spiritual hosts of wickedness in the heavenly places.*

---

[67] Rikki Schlott, "'I Literally Lost Organs:' Why Detransitioned Teens Regret Changing Genders," *New York Post* (June 2022), accessed September 11, 2023, https://nypost.com/2022/06/18/detransitioned-teens-explain-why-they-regret-changing-genders.

[68] "Influencer," *Merriam-Webster*, accessed September 7, 2023, https://www.merriam-webster.com/dictionary/influencer.

> Therefore take up the whole armor of God, that you may be able to withstand in the evil day, and having done all, to stand. (Ephesians 6:11–13, emphasis supplied)

Let me give you some examples of what our children can learn from these "influencers" on social media:

1. If you think you might be trans, you are.

    "Trans" is a state of mind… It is an important social identity, over and above (and even without) the psychological condition once thought to undergird it… The important thing is the social identity, not any diagnosis. Understood this way, trans is something you might want to become even if you aren't suffering from gender dysphoria. Then again, many influencers define "dysphoria" so broadly that nearly every teen would seem to have it… Having cast gender dysphoria aside, trans influencers describe symptoms that are vague and ubiquitous: *feeling different, not really fitting in, and not feeling feminine or masculine enough.*

2. If your parents loved you, they would support your trans identity.

    Jett Taylor is a well-known trans influencer. He said, "True love is unconditional love. Love without restrictions. For you not to accept someone as they truly are is you not truly loving them." There's nothing crueler and more toxic to trans girls than parents who failed to jump on board with each step of gender transition and every tenant on gender ideology.

3. If you're not supported in your trans identity, you'll probably kill yourself.

    Suicide rates among the transgender-identified are, indeed, alarmingly high. Nearly every trans influencer believes, therefore, that anything parents do to make their trans-identified adolescent's life harder is unforgivably cruel. There's no doubt that there's mental anguish in those suffering from gender dysphoria. But extending compassion is not

the same as giving in to demands, particularly to demands that a parent believes are not in the child's best interests.
4. Deceiving parents and doctors is justified if it helps with the transition.

Trans influencers typically take a by-any-means-necessary approach to procuring cross-sex hormones. Whatever you do, whatever you have to say—do it. Your life is on the line. "Find out what they want to hear…and then tell them just that."[69]

It's about educating us

"Hi, sweetie! What did you learn in school today?" This is a question many of us you to got from our parents "back in the day." "Oh, the usual, social studies was boring, but we learned about fractions in math, and I gave my book report in English class." While this is part of what kids are still learning today, a child may come home with a different view of who and what they are. This is especially true for children of Christian parents. During my research, I learned about the Genderbread Person. This is a tool created by transgender activists to teach children about sex and gender. A sample of this is below. (Photo: Sam Killerman/It's Pronounced Metrosexual).[70]

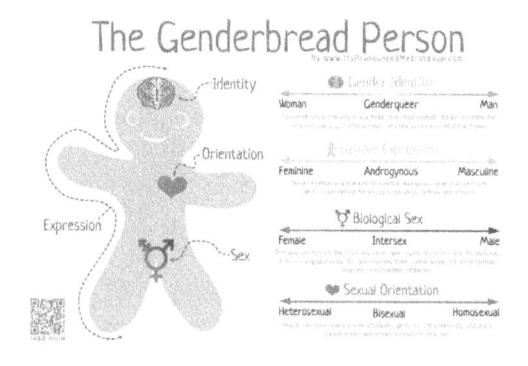

The Genderbread Person

---

[69] Shrier, 44–52.
[70] "The Genderbread Person," accessed September 11, 2023, https://www.itspronouncedmetrosexual.com/2018/10/the-genderbread-person-v4.

Today, transgender "allies" in good standing don't use the Genderbread Person in their classrooms but opt for the "Gender Unicorn,"⁷¹ which was created by the Trans Student Educational Resource. It has a body shape that doesn't appear either male or female; and instead of a "biological sex," it has a "sex assigned at birth."⁷² See below:

The Gender Unicorn — Graphic by TSER

- Gender Identity: Female/Woman/Girl, Male/Man/Boy, Other Gender(s)
- Gender Expression: Feminine, Masculine, Other
- Sex Assigned at Birth: Female, Male, Other/Intersex
- Physically Attracted to: Women, Men, Other Gender(s)
- Emotionally Attracted to: Women, Men, Other Gender(s)

To learn more, go to: www.transstudent.org/gender
Design by Landyn Pan and Anna Moore

In June 2019, the policy making arm of the California teachers association (CTA) met in Los Angeles at the Westin Bonaventure Hotel. On the agenda for the public school teacher's union's quarterly meeting or a number of routine items: the recent election of new officers, the union's continuing efforts to monitor new charter-school activity. And the delegates voted on New Business Item, #6/19–12, requiring "immediate action this was a proposal to allow trans identified minor students to leave campus

---

⁷¹ "Gender Unicorn," accessed September 11, 2023, https://transstudent.org/gender.

⁷² Ryan T. Anderson, Ph.D., "Transgender Ideology Is Riddled with Contradictions. Here Are the Big Ones," *The Heritage Foundation* (February 2018), accessed September 11, 2023, https://www.heritage.org/gender/commentary/transgender-ideology-riddled-contradictions-here-are-the-big-ones.

> during school hours to obtain gender hormone treatments *without parental permission.*"⁷³

I want to be careful here because I have several friends who are teachers; and, acknowledging my own limitations on teaching children, I know that teachers have a hard task, so my hat off for our nation's teachers. That being said, I am concerned about some of the resource's teachers are forced to use today when teaching about sex and gender. On the page "Educators 4SC," there is an article titled "Teaching about LGBTQ+ World History," which is introduced by saying,

> Despite the landmark Supreme Court decision in 2016 which legalized same-sex marriage in the United States, homophobia, transphobia, and other forms of LGBTQ+ discrimination are very much alive and well. LGBTQ+ students face challenges in school that their peers do not, and are often the victims of verbal and physical harassment. The National School Climate survey found that fifty-five percent of LGBTQ+ students report feeling unsafe at school because of their sexual orientation, while thirty-eight percent report feeling unsafe due to their gender identity or expression. Creating a safe school culture begins with affirming their history in the classroom, and this is why teaching LGBTQ+ history is so important.⁷⁴

---

[73] Shrier, 59.
[74] "Teaching about LGBTQ+ World History," *Educator 4SC*, accessed September 11, 2023, https://educators4sc.org/teaching-about-lgbtq-world-history/?hsa_grp=127120961752&hsa_ver=3&utm_campaign&hsa_cam=14471342605&hsa_net=adwords&hsa_kw=teaching%20lgbtq%20in%20schools&hsa_ad=542604723008&hsa_tgt=kwd-1145509453895&hsa_mt=b&hsa_acc=2755491261&hsa_src=g.

There is no question about the fact that we all must do what we can to make sure that all children are safe in our schools. There is absolutely no room for bullying or any kind of discrimination against anyone, and this includes those who are LGBTQ+. However, it is possible that the authorities and the powers that be are taking this to the extreme. Part of the lesson plans provided by the Educators 4SC site include "Teaching LGBTQ history," "LGBTQ+ foundation lesson plans," "Unheard voices," and "Stories of LGBTQ history." Additional resources include articles that will help teachers, such as "Teaching and Learning about Gay History and Issues" and "Incorporating LGBTQIA+ in History Lessons," among others. There are also books that could be incorporated into their teaching, such as *A Queer History of the United States, Sapphistries: A Global History of Love between Women,* and *We Are Everywhere: Protest, Power, and Pride in the History of Queer Liberation.*[75]

"Hi, sweetie! What did you learn in school today?" For those of us looking at the world through a biblical lens, it has changed a lot more than we were expecting and, unfortunately, not in a good way. Our children, and even adults today, are being bombarded with the LGBTQ+ ideology everywhere. This should not surprise us because Satan's strategy is to saturate us with sin so as to convince us that there isn't anything wrong with it. Satan is getting desperate. This is why Peter and John admonish us, saying, "Be sober, be vigilant; because your adversary the devil walks about like a roaring lion, seeking whom he may devour... Woe to the inhabitants of the earth and the sea! For the devil has come down to you, having great wrath, because he knows that he has a short time" (1 Peter 5:8, Revelation 12:12).

The psychology of it all

A woman walks into a therapist's office, dragging her teenage son. "Doctor," she says, "please help! My son thinks he's a chicken."

---

[75] Ibid.

The son says, "If there's one thing I can tell you about chickens, it's that we know who we are."

"Where is your proof?" the woman demands of her son. "You have no feathers."

"True," the son replies. "I went through the wrong puberty."

The woman turns to the therapist and says, "You see what I mean? He's lost his mind!"

The therapist replies, "You're the one arguing with the chicken."

It is a corny joke, I know. But this is, roughly, the scenario created by "affirmative care," the prevailing medical standard for the treatment of transgender patients. The standard asks—against much evidence and sometimes contrary to their beliefs on the matter—that mental health professionals "affirm" not only the patient self-diagnosis of this dysphoria but also the accuracy of the patient's perception. The therapist must agree, in other words, that a male patient with gender dysphoria who identifies as a woman *really is* a woman.[76]

For the sake of review, let us see how mental health professionals define issues of gender and how they are treated. This is straight from the American Psychiatric Association.

The term *transgender* refers to a person whose sex assigned at birth (i.e., the sex assigned at birth, usually based on external genitalia) does not align with their gender identity (i.e., one's psychological sense of their gender). Some people who are transgender will experience "gender dysphoria," which refers to psychological distress that results from an incongruence between one's sex assigned at birth and one's gender identity. Though gender dysphoria often begins in childhood, some people may not experience it until after puberty or much later.

The *Diagnostic and Statistical Manual of Mental Disorders, Fifth Edition, Text Revision* (DSM-5-TR) 1 provides for one overarching diagnosis of gender dysphoria with separate specific criteria for children and for adolescents and adults.

The DSM-5-TR defines "gender dysphoria" in adolescents and adults as a marked incongruence between one's experienced/expressed

---

[76] Shrier, 97.

gender and their assigned gender, lasting at least six months, as manifested by at least two of the following:

- A marked incongruence between one's experienced/expressed gender and primary and/or secondary sex characteristics (or in young adolescents, the anticipated secondary sex characteristics)
- A strong desire to be rid of one's primary and/or secondary sex characteristics because of a marked incongruence with one's experienced/expressed gender (or in young adolescents, a desire to prevent the development of the anticipated secondary sex characteristics)
- A strong desire for the primary and/or secondary sex characteristics of the other gender
- A strong desire to be of the other gender (or some alternative gender different from one's assigned gender)
- A strong desire to be treated as the other gender (or some alternative gender different from one's assigned gender)
- A strong conviction that one has the typical feelings and reactions of the other gender (or some alternative gender different from one's assigned gender)
- The DSM-5-TR defines "gender dysphoria" in children as a marked incongruence between one's experienced/expressed gender and assigned gender, lasting at least six months, as manifested by at least six of the following (one of which must be the first criterion):
- A strong desire to be of the other gender or an insistence that one is the other gender (or some alternative gender different from one's assigned gender)
- In boys (assigned gender), a strong preference for cross-dressing or simulating female attire; or in girls (assigned gender), a strong preference for wearing only typical masculine clothing and a strong resistance to the wearing of typical feminine clothing
- A strong preference for cross-gender roles in make-believe play or fantasy play

- A strong preference for the toys, games, or activities stereotypically used or engaged in by the other gender
- A strong preference for playmates of the other gender
- In boys (assigned gender), a strong rejection of typically masculine toys, games, and activities and a strong avoidance of rough-and-tumble play; or in girls (assigned gender), a strong rejection of typically feminine toys, games, and activities
- A strong dislike of one's sexual anatomy
- A strong desire for the physical sex characteristics that match one's experienced gender[77]

I want to point out in the above list of gender dysphoria as experienced by children that part of the problem may be, as already mentioned in this chapter, misunderstandings about gender roles. However, notice the recommended treatment below.

> Support for people with gender dysphoria may include open-ended exploration of their feelings and experiences of gender identity and expression, without the therapist having any pre-defined gender identity or expression outcome defined as preferable to another. *Psychological attempts to force a transgender person to be cisgender (sometimes referred to as gender identity conversion efforts or so-called "gender identity conversion therapy") are considered unethical* and have been linked to adverse mental health outcomes. Support may also include affirmation in various domains. Social affirmation may include an individual adopting pronouns, names, and various aspects of gender expression that

---

[77] "What Is Gender Dysphoria?" *American Psychiatric Association*, accessed September 11, 2023, https://www.psychiatry.org/patients-families/gender-dysphoria/what-is-gender-dysphoria.

> match their gender identity. Legal affirmation may involve changing name and gender markers on various forms of government identification. Medical affirmation may include pubertal suppression for adolescents with gender dysphoria and gender-affirming hormones like estrogen and testosterone for older adolescents and adults. Medical affirmation is not recommended for prepubertal children. Some adults (and less often adolescents) may undergo various aspects of surgical affirmation.[78] (emphasis supplied)

It could be that some mental health professionals have some qualms with the guidelines presented above. Yet, if they are to practice mental health medicine, they must adhere to them.

Psychologists are encouraged to adapt or modify their understanding of gender, broadening the range of variation viewed as healthy and normative. By understanding the spectrum of gender identities and gender expressions that exist and that a person's gender identity may not be in full alignment with the sex assigned at birth, psychologists can increase their capacity to assist transgender and gender-nonconforming patients, their families, and their communities.[79]

Abigail Shrier presents a humorous illustration to make the point about how ludicrous the above guidelines have become.

> Imagine we treated anorexics this way. Imagine a girl—5'6" tall, 95 pounds—approaches your therapist and says: "I know that I'm fat. Please call me 'fatty.'" Imagine the APA (American Psychological Association) encourages its doctors to "modify their understanding" of what constitutes "fat" to include this emaciated

---
[78] Ibid.
[79] "Guidelines for Psychological Practice with Transgender and Gender Nonconforming People," *American Psychological Association*, December 2015, 834–835.

girl. Imagine the APA encouraged therapists to respond to such patients, "If you feel fat, then you are. I support your lived experience. OK, fatty?"[80]

This is where we are today. I will say I have no qualms with adults making these life-changing adjustments to themselves, however misguided they may be. But children and teenagers do not know what they are doing. As a parent of two young adults, having graduated from the "teen parent" school of hard knocks, I can tell you that they often used their feelings to make decisions; and then two days later, those feelings, which were so powerful, now have changed. "Teenagers test boundaries. They press limits. They question authority."[81]

There is a lot more we could say in this chapter. Clearly, there are many complexities when it comes to LGBTQ+ ideology and how mental health professionals diagnose and treat them. I will also say that, as Christians, we should not put everyone under the same umbrella, which is why as a church we need to talk about this issue and not be afraid of talking to individuals who are struggling with gender dysphoria and sexual orientations issues or who have fully transitioned. That said, there are many inconsistencies, and we cannot simply sweep them under the rug. Furthermore, we cannot take the words of "scientists" and "medical professionals" on everything, because as we have seen in the last few years, they constantly change their minds. Thus, our textbook on these matters ought to be the infallible and unchangeable word of God.

Before ending this chapter, there is a challenge on the horizon that many have not thought about, and that undeniably will come around.

---

[80] Shrier, 99.
[81] Ibid., 108.

THE PRESENT TRUTH AND THE LGBTQ+ MOVEMENT

What's next?

As mentioned earlier in the chapter, sin does not just all of a sudden pop into our minds. We do not simply wake up one morning and say, "I am going to commit this sin or that one." When we commit a willful sinful act, we have slowly but surely placed ourselves in that position. The apostle James says it this way:

> Let no one say when he is tempted, "I am tempted by God"; for God cannot be tempted by evil, nor does He Himself tempt anyone. But each one is tempted when he is drawn away by his own desires and enticed. Then, when desire has conceived, it gives birth to sin; and sin, when it is full-grown, brings forth death. (James 1:13–15)

The transgender ideology and lifestyle that we are seeing today came as a result of missteps, phases, and compromises. One can argue that desire has conceived and has given birth to sin. But will other sinful ideologies and lifestyles be born? Is there a risk of this?

I realize there is going to be some serious disagreement on what I will share below, but is it something we ought to be thinking about, considering what we have learned in this chapter?

Pedophilia is viewed as among the most horrifying social ills. But scientists who study the sexual disorder say it is also among the most misunderstood. When most of the public thinks of pedophilia, they assume it's synonymous with child sexual abuse, a pervasive social problem that has exploded to crisis levels online. Researchers who study pedophilia say the term describes an attraction, not an action, and using it interchangeably with "abuse" fuels misperceptions. The American Psychiatric Association's *Diagnostic and Statistical Manual of Mental Disorders* said pedophilia is defined by "recurrent, intense sexually arousing fantasies, sexual urges, or behaviors involving sexual activity with a prepubescent child or children." Scientists have in recent decades improved their understanding of pedophilia's causes, prenatal and early childhood risk factors, and how pedophiles can better control impulses.

One of the most significant findings is that scientists who study the disorder say pedophilia is determined in the womb, though environmental factors may influence whether someone acts on an urge to abuse. "The evidence suggests it is inborn. It's neurological," said James Cantor, a clinical psychologist, sex researcher, and former editor-in-chief of *Sexual Abuse: A Journal of Research and Treatment*. "Pedophilia is the attraction to children, regardless of whether the (person) ever… harms."

Michael Seto, forensic research director at the Royal Ottawa Health Care Group in Canada, said there is more neuroscientific knowledge of pedophilia than ever before. MRI research shows how sexual interests develop in the brain. "I think as a field, we've accepted the idea that this is not something that people choose," Seto said. "*Pedophilia is something people are born with or at least have a predisposition to…*" Research also offers insights into risk factors. Seto said men with pedophilia have a much higher incidence of early childhood head injury. One study on diagnosed pedophiles showed they are more likely to report their mothers had received psychiatric treatment, *which suggests the disorder may be influenced by genetic factors.*[82]

Those who are familiar with social media may know the meaning of TEDx. Basically, these are talks on various subjects that are recorded and presented via YouTube. In 2018, a woman by the name of Mirjam Heine presented her talk in which she argued that pedophilia should be accepted as an unchangeable sexual orientation. This is part of what she said, "According to current research, pedophilia is an unchangeable sexual orientation just like, for example, heterosexuality. No one chooses to be a pedophile. No one can cease being one," Heine argued. "The difference between pedophilia and other sexual orientations is that living out this sexual orientation will end in a disaster." She also said that accepting pedophiles and encourag-

---

[82] Alia E. Dastagir, "The Complicated Research behind Pedophilia," *USA Today* (January 2022), accessed September 11, 2023, https://www.usatoday.com/story/life/health-wellness/2022/01/10/pedophiles-pedophilia-sexual-disorder/8768423002.

ing them to not pursue their desires will help end their "suffering." She said,

> We shouldn't increase the sufferings of pedophiles by excluding them, by blaming and mocking them. By doing that, we increase their isolation, and we increase the chance of child sexual abuse. We should accept that pedophiles are people who have not chosen their sexuality and who, unlike most of us, will never be able to live it out freely... Most of us feel discomfort when we think about pedophiles. But *just like pedophiles, we are not responsible for our feelings. We do not choose them but we are responsible for our actions.*[83] (emphasis supplied)

Does this sound familiar? Of course, it does, these are some of the same arguments made by LGBTQ+ activists. But it is different, they will argue. Alicia Johnston, who argues for acceptance of same-sex marriage in the Adventist Church, says,

> Same-gender marriage is not intrinsically evil. It doesn't compare to anything else we consider a sin. God's love is not revealed through alcoholism, adultery, divorce, *pedophilia*, incest, or bestiality. Many times, I've heard those compared to same-gender marriage. It's false on the face of it. No analogy rightly compares this love to sin.[84] (emphasis supplied)

---

[83] Bailey Vogt, "TEDx Speaker Argued That Pedophilia Should Be Accepted as 'An Unchangeable Sexual Orientation,'" *Metro Weekly* (July 2018), accessed September 11, 2023, https://www.metroweekly.com/2018/07/tedx-speaker-argues-that-pedophilia-should-be-accepted-as-an-unchangeable-sexual-orientation.

[84] Johnston, 221.

But this would be a matter of opinion. If those struggling with pedophilia are making the same arguments as those who argue for the LGBTQ+ ideology and lifestyle, who is she to say they are wrong? If I were to argue, as I will later in the book, that God's love is not revealed in a same-gender marriage, she would say I am wrong and that I am being judgmental. Yet she is doing the same thing for those struggling with pedophilia, which, as we have seen, is classified as a mental disorder by the DSM-5, just like gender dysphoria used to be.

What changed? Society did, and with it, what medical professionals used to believe. You see, my opinion is that mental health professionals have changed their views because they need to be politically correct. They do not want to be accused of being a homophobe, which, these days, is seen as one of the greatest insults. Not only is it insulting, but these days, such an accusation can land you in the unemployment line.

Will the same thing happen with pedophilia? Now please do not misinterpret me. I am not saying that those who are struggling with gender dysphoria and sexual orientation issues or those who have transitioned are just as bad as pedophiles. Nor am I defending pedophiles. I am just simply pointing out that understanding the nature of sin, which advances step by step, is getting worse with every step, and seeing the changes in our society that have placed us where we are today with respect to its views on LGBTQ+ ideology and lifestyle, it isn't a big stretch for the eventual acceptance of pedophilia as a mental disorder and for society clamoring for their acceptance and affirmation. The writing is on the wall.

CHAPTER 2

Transgenderism
A Christian Perspective

A MAN WAS WALKING THROUGH an art gallery when he came upon a picture of the Lord Jesus dying upon the cross. He stopped and looked at the beautiful portrait of Calvary's love. As he stared into the face of Christ so full of agony, the gallery guard tapped him on the shoulder. "Lower," the guard said. "The artist painted this picture to be appreciated from a lower position." So the man bent down. And from this lower position, he observed new beauties in the picture not previously shown. "Lower," said the guard. "Lower still." The man knelt down on one knee and looked up into the face of Christ. The new vantage point yielded new beauties to behold and appreciate. But motioning with his torch toward the ground, the guard said, "Lower. You've got to go lower." The man now dropped down to two knees and looked up. Only then as he looked up at the painting from such a low posture could he realize the artist's intended perspective. Only then could he see the full beauty of the cross.[1]

A synonym for the word *perspective* is "point of view" or "worldview." American author and poet Myrtle Reed once said, "It all

---

[1] David Moore, "The Right Perspective," *Sermon Central* (December 2008), accessed September 6, 2023, https://www.sermoncentral.com/sermon-illustrations/70197/the-right-perspective-by-sermon-central.

depends on the way you look at it. The point of view is everything in this world."² So what is, in essence, a worldview?

> It's the lens through which you interpret all your experience and through which you make decisions. It's your colored glasses you wear, even if you don't know you're wearing them. More technically, according to David Noebel, author of Understanding the Times (Focus on the Family), a worldview is… "The framework from which we view reality and make sense of life and the world. [It's] any ideology, philosophy, theology, movement or religion that provides an overarching approach to understanding God, the world and man's relations to God and the world."³

You will find that how we evaluate the complexities surrounding gender dysphoria and the LGBTQ+ movement is dependent on our worldview.

> Transgenderism offers a different story about reality… Humans are not made in the image of God as essentially sexed beings. The two-sexed system of male and female is considered ideological rather than a natural occurrence. Thus, humans have a fluid biological nature. Freedom is not found in orienting one's life to God's truth as revealed in nature and Scripture, but in having self-determination and societal support for one's chosen gender self-expression.⁴

---

[2] Myrtle Reed, *QuoteFancy*, accessed September 6, 2023, https://quotefancy.com/myrtle-reed-quotes.
[3] "What Is a Worldview and Why It Matters?" (January 2018), accessed September 6, 2023, https://truthstory.org/blog/what-is-a-worldview-why-it-matters.
[4] Sean McDowell, "The Worldview behind Transgenderism," (April 2019), accessed September 6, 2023, https://seanmcdowell.org/blog/the-worldview-

On the other hand, "the Bible records the original created order as male and female" (Genesis 1:27; 5:2). This gender binary is linked to God's mandate for human beings to populate the earth (Genesis 1:28). Although we will expand more on this later, we could say, "Created in God's image and likeness, male and female, our sexuality is a gift from God that we offer back, in love, to Him. *Transgenderism violates God's design.*"[5]

In the book *Understanding Gender Dysphoria*, already cited, Mark Yarhouse presents three frameworks that, in his mind, will help us understand gender identity issues. While I do not fully subscribe to all he presents, these frameworks are worth mentioning.

The integrity framework

This framework views sex and gender and, therefore, gender identity conflicts in terms of "the sacred integrity of maleness and femaleness stamped in one's body. Cross gender identification is a concern in large part because it threatens the integrity of male-female distinctions. Proponents of this view would cite many biblical passages (e.g., Deut. 22:5; 23:1). Even if there was some concession that some of the Old Testament biblical prohibitions were related to avoiding pagan practices of their neighbors, the overall themes from scripture support the importance of complementary male-female differences from creation" (e.g., Gen. 2:21–24)… In other words, from this perspective, the same-sex sexual behavior is sin in part because it does not merge or join two persons into an integrated sexual whole; the "essential maleness" and "essential femaleness" are not brought together as intended from creation.[6]

---

behind-transgenderism.
[5] "Transgenderism: Our Position," *Focus on the Family* (February 2018), accessed September 6, 2023, https://www.focusonthefamily.com/get-help/transgenderism-our-position.
[6] Mark A. Yarhouse, *Understanding Gender Dysphoria: Navigating Transgender Issues in a Changing Culture* (Downers Grove, IL: IVP Academic, 2015), 46.

The disability framework

This framework views gender dysphoria as a result of living in a fallen world in which the condition—like so many mental health concerns—is a nonmoral reality. Whether we consider brain sex theory or any other explanatory framework for the origin of the phenomenon, the causal pathways and existing structures are viewed by proponents of the disability framework as not functioning as originally intended. If the various aspects of sex and gender are not aligning, then that nonmoral reality reflects one more dimension of human experience that is not the way it's supposed to be.[7] Thus, because it could be argued mental health disease is a result of sin, gender dysphoria is a disability, but like other mental health ailments, it is nonmoral, that is, it is not a sin.

The diversity framework

This framework views transgender issues as something to be celebrated, honored, or revered. The social-cultural context of the West is rapidly moving in this direction. This framework highlights transgender issues as reflecting identity and culture to be celebrated as an expression of diversity. Current models that celebrate transgender identity and community reflect this framework. This understanding also frequently cites historical examples in which gender-variant expressions have been documented and held in higher esteem. Proponents of this framework wish to recast sex as just as socially constructed as gender.[8]

> We believe it is indispensable to deconstruct the binary sex/gender system that shapes the western world so absolutely that in most cases it goes unnoticed. For "other sexualities to be possible" it is indispensable and urgent that

---

[7] Ibid., 48.
[8] Ibid., 50.

we stop governing ourselves by the absurd notion that only two possible body types exist, male and female, with only two genders inextricably linked to them, man and women. We make trans and intersex issues our priority because their presence, activism and theoretical contributions show us the path to a new paradigm that will allow as many bodies, sexualities and identities to exist as those living in this world that might wish to have, with each one of them respected, desired, celebrated.[9]

I would like to suggest a framework that encompasses both the integrity and the disability frameworks. Clearly, as we shall see later, God created a pattern when He made a male and a female. Thus, changing what God created—in this case, engaging in same-sex sexual relations—is a sin, as it is contrary to God's desire and intention. It certainly goes against scripture. Now sin did bring sickness, both physical and mental. While some argue that gender dysphoria is a mental illness (as it was classified before in the *Diagnostic and Statistical Manual of Mental Disorders*), the challenge comes when it is seen just as a mental illness. Nobody would fault a person suffering from depression, anxiety, schizophrenia, etc. for committing a sin; these are mental illnesses that can be treated psychologically and, in some cases, with medications. Gender dysphoria, as it was classified before, is a mental illness. Nothing wrong with that, so it should be treated as any other mental illness. The moral issue comes from the actions taken because of the mental illness. A person experiencing gender dysphoria, like any other illness, may struggle as they are treated for the condition. However, if the individual acts on these feelings (those within the LGBTQ+ ideology), whether committing

---

[9] International Gay and Lesbian Human Rights Commission, *Institutional Memoir of the 2005 Institute for Trans and Intersex Activist Training* (2005), accessed September 6, 2023, https://iglhrc.org/sites/default/files/367-1.pdf.

to a same-sex sexual relationship or hormone treatment and/or sex reassignment surgery, that is when it becomes a moral issue.

The fact that most proponents of the LGBTQ+ ideology classify their feelings and experiences as either just a mental illness or as a natural God-ordained order of things creates a spiritual conundrum. Jesus died to save us from our sins. The apostle John wrote, "If we confess our sins, He is faithful and just to forgive us our sins and to cleanse us from all unrighteousness" (1 John 1:9). So when a person has already repented (see Acts 3:19) and confessed their sin, we can be sure that the sin, whatever that sin is, has been forgiven. But what if I do not repent and confess? Will my sin be forgiven? The answer is no; and it is here that those who subscribe to the LGBTQ+ ideology enter a dangerous territory because, in their minds, the feelings and actions resulting from those feelings are not sinful. If it is not a sin, they have nothing to repent of and confess.

We have talked about seeing the world through a biblical lens, that is, having a biblical worldview. One of the things that proves to me that the Bible is reliable is that it tells it like it is. God is not afraid to hurt our feelings (that is never His intention) when He tells us what He believes is best for us. When we develop an intimate relationship with God, when we recognize Him as our Heavenly Father, we understand that we are not always going to like what He tells us. We are not always going to agree with Him because our sinful nature causes us to want to have control of our lives and a "nobody tells me what I can do" attitude. However, since we have this relationship with Him, even if we do not agree, even when we do not like what He is telling us through His word, we choose to do it His way because we recognize that He knows better than us.

Unfortunately, many feel that God's job is to make us happy. They dismiss any idea of a God Who has rules because rules spoil the fun. Those who push for the church to affirm the LGBTQ+ lifestyle argue that not doing so places a burden on them. If the burden isn't bearable, it must not come from God. Alice Johnston says,

> It matters whether theology is bearable. Does it work in the practical, day to day lives

of Christians? ... At some point, we must look directly at the result of our theology and ask whether it's life giving. We must not make excuses or turn away from the suffering of others. We must not pick and choose the stories that fit our theology, amplifying narratives that make us feel good about our theology and muting the multitude of those who experiences present a challenge. We know they are a burden if they prop up the status quo, bringing stability to the organization, and reduce change for religious leaders, but don't bring life... When someone places a burden on you, you can tell because they describe God as an eternal miser. *Their vision of God is that withholding parent who wants your obedience, not your joy.*[10] (emphasis supplied)

While I agree that we should not pick and choose our stories to help us feel good about ourselves and our theology, she assumes this is the reason the Seventh-day Adventist church does not affirm the LGBTQ+ lifestyle. Since the church's stance on the issue is contrary to her desire, it is a burden, and she assumes those placing the burden (the church and its leaders) view God as a miser because it does not cause them joy. Furthermore, she places obedience against joy. This is a very secular way of thinking as if "God just wants to take away our fun." Since we have a sinful nature, obedience to God may sometimes seem like it's going against our grain, as it were. But because we love God, we choose to obey Him (John 14:15); and because it is a love response, there is joy in obedience.

Living the Christian life is a paradox. Those who surrender to God can testify that as they surrender to Him, they experience joy. But full surrender requires sacrifice; it isn't easy because surrendering

---

[10] Alicia Johnston, *The Bible and LGBTQ Adventists: A Theological Conversation about Same-Sex Marriage, Gender, and Identity*, (Affirmative Collective, 2022), 189–190.

goes against our nature and our desire to have control over our lives. This is especially true when it comes to the modern belief about our bodies and who has the right to decide what we do with them. John Stuart Mill said, "Over himself, over his own body and mind, the individual is sovereign."[11] Jonathan Grant expressed it this way,

> Modern authenticity encourages us to create our own beliefs and morality, the only rule being that they must resonate with who we feel we really are. The worst thing we can do is to conform to some moral code that is imposed on us from outside—by society, our parents, the church, or whoever else. It is deemed to be self-evident that any such imposition would undermine our unique identity… The authentic self believes that personal meaning must be found within ourselves or must resonate with our one-of-a-kind personality.[12]

This thinking flies against the clear word of the apostle Paul, who said, "Or do you not know that your body is the temple of the Holy Spirit who is in you, whom you have from God, and *you are not your own*? For you were bought at a price; therefore, glorify God in your body and in your spirit, which are God's" (1 Corinthians 6:19–20, emphasis supplied).

The reality is that surrender requires sacrifice. Jesus said it best: "If anyone desires to come after Me, let him deny himself, and take up his cross, and follow Me" (Matthew 16:24). We do need a little context to understand this passage. In the previous passages, we find

---

[11] John Stuart Mill, *On Liberty*, ed. Elizabeth Rapaport (Indianapolis, IN: Hackett, 1979), 9.

[12] Jonathan Grant, *Divine Sex* (Grand Rapids, MI: Brazos Press, 2015), 30.

Peter trying to convince Jesus to give up on His plan that called for Him to suffer.

> From that time Jesus began to show to His disciples that He must go to Jerusalem, and suffer many things from the elders and chief priests and scribes, and be killed, and be raised the third day. Then Peter took Him aside and began to rebuke Him, saying, "Far be it from You, Lord; this shall not happen to You!" But He turned and said to Peter, "Get behind Me, Satan! You are an offense to Me, for you are not mindful of the things of God, but the things of men." (Matthew 16:21–23)

In verse 24, Jesus describes to Peter (and the rest of the disciples) what it truly means to be a disciple. First, a disciple must *deny* himself. The word deny comes from the Greek word *aparneomai*, which means to repudiate or disregard oneself. That is, a disciple renounces himself and submits to Jesus. A disciple puts his/her wishes in the back burner, if you will, and what Jesus requires comes first. Then a disciple must take up his cross.

> A criminal condemned to die by crucifixion literally did "take up his cross," or at least the crossbar to it, which he carried to the scene of execution, and it is probably this to which Christ here alludes. In the context in which Christ here mentions cross bearing, it seems that he refers, not so much to the minor difficulties and obstacles to be encountered by disciples, but rather to the need of being ready to face death itself… If Peter is to continue as a disciple, he must be willing to pay the price, as, indeed he eventually did.[13]

---

[13] "Take Up His Cross" [Matthew 16:24], *Seventh-day Adventist Bible Commentary (SDABC)*, rev. ed., ed. Francis D. Nichol (Washington, DC: Review & Herald,

It is then that a disciple is ready to follow Jesus. "The would-be disciple must first renounce himself, his own plans, his own desires; then he must be willing to bear any cross that duty calls him to 'take up.' Finally, he must follow in the footsteps of Jesus."[14]

While very eloquent, Johnston, commenting on the cross a disciple is called to bear, simply says, "Contrasted to burdens, taking up our crosses is entirely about sacrificing for those we love. This is the cross. It is a sacrifice motivated by love for others."[15] There is no question that, as Christians, we must love others and that at times loving others can be classified as a sacrifice, especially for those who "rub us the wrong way." But limiting the words of Jesus in Matthew 16:24 to that is ignoring the context of the passage. She is not the only one who has done this. In the book *The Bible and the Transgender Experience*, Linda Tatro Herzer explains her interpretation of Matthew 16:24:

> The injunction "take up your cross" does not mean to choose to suffer the pain of denying your true self. Nor does it mean that we are to deny our own needs and suffer the pain of doing and doing and overdoing for others. What Jesus means here is that we are to be willing to suffer the pain that comes from not playing by all of society's rules, the pain we'll experience as a result of rejecting misguided human values in order to follow Christ's teachings. What Jesus is referring to is the kind of pain Martin Luther King experienced when he challenged the value systems of America in the 1950s and '60s, the kind of pain transgender people suffer when they come out in our society today. Here Jesus is telling his followers that this is what we're signing up for when

---

1976—1980), 5:435.
[14] Ibid.
[15] Johnston, 190.

we deny our misguided, false selves and challenge the world's values by taking up our crosses and following him.[16]

Notice that she interprets the passage with one goal in mind, justifying gender variance, which is the premise of her book. She wants to advocate for the transgender movement, so she interprets the passage with that end in mind. As we will see in this chapter, this is what LGBTQ+ advocates do, at least those who want to use the Bible to justify their claims. In essence, they are grasping at straws. There are a series of Bible passages that address the LGBTQ+ lifestyle. Obviously, the Bible does not address the nuances and the complexities of being gay, lesbian, bisexual, and the more recent transgender lifestyle; but it provides enough information to help us understand that this is a moral issue and that, with all the love in our hearts, must be exposed. Furthermore, if the LGBTQ+ lifestyle is affirmed by the church, it will present a danger to the proclamation of the Present Truth and the Three Angels' Messages, and Satan would want nothing more.

Genesis 1–2

It makes sense that, as we look at the passages addressing the subjects of what it means to be a male and a female and gender issues, we start with the story of creation.

> Then God said, "Let Us make man in Our image, according to Our likeness; let them have dominion over the fish of the sea, over the birds of the air, and over the cattle, over all the earth and over every creeping thing that creeps on the earth." So God created man in His own image;

---

[16] Linda Tatro Herzer, *The Bible and the Transgender Experience: How Scripture Supports Gender Variance* (Cleveland, OH: The Pilgrim Press, 2016), 76–77.

in the image of God He created him; male and female He created them. (Genesis 1:26–27)

The sexual distinction between male and female is fundamental to the issues revolving around the LGBTQ+ ideology. While the creation story is very clear and should be no source of argument, unfortunately, some people have stretched their interpretation of it so far that, if you would listen to their explanations, you would respond, "What?"

Herzer explains that Genesis is written in a poetic fashion. As such, she believes that its author "was not trying to write a scientific explanation of the creation of all things."[17] To prove her point, she quotes Genesis 1:3–5, "Then God said, 'Let there be light'; and there was light. And God saw the light, that it was good; and God divided the light from the darkness. God called the light Day, and the darkness He called Night. So the evening and the morning were the first day." She then says, "Taking this poetic passage literally and believing that it explained all the realities that God created regarding a twenty-four-hour period would result in us believing that there is nothing other than night or day. Of course, we know from experience that there is also dusk and dawn, those times a day when it is not totally day, but it is not totally night either."[18]

She then quotes verses 9–10,

> Then God said, "Let the waters under the heavens be gathered together into one place, and let the dry land appear"; and it was so. And God called the dry land Earth, and the gathering together of the waters He called Seas. And God saw that it was good.

---

[17] Ibid., 52.
[18] Ibid.

She further says,

> Again, taking this poetic passage literally and believing that it explained all the realities God created regarding land and sea would result in us believing that there is no such thing as shorelines or marshes, which can be under water during one part of a day and dry land hours later, depending on the tides. However, again we know from experience that this is not the case.[19]

This leads her to conclude,

> Some say that Genesis 1:27 means that God created only male and female. But might there be a dawn in a dusk, a shoreline and a marshland in the realm of male and female? The reports of modern medicine answer the question with a resounding yes![20]

By this, she means that there must be variations to the sexes, which explains those who are lesbians, gay, bisexual, and transgender. All these fall into these variations, and in her mind, they must be God ordained.

Johnston makes a similar argument when she highlights the Bible's use of Hebrew merisms.

> A merism is a rhetorical device (or figure of speech) in which a combination of two contrasting parts of the whole refer to the whole... Merisms are common in the Old Testament. For example, in Genesis 1:1, when God creates "the heavens and the earth" the two parts (heavens

---

[19] Ibid., 53.
[20] Ibid., 54.

and earth) do not refer only to the heavens and the earth. Rather, they refer to the heavens, the earth and everything between them: God created the entire world, the whole universe.[21]

She writes,

> God separated the light of day from the darkness of night (Gen. 1:4,5). But we know that there is also an in-between time of twilight when the sun sets and rises. These emerge from the spaces of overlap, when one aspect of God's creation touches another. Does that mean sunsets and sunrises are outside of God's will? Of course not. These words were not intended to exclude sunsets from God's creative intent simply because they aren't day or night. Neither are sunsets an accident. The author simply did not include every possibility. Day and night are excellent examples of God's creation, not the only options… Many use Genesis 1:27 to indicate that "male and female" is all God created. This interpretation ignores the possibility of a Hebrew merism and is inconsistent with the rest of the creation narrative. The creation categories simply are not intended to explain all that can be, all that should be, or all that can morally and ethically be considered good.[22]

Notice how Johnston, a former Seventh-day Adventist pastor, questions the creation narrative to justify the belief that the Bible somehow supports the idea that God created gender variance. So

---

[21] "Merism," *Wikipedia*, accessed September 12, 2023, https://en.wikipedia.org/wiki/Merism.
[22] Johnston, 61–63.

what does the creation story really tell us about gender? Here it is again:

> Then God said, "Let Us make man in Our image, according to Our likeness; let them have dominion over the fish of the sea, over the birds of the air, and over the cattle, over all the earth and over every creeping thing that creeps on the earth." So God created man in His own image; in the image of God He created him; male and female He created them... And the Lord God caused a deep sleep to fall on Adam, and he slept; and He took one of his ribs, and closed up the flesh in its place. Then the rib which the Lord God had taken from man He made into a woman, and He brought her to the man. And Adam said: "This is now bone of my bones and flesh of my flesh; She shall be called Woman, Because she was taken out of Man." Therefore a man shall leave his father and mother and be joined to his wife, and they shall become one flesh (Genesis 1:26–27, 2:21–24).
>
> In Genesis 1 heterosexuality is at once proclaimed to be the order of creation. Human sexuality according to the Edenic divine paradigm finds expression in heterosexual marital form. Genesis 2:24 presents a succinct theology of marriage: "Therefore a man shall leave his father and mother and be joined to his wife, and they shall become one flesh." The introductory "therefore" ['al-kên] indicates that the relationship of Adam and Eve is upheld as the pattern for all human

sexual marriage relationships of a man and a woman as the Edenic model for all time.[23]

It is worthwhile mentioning that from God's perspective, creation was perfect. "Then God saw everything that He had made, and indeed it was very good. So the evening and the morning were the sixth day" (Genesis 1:31).

> When we look at the Bible, we see…there was a Designer, and He had a plan for how He was going to make the world. *There was a blueprint that God had in mind.* God's creation was very good. It was not average, and it was not purposeless. God's act of creating was successful in every part, and it was intentional in every part. The God of the Bible is not a God of chaos or randomness, but of order and purpose.[24]

What we see in the Genesis creation account is that God established a pattern, a blueprint, as Walker suggested. As such, human beings have no business in trying to change it. Those who question it or try to explain it away are suggesting, in spite of their intentions, that God made a mistake. A common statement we hear from LGBTQ+ activists is that "people should become what God created them to be." So the implication is that, for example, if a male transitions into a female, God intended that person to be a female. If that is the case, why was he born a male?" Why didn't God create him as a female in the first place? There are many ambiguous answers to these questions, unless, of course, we answer them using the biblical lens.

---

[23] Richard M. Davidson, "Homosexuality in the Old Testament," in *Homosexuality, Marriage, and the Church: Biblical, Counseling, Religious Liberty Issues,* ed. Roy E. Gane, Nicholas P Miller, and H. Peter Swanson (Berrien Springs, MI: Andrews University Press, 2012), 5–6.

[24] Andrew T. Walker, *God and the Transgender Debate: What Does the Bible Actually Say About Gender Identity?* (Turkey: The Good Book Company, 2022), 50.

The truth is that the Hebrew words for *male* (*zakar*) and *female* (*neqebah*) are adjectives that indicate the sex of the two individuals. This is not a Hebrew merism, as suggested by Johnston. Thus, God defines the purpose of what He has created. Genesis 2:21–24 gives us a quick summary from the creation of Eve to her marriage to Adam. Furthermore, we see that Adam is identified as a male and Eve as a female; there is nothing ambiguous about this. Genesis 2 shows us that Eve was a complement to Adam. Thus, God could command them to "Be fruitful and multiply; fill the earth and subdue it" (Genesis 1:28), which is only possible with a male and a female coming together. If the Genesis narrative was simply a poem describing all the possibilities, as suggested by Johnston and Herzer, Genesis 1:28 would not make sense in the context of the story.

Ellen White says it this way:

> God celebrated the first marriage. Thus the institution has for its originator the Creator of the universe. "Marriage is honorable" (Hebrews 13:4); it was one of the first gifts of God to man, and it is one of the two institutions that, after the Fall, Adam brought with him beyond the gates of Paradise. *When the divine principles are recognized and obeyed in this relation, marriage is a blessing; it guards the purity and happiness of the race*, it provides for man's social needs, it elevates the physical, the intellectual, and the moral nature.[25] (emphasis supplied)

Notice that marriage between a male and a female is a divine principle, and when this is recognized and followed as such, then marriage will be a blessing. The implication is clear, any deviation from that divine principle will not result in a blessing because it is contrary to the principles or pattern established by God. "Scripture

---

[25] Ellen G. White, "The Creation," *Patriarchs and Prophets* (Silver Spring, MD: 2018), 47.

clearly defines human beings as male and female, not by accident, but by divine purpose. Furthermore, this purpose, along with every other aspect of God's creation, it's declared by the creator to be 'good.' This means that human flourishing and happiness will take place *only when the goodness of God's creation is honored as God intended.*"[26]

So what happened? Why do we have so many people struggling with gender identity? And what about intersex people? The existence of intersex people is often used as an argument against the belief that God created a male and a female. As mentioned in chapter 1, *intersex* is a term to describe conditions (e.g., congenital adrenal hyperplasia) in which a person is born with sex characteristics or anatomy that do not allow clear identification as male or female. The cause of an intersex condition can be chromosomal, gonadal, or genital.[27] What about them? The reason for all gender variance is that the creation narrative did not end in Genesis 2. Unfortunately, from Genesis 3 on, we read about the fall and its results.

"And the Lord God commanded the man, saying, 'Of every tree of the garden you may freely eat; but of the tree of the knowledge of good and evil you shall not eat, for in the day that you eat of it you shall surely die'" (Genesis 2:16). But what did Adam and Eve do? They ate the fruit of the tree.

> The tree represents the fact that God alone has the authority to define what is good and what is evil, what is right and what is wrong. And by taking that fruit, human beings are saying, No! We are not accepting that God alone is God. We are going to take that authority for ourselves. We are going to decide what is right and what is wrong. Satan, who appears in the story as a snake, temps the man and woman with the promise that they can be like God. And what is

---

[26] R. Albert Mohler Jr., *We Cannot Be Silent: Speaking Truth to a Culture Redefining Sex, Marriage, and the Very Meaning of Right and Wrong* (Nashville, TN: Nelson Books, 2015), 107.

[27] Yarhouse, 21.

> it to be like God? It is to set the rules, to being in charge, to decide what is right and wrong… God's originally perfect creation is no longer as it was designed to be. The act of eating the fruit was a bid for "freedom" but it didn't deliver what Satan promised. The bible's insight that we are all both created and broken is vital for understanding not just transgender questions but every kind of human affliction—physical or psychological. We have all been profoundly impacted by the fall.[28]

Sin is the culprit of all the world's woes. Sin is rebellion, and one way we show our rebellion against God is by refusing to go along with the way in which He has made the world, such as in the division of the sexes.

> The brokenness of the world explains why sinners will often either deny the distinctions between the male and the female or exaggerate them beyond what scripture reveals. Sex, gender, marriage, and family all come together in the first chapters of scripture in order to make clear that every aspect of our sexual lives is to submit to the creative purpose of God and be channeled into the exclusive arena of human sexual behavior—marriage—defined clearly and exclusively as a lifelong, monogamous union *of a man and a woman*. The reality of human sinfulness explains why so many of these issues are confused and why we should expect confusion in this world. The effects of sin also explain why there are those deeply troubled about something as fundamental

---

[28] Vaughan Roberts, *Transgender* (India: The Good Book Company, 2021), 46–47.

as their gender... The brokenness of the world also explains why sinners have constructed entire ideologies, theories, and systems of thought in order to justify their sin. This is exactly what Paul indicted in Romans 1 when he described suppressing the truth in unrighteousness and exchanging the truth of God for a lie.[29]

But not all is lost. The fact that sin is the cause of all the confusion regarding gender identity tells us that there is hope. The hope comes from the fact that Jesus died to save sinners like you and me. Contrary to what some saints may believe, LGBTQ+ ideology is not "the sin," as if no redemption was available for those who have decided to live out their gender confusion. The solution to their problem is the same solution as ours. Jesus!

Since we have started with creation, I think it is valuable to see what Jesus said with respect to the passages discussed above.

Matthew 19:3–12

Throughout the gospels, we read about a few incidents in which the religious leaders wanted to trick Jesus into saying something that they could use to condemn Him. Jesus, of course, knew their hearts and always used the truth of His word as a way of escape, as a way to clarify misconceptions, and as a way to show valuable lessons. In Matthew 19, we read about one such incident. "The Pharisees also came to Him, testing Him, and saying to Him, 'Is it lawful for a man to divorce his wife for just any reason'" (Matthew 19:3)? It is important to see that the text clearly says that the issue in question was divorce; thus, it was related to marriage.

"God celebrated the first marriage. Thus the institution has for its originator the Creator of the universe. 'Marriage is honorable' (Hebrews 13:4); it was one of the first gifts of God to man, and it is

---

[29] Mohler, 107–108.

one of the two institutions that, after the Fall, Adam brought with him beyond the gates of Paradise."[30] There should be no discussion about the fact that marriage as created by God was between one man and one woman. Jesus's response makes this clear:

> And He answered and said to them, "Have you not read that He who made them at the beginning 'made them male and female,' and said, 'For this reason a man shall leave his father and mother and be joined to his wife, and the two shall become one flesh'? So then, they are no longer two but one flesh. Therefore what God has joined together, let not man separate." (vv. 4–6)

Jesus directs His inquisitors not only to scripture but to the story of creation. This is important because the question was about divorce. Thus, the minds of the religious Pharisees were in the law of Moses (see verse 7). Jesus takes them further back, to the very beginning. "He who made them," who is the He? Jesus, of course. "For by Him all things were created that are in heaven and that are on earth, visible and invisible, whether thrones or dominions or powers. All things were created through Him and for Him" (Colossians 1:16). Who better than Jesus, the Creator Himself, to know how things were actually done? He says He created them male (*ar'-hrane*) and female (*thay'-loos*). Both these words are adjectives; thus, they are words that describe. The word *ar'-hrane* occurs nine times in the New Testament and each time it refers to a being who is male, a man. The word *thay'-loos* five times, meaning a woman with nursing breasts ("one who gives suck").[31]

---

[30] White, 47.
[31] "730, arsen, 2338, thēly," Bible Hub, https://biblehub.com/text/matthew/19-4.htm.

Because God created them male (one man) and female (one woman), the man is to leave his home, join his wife (a female), and become one flesh through the sexual union.

Same sex intercourse radically offends against God's intentional creation of humans as a uniquely complementary sexual pair, "male and female" (Gen. 1:27), the image of sexual differentiation as a taking from the original human (Gen. 2:21–24), and the definition of marriage as a union between a man and a woman (Gen 2:24). Since Jesus himself defined these texts as foundational for matters of human sexual ethics (Matt. 19:4–6, Mark 10:6–8), Jesus' church must treat an offense against them as a major violation of Christian sexual ethics. Genesis 1:27 brings into close connection the "image of God" and the creation of humans as "male and female": "in the image of God he (God) created [the human]; male and female he created them." The language of Genesis 1:27 suggests two points of importance:

First, though animals too participate in sexual differentiation and pairing, human sexual differentiation and pairing is uniquely integrated into God's image. This makes it possible for humans to enhance or to efface that image through their sexual behavior. The alternative is to argue, falsely, that one's sexuality is wholly disconnected from God's image, thereby making it possible for one to engage in every kind of sexual misbehavior, including adultery, bestiality, and pedophilia, without doing any harm to the imprint of God's image. Secondly, a male-female sexual pairing manifests the fullness of the imprint of God's image on the sexual dimension

> of human life… *Since male and female combined constitute the totality of the sexual spectrum, it is axiomatic that a union of male and female establishes a sexual whole.*[32] (emphasis supplied)

Again, what we see here, and from the words of Jesus in Matthew 19, is that the creation of a male and a female was God's blueprint to marriage and sexual relations. To interpret this in any other way is not only to ignore the context but to take huge leaps in logic. Let me give you a few examples of these leaps. In speaking about the beauty and variety in the universe, Justin Sabia-Tanis applies this to human beings and gender.

> When we consider human beings, we should see ourselves through the same lenses with which we read the rest of the creation story—that is, that we too are part of a marvelous story in which diversity and variation play a critical role. Human beings share more than 99% of our DNA; we have a lot in common. But we also exhibit tremendous differences in color, size, shape, outlook, features, and so on. This is part of God's plan. Gender is one more facet of this natural variation intended by God as a feature of life on earth. *Male and female define two categories of human, but they are not meant to be exclusive boxes that limit our individual expression.*[33] (emphasis supplied)

---

[32] Robert A. J. Gagnone, "The Scriptural Case for a Male-Female Prerequisite for Sexual Relations: The New Testament Perspective, in *Homosexuality, Marriage, and the Church: Biblical, Counseling, Religious Liberty Issues*, ed. Roy E. Gane, Nicholas P Miller, and H. Peter Swanson (Berrien Springs, MI: Andrews University Press, 2012), 65–66.

[33] Justin Sabia-Tania, "Holy Creation, Wholly Creative: God's Intention for Gender Diversity," in *Understanding Gender Identities*, ed. James K. Beilby and Paul Rhodes Eddy (Grand Rapids, MI: Baker Academic, 2019), 196–197.

Alicia Johnston is a proponent of "affirming theology." Thus, the church (in this case, the SDA Church) should be "affirming our (LGBTQ+) sexuality and gender in the same way cisgender heterosexual people are affirmed."[34] She addresses the issue of male and female as God's blueprint (she doesn't agree with it), so she explains,

> The significant difference between seeing Genesis as the model and seeing Genesis as the beginning is this: Models are rarely built upon and added to, but beginnings always are. Models should be strictly followed. Beginnings tell us something about who we are. Beginnings guide us; they teach us about realities that can never change, but not every detail is a rule or prophecy. Those who believe in affirming theology believe that Adam and Eve are not models to be emulated… We shouldn't all be farmers. Living in a house is just fine. Not everyone will get married. A small number of people might even marry someone of the same gender. Adam and Eve give us a way of understanding how this whole thing started and some of the beautiful gifts we've been given—gifts like nature, meaningful work, the Sabbath, and marriage.
>
> Those who see Genesis as a model struggle to give specific, textual reasons for applying parts of the narrative as rules while not applying other parts. Why don't we all live in nature under the stars rather than in cities and houses? Why do the specifics of Adam and Eve's genders constrain marriage, but the specifics are their professions don't? Even though Genesis says, "it is not good for man to be alone," why is celibacy acceptable? Why is same sex-marriage forbidden

---

[34] Johnston, 13.

simply because it is not in Eden when so much of our daily lives were not literally present in Eden either?[35]

Notice that interpreting Genesis as simply a description of the beginning allows her to conclude that her views on sexuality (she is bisexual) are okay. What if everyone simply viewed the whole Bible that way? The danger is apparent. Considering the Sabbath is so closely connected to the creation of marriage, someone may say that the Sabbath was not a pattern or a model but a description of the need to have a day of rest. Since Adam and Eve are not a model and one can marry a person of the same sex, the Sabbath is not a model either, and "I can rest any day of the week." Do you see how dangerous these leaps in logic can be? This is an example on how buying into this LGBTQ+ ideology hinders the distinctive message of Seventh-day Adventists and the Present Truth (more on this later).

In His response to the Pharisees, Jesus quotes Genesis 2:24, "Therefore a man shall leave his father and mother and be joined to his wife, and they shall become one flesh." The Hebrew to the word *joined* is *dabaq*, which means to cling or cleave. This clinging is to take place only in the context of marriage between a man and a woman.

> Genesis 2:21–24 add to this point with a beautiful picture of the reality that man and woman are complementary sexual other halves. Four times in three verses the narrator emphasizes that something is "taken from" the *ā-dām*, or undifferentiated human. The sole differentiation produced by the removal of a "side" from the original human is that differentiation of sexes ("side" may be a better translation than "rib" of the Hebrew *tsela*). The principle of two sexes becoming one flesh is thus grounded in the pic-

---

[35] Ibid., 53.

ture of two sexes becoming one flesh. What is required in the storyline of Genesis (2:21–24) is not merely a joining or merger of two persons but a rejoining of two sexes into one… *The image conveys the essential point that a man and a woman are the two essential and complementary parts in a holistic picture of human sexuality.* Jesus gave priority to Genesis 1:27 and 2:24 as the prime texts for defining normative and prescriptive sexual ethics. Indeed, He predicated His "two and only two" rule for the number of persons in a sexual bond on the twoness of the sexes ordained at creation… The picture in Genesis 2:21–24 of a woman being formed from what is pulled from the man illustrates the point that the missing element from one sex is not another of the same sex but rather someone of the only other sex. The story conveys the self-evident point that on a sexual level men and women are configured bodily—and here I mean "bodily" in a holistic sense—as open-ended to a person of the only other sex, not a person of the same sex.[36] (emphasis supplied)

After Jesus's response to their initial question, the Pharisees respond, "Why then did Moses command to give a certificate of divorce, and to put her away" (v. 7)? Let us remember that their original question was about divorce and that their intention was to trick Jesus. This is why the question in verse 3 is "Is it lawful for a man to divorce his wife *for just any reason*" (emphasis supplied)? Moses did instruct the children of Israel about divorce, saying, "When a man takes a wife and marries her, and it happens that she finds no favor in his eyes because he has found some uncleanness in her, and he writes her a certificate of divorce, puts it in her hand, and sends

---

[36] Gagnone, 66–67, 69.

her out of his house" (Deuteronomy 24:1). However, the Jews had taken this instruction to the extreme and "understood this Mosaic precept to mean that a man might divorce his wife for almost any reason."[37] Jesus responds, "Moses, because of the hardness of your hearts, permitted you to divorce your wives, but from the beginning, it was not so. And I say to you, whoever divorces his wife, except for sexual immorality, and marries another, commits adultery; and whoever marries her who is divorced commits adultery" (vv. 8–9). Jesus again goes back to the beginning. "God has never repealed the law of marriage he enunciated in the beginning. It was not God's plan that divorce should ever be necessary."[38]

It would seem that Jesus's response on the matter of divorce disappointed the disciples. I suppose that as Jews, they, too, wanted to be able to divorce their wives for any reason whatsoever. So Jesus burst their bubble. Jesus responds to them by mentioning eunuchs and LGBTQ+ activists point to the mention of eunuchs as biblical proof that gender variance not only existed in Bible times but that it was affirmed by God.

What about Eunuchs?

> But He said to them, "All cannot accept this saying, but only those to whom it has been given: For there are eunuchs who were born thus from their mother's womb, and there are eunuchs who were made eunuchs by men, and there are eunuchs who have made themselves eunuchs for the kingdom of heaven's sake. He who is able to accept it, let him accept it." (Matthew 19:11–12)

---

[37] "Uncleanness" [Deuteronomy 24:1], *Seventh-day Adventist Bible Commentary (SDABC)*, rev. ed., ed. Francis D. Nichol (Washington, DC: Review & Herald, 1976–1980), 1:1037.

[38] "From the beginning" [Matthew 19:8], *Seventh-day Adventist Bible Commentary (SDABC)*, rev. ed., ed. Francis D. Nichol (Washington, DC: Review & Herald, 1976–1980), 5:454.

Following the context, in verses 11–12, Jesus is talking about celibacy, which makes sense because the disciples say in verse 10, "If such is the case of the man with his wife, it is better not to marry." In other words, if marriage binds a man so tightly, as Jesus explained in verses 8–9, it is better to remain celibate.

Jesus, however, tells them that celibacy is not a general rule and that only those to whom special grace is given can remain celibate. Celibacy is a call from God. Then he gives an example, eunuchs. A eunuch was "a castrated person, or one who voluntarily abstains from marriage."[39] Jesus presents three kinds of eunuchs: those born that way, those made by men, and those who made themselves eunuchs. First, Jesus appears to be "describing certain persons who suffered from a congenital defect, and thus one for which they were not to be considered responsible."[40] "Others are so because they were castrated by men; oriental rulers often subjected the harem attendants to surgery to make them eunuchs."[41] It is worth mentioning that some eunuchs apparently married. An example is Potiphar. We read in Genesis 37:36, "Now the Midianites had sold him (Joseph) in Egypt to Potiphar, an officer of Pharaoh and captain of the guard." The Hebrew word for *officer* is the word *saris*, which means "eunuch."[42] We know that Potiphar was married because his wife took a liking to Joseph, which was the reason the latter was imprisoned.

Jesus, however, seems to emphasize the third category, those who made themselves eunuchs.

> These men could be married, and they had no physical impairment. Yet in dedication to the king and his Kingdom, they willingly forego marriage in order to give themselves to the cause

---

[39] "2135, eunouchos," Bible Hub, https://biblehub.com/greek/2135.htm.
[40] "Some Eunuchs" [Matthew 19:12], *Seventh-day Adventist Bible Commentary (SDABC)*, rev. ed., ed. Francis D. Nichol (Washington, DC: Review & Herald, 1976–1980), 5:455.
[41] "Eunuchs" [Matthew 19:12], *Believer's Bible Commentary* ed. William Macdonald (China: Thomas Nelson 2016), 1196.
[42] "5631, saris," Bible Hub https://biblehub.com/hebrew/5631.htm.

> of Christ without distraction… Their celibacy is not physical but a matter of voluntary abstinence. Not all men can live such a life; only those divinely empowered.[43]

Not all men can understand and accept this, except for those to whom it is given, that is, only those who are called.

LGBTQ+ activists, as said previously, take huge acrobatic leaps of logic when speaking of these passages. Notice this:

> The context in which Jesus makes these statements about eunuchs is a discussion about marriage and divorce. This suggests that the gender variance Jesus is referring to here is the gender nonconforming act of not marrying… Consequently, in order to understand this verse about someone being born a eunuch we must ask ourselves, "Why wouldn't someone—from birth—not want to, or not be able to, get marriage so they could procreate and have legitimate heirs, especially in a culture where having children was a sign of God's blessing and the means by which family inheritance were passed down?" Perhaps the most obvious answer…*is because they are gay, so from birth they have no interest in heterosexual marriage. Another possible answer is that they were born transgender,* so they have no interest in carrying out the roles and expectations typically assigned to someone with their genitals. A third possibility is that they might be intersex, persons who may have thought, because of the emphasis placed on procreation in Jesus' day, that they should not marry if their genitals, and thus

---

[43] Macdonald, *Believer's Bible Commentary,* 1196–1197.

perhaps their reproductive capabilities, were not typically male or female.[44]

This is an example of taking the issues of today and reading them into the passage. Instead of looking at the context of the passage and extracting the principles from it in order to help us understand the issues of today, they do the reverse. Since, in this case, Herzer wants to justify her belief, she interprets the passage as if Jesus was specifically talking about LGBTQ+ issues.

Johnston does not take as big of a leap as Herzer does; she explains eunuchs this way:

> Eunuchs were important people in the Ancient Near East and were often outside of typical gender norms. They were sometimes trusted advisers since they didn't have ambitions for their own progeny. The Hebrew word for "eunuch" is the same as the word for "trusted advisor." Eunuchs often watched over women in the court, guarding and helping them (Esther 2:14) because there was no concern that they could produce an illegitimate heir. A religion that requires circumcision on the eighth day, as Judaism does (Gen. 17:12), is one in which the genitalia of all children are examined. Eunuchs were inevitably identified, and decisions were made about intersex infants. The legal code of the Torah provides guidance. Eunuchs were excluded. Even if they were Levites, they were not allowed to serve as priests. Being a eunuch was considered a "defect" (Lev. 21:16–20).[45]

---

[44] Herzer, 45–46.
[45] Johnston, 79.

Here Johnston provides accurate information, yet in her book, it seems that she equates the eunuchs with those in the transgender community. "Many transgender and intersex people find hope in the way God restored and honored eunuchs."[46] She quotes Isaiah 56:3–5 as evidence:

> Do not let the son of the foreigner who has joined himself to the Lord speak, saying, "The Lord has utterly separated me from His people"; Nor let *the eunuch* say, "Here I am, a dry tree." For thus says the Lord: "*To the eunuchs* who keep My Sabbaths, and choose what pleases Me, and hold fast My covenant, even to them I will give in My house and within My walls a place and a name Better than that of sons and daughters; I will give them an everlasting name That shall not be cut off." (emphasis supplied)

In context, Isaiah 56 speaks of the salvation of the Gentiles.

> In anticipation of God's deliverance, the exiles are urged to practice justice and righteousness and keep the Sabbath. Neither the foreigner nor the eunuch should fear that they will be barred from any of the benefits of Christ's Kingdom. In fact, those who obey the word of the Lord will have preferred positions.[47]

Nobody is arguing against the fact that God shows mercy to everyone. Salvation is offered and given to all those who want it. Eunuchs who, as Johnston accurately stated, were excluded from serving because of their defects are accepted, as described by Isaiah. However, one must keep in mind that the reason eunuchs were

---

[46] Ibid., 78.
[47] Macdonald, *Believer's Bible Commentary*, 901.

excluded, according to the legal code, was that the services in the temple—the ceremonial law, if you will—were an object illustration of the plan of salvation. For example, the Passover lamb could not have any defects: "Your lamb shall be without blemish, a male of the first year. You may take it from the sheep or from the goats" (Exodus 12:5). "Whatever has a defect, you shall not offer, for it shall not be acceptable on your behalf" (Leviticus 22:20). The lamb represented Jesus, the perfect and sinless Lamb of God. This may be one reason for the exclusion of eunuchs.

Another reason is that "such mutilations were part of the religious and cultic practices of the nations. The most probable reason for their exclusion from the assembly of the Lord was their divided loyalties."[48] Regardless of the reasons, Isaiah reminds us that God is merciful. Yet it is important to point out that Isaiah says, "*To the eunuchs* who keep My Sabbaths, and choose what pleases Me, and hold fast My covenant, even to them I will give in My house…" Notice that the eunuchs had to walk in obedience. So even if we could equate the experience of the eunuchs with those who are transgender, this does not give carte blanche for them to live out their lifestyle as they please because God is merciful. That is not faith but presumption. God desires everyone to be saved (1 Timothy 2:4), but the gospel calls us to a change in lifestyle: "And do not be conformed to this world, but *be transformed by the renewing of your mind,* that you may prove what is that good and acceptable and perfect will of God" (Romans 12:2, emphasis supplied).

Another example often quoted by LGBTQ+ activists is found in Acts 8:25–39, where we find the story of Phillip and the Ethiopian eunuch. It may be safe to assume that this Ethiopian eunuch belonged to those "made by men." He was clearly interested in the Hebrew scriptures, for he was reading from Isaiah 53. God wanted to save this man, so He sent Phillip to him so he could accomplish this through his servant. Phillip preached Jesus to the eunuch, and

---

[48] Ángel Manuel Rodríguez, "Deuteronomy 23:1–4, and Isaiah 56:3–8," *Biblical Research Institute*, accessed September 14, 2023, https://www.adventistbiblicalresearch.org/materials/deuteronomy-231-4-and-isaiah-563-8.

the latter accepted the gospel and Jesus as Savior and Lord. This led him to want to be baptized, and so he was (v. 38). If this eunuch had been castrated, this did not mean that now he had to find a way to correct the defect. God accepted and forgave him, which implies that if there was a sin committed, the eunuch had repented and confessed it (1 John 1:9). This is the same thing that all of us must do. Now, in the case of say, an intersex person, when this person accepts Jesus, if there is something that can be corrected (medicine is obviously more advanced today than in Bible times), then the correction is to be done; if there is nothing that can be done, God doesn't reject him. The same is true with transgender people. If a transgender man or woman comes to the church, the gospel is proclaimed to them, and they accept Jesus and want to be baptized, even if they had already transitioned. It does not mean that God holds His acceptance of them until they have corrected their mistake. I would say that if they have transitioned, then they should make every effort to appear as the sex they were born with and, if surgeries had taken place, that they should take the appropriate steps to transition back to what God intended, although, in some cases, this may not be possible. However, their acceptance by God takes place the moment they accept Jesus. God then provides the power, through the Holy Spirit to be transformed (Ephesians 3:16–20, 2 Timothy 1:7). This is not only true for those struggling with gender dysphoria, sexual orientations issues, and transgenders but for all of us, "for all have sinned and fall short of the glory of God" (Romans 3:23).

But unfortunately, we cannot do much for those who do not want to see it this way. In her comment about the story of the Ethiopian eunuch, Herzer writes,

> The Bible clearly shows a change in attitude towards the inclusion of eunuchs in God's assembly…from Deuteronomic prohibition, to Isaiah's prophecy of inclusion, to the baptism of the Ethiopian eunuch recounted in the book of Acts. Such a movement from exclusion to inclusion mirrors the entire contextual trajectory of

the scriptures in general... The fact that the Bible itself shows a historical movement and shift in the Israelites understanding of how God would have them relate to the gender variant people of their day suggests that God may also have an accepting, affirming, and inclusive attitude toward the gender variant people of our day.[49]

However, Ellen White says, "This Ethiopian represented a large class who need to be taught by such missionaries as Philip—men who will hear the voice of God and go where He sends them."[50] Thus, if the experience of eunuchs equates to that of transgender or intersex people, this means that the gospel must be taught to them, and if they accept it, then they can be baptized, but as mentioned above, there must be a transformation. This is what baptism means in the first place.

> Or do you not know that as many of us as were baptized into Christ Jesus were baptized into His death? Therefore we were buried with Him through baptism into death, that just as Christ was raised from the dead by the glory of the Father, even so we also should walk in newness of life. For if we have been united together in the likeness of His death, certainly we also shall be in the likeness of His resurrection, knowing this, that our old man was crucified with Him, that the body of sin might be done away with, that we should no longer be slaves of sin. For he who has died has been freed from sin. (Romans 6:3–7)

---

[49] Herzer, 24–25.
[50] Ellen G. White, *The Acts of the Apostles* (Nampa, ID: Pacific Press Publishing Association, 2005, 109.

Deuteronomy 22:5

"A woman shall not wear anything that pertains to a man, nor shall a man put on a woman's garment, for all who do so are an abomination to the Lord your God." Deuteronomy 22:1–12 addresses various practical laws, some pertaining to people and some to animals. Some of these make no sense to us because Israel was an agrarian society. In fact, verse 5 seems to be out of place, but that is my finite mind talking. Regardless, there is a principle in this verse that does apply to us.

> The command for a woman not to wear what pertains to man probably refers to the heathen custom...for immoral purposes, men wearing women's clothes, aping their manners, and offering their bodies for immoral purposes. The word translated "that which pertaineth" is used of many articles other than clothing, such as "jewels" (Gen. 24:53), "weapons" (Gen. 27:3), "stuff" (Gen. 31:37), "armour" (1 Sam. 14:1, 6), "bag" (1 Sam. 17:40), "furniture" (Nahum 2:9). God made man male and female, and the distinction thus ordained is to be honored and obeyed. The desire to minimize this distinction grows from the low ideals and contributes to immorality.[51]

Because of the varied interpretations of "that which pertaineth," Herzer makes this interpretation, which contains more leaps in logic:

> A careful consideration of the immediate context suggests that what God was telling people to do in Deuteronomy 22:5 was to not dress

---

[51] "Not Wear" [Deuteronomy 22:5], *Seventh-day Adventist Bible Commentary (SDABC)*, rev. ed., ed. Francis D. Nichol (Washington, DC: Review & Herald, 1976–1980), 1:1030.

> in a way that would hide their true identity and deceive others in a harmful way. Knowing that this is the intent of this verse helps us understand why there are no objections at Halloween when people dress in the clothing of the opposite gender because everyone understands that cross-dressing is being done with no intention to harm others. It also explains why back in Shakespeare's day, there were no objections when men dressed in women's clothes to portray female characters on the stage because the culture of that time did not yet allow women to be actors. Likewise today, when gender variant people dress in clothes that do not match the gender they were assigned at birth, there should be no objections based on this biblical passage, since they are not dressing to hide themselves so they can harm others. In fact, just the opposite is true! Gender variant individuals carefully choose their clothing so as to not hide themselves so people can know and interact with them according to their truth. Therefore, understood in its immediate context, this verse that appears to be a law against cross dressing *actually becomes an exhortation to modern day gender variant individuals not to hide themselves, but to dress in the clothes that truly reflect their internal sense of themselves!*[52] (emphasis supplied)

Notice how suddenly every story in the Bible is addressing LGBTQ+ issues. Much of the emphasis in Herzer's explanation has to do with feelings and emotions, which, while having their place, are untrustworthy and subject to change by life's circumstances: "The heart is deceitful above all things, and desperately wicked; Who can know it" (Jeremiah 17:9)? "He who trusts in his own heart is a fool,

---

[52] Herzer, 38–39.

but whoever walks wisely will be delivered" (Proverbs 28:26). Notice that Solomon tells us that it is possible to follow our hearts and not walk wisely. Respectfully, I believe this is what LGBTQ+ activists are doing.

When we read about the rules and regulations God provided for the children of Israel, we cannot ignore that God's intention for them was that they would be holy. Leviticus 20 speaks about the penalties for breaking God's law. God admonishes His people against worshiping idols (vv. 1–5); turning to mediums and psychics (v. 6); honoring parents (v. 9); committing adultery (v. 10); homosexual practices, "If a man lies with a male as he lies with a woman, both of them have committed an abomination. They shall surely be put to death" (v. 13); etc. The chapter ends by giving one reason for God's people to follow His laws, "And *you shall be holy to Me, for I the Lord am holy*, and have separated you from the peoples, that you should be Mine" (v. 26, emphasis supplied). The holiness of His people was part of God's plan for day one. "Now therefore, if you will indeed obey My voice and keep My covenant, then you shall be a special treasure to Me above all people; for all the earth is Mine. And you shall be to Me a kingdom of priests and a holy nation" (Exodus 19:5–6). Notice holiness comes from obeying God, doing things His way, not ours.

Many of the arguments made by LGBTQ+ proponents have to do with these prescriptions that were just for the children of Israel because God did not want them to behave like the heathen nations around them and that they were culturally conditioned. But is holiness a cultural issue? Is holiness something relegated to just the children of Israel? Of course not! The apostle Peter said, "Therefore gird up the loins of your mind, be sober, and rest your hope fully upon the grace that is to be brought to you at the revelation of Jesus Christ; *as obedient children, not conforming yourselves to the former lusts, as in your ignorance*; but as He who called you is holy, you also be holy in all your conduct, because it is written, *"Be holy, for I am holy"* (1 Peter 1:13–16, emphasis supplied). Peter is quoting from Exodus 19. Thus, he also connects holiness with obeying God. His words apply to the Christian church today, that is, we are to be holy.

The Hebrew for *holy* in Exodus 19 is the word *qadosh*, which is also translated as "sacred." It is the same word we find in Genesis 2:3 in speaking about the Sabbath. God sanctified the seventh-day Sabbath, that is, He set it apart from all the others. Thus, when we think about God's command for His people today to be holy, He is saying He wants us to stand apart, to be different, not to be like everyone else. It is the same meaning that is given in 1 Peter 1:16. The word *holy* comes from the Greek word *hagios*, which means "set apart by (or for) God, holy, sacred."[53] Notice also that Peter counsels us not to be like we were before coming to the knowledge of the gospel. This implies a change; a transformation has taken place, and he does not want us to go back to what we once were. The idea that a person can be a practicing Christian and subscribe to the LGBTQ+ ideology and lifestyle is incongruent with the word of God. The desire of some, like Alicia Johnston, that the church affirms LGBTQ+ ideology is asking the church to condone sin and not require a change when coming to Christ. In fact, she believes that the church has too many rules. Speaking about the church organization she says,

> The institution is the problem. It constrains member's compassion. If Adventist individuals felt the moral responsibility to *make their own decisions*, everything would be different. In this instance, Adventist people are better than their institution. Adventist people would suffer longer and study deeper if the decisions rested on them alone. This is the problem…[54]

I assume the perfect church, for this former Adventist pastor, is a church where everyone makes their own rules. It doesn't matter what one believes, just come and worship, and love one another… That's all that matters. I am sure she would correct me for making

---

[53] "40, hagios," Bible Hub https://biblehub.com/greek/40.htm.
[54] Johnston, 329.

that statement, perhaps she would say, "The church needs to have rules, except when it comes to LGBTQ+ issues."

But compromise with the world is a big problem. Ellen White said it this way,

> Many who call themselves Christians are mere human moralists. They have refused the gift which alone could enable them to honor Christ by representing Him to the world. The work of the Holy Spirit is to them a strange work. They are not doers of the word. The heavenly principles that distinguish those who are one with Christ from those who are one with the world have become almost indistinguishable. The professed followers of Christ are no longer a separate and peculiar people. The line of demarcation is indistinct. The people are subordinating themselves to the world, to its practices, its customs, its selfishness. The church has gone over to the world in transgression of the law, when the world should have come over to the church in obedience to the law. Daily the church is being converted to the world.[55]

But many in the Christian world, certainly in the Seventh-day Adventist Church, want to be like everyone else. I am reminded of the story found in 1 Samuel 8. The children of Israel were demanding to have a king. They told the prophet Samuel, "Now make us a king to judge us *like all the nations*" (1 Samuel 8:5, emphasis supplied). This is what we are seeing today. "Acceptance of homosexuality is rising across the broad spectrum of American Christianity, including among members of churches that strongly oppose homosexual relationships as sinful, according to an extensive Pew Research Center

---

[55] Ellen G. White, *Christ's Object Lessons* (Silver Spring, MD: Ellen G. White Estate) 315.

survey of U.S. religious beliefs and practices."[56] This survey was conducted eight years ago; we may imagine that today the results would show that even more Christians have "become assimilated." Research conducted in 2019 revealed that "More than six in ten (62%) Americans say they have become more supportive toward transgender rights compared to their views five years ago. By contrast, about one-quarter (25%) say their views are more opposed compared to five years ago."[57]

This is probably seen as progress by some but not by those who understand the "Great Controversy" and maintain a biblical worldview.

Romans 1:24–27

The book of Romans, in my opinion, provides the clearest picture of how God views same-sex relationships. Here is what the apostle Paul says in the above passages:

> Therefore God also gave them up to uncleanness, in the lusts of their hearts, to dishonor their bodies among themselves, who exchanged the truth of God for the lie, and worshiped and served the creature rather than the Creator, who is blessed forever. Amen. For this reason God gave them up to vile passions. For even their women exchanged the natural use for what is against nature. Likewise also the men, leaving the natural use of the woman, burned in

---

[56] Carlye Murphy, "Most US Christian Groups Grow More Accepting of Homosexuality," *Pew Research Center* (December 2015), accessed September 14, 2023, https://www.pewresearch.org/short-reads/2015/12/18/most-u-s-christian-groups-grow-more-accepting-of-homosexuality.

[57] Robert P. Jones, Ph.D., "America's Growing Support for Transgender Rights" *PRRI* (June 2019), accessed September 14, 2023, https://www.prri.org/research/americas-growing-support-for-transgender-rights.

their lust for one another, men with men committing what is shameful, and receiving in themselves the penalty of their error which was due.

Verse 24 starts with the word *therefore*, which suggests that Paul is making a conclusion based on what he has already said. Thus, we must look at the context. The book of Romans is a jewel in the New Testament, as it provides the reader with a clear answer to "What is the Gospel?" and "What does it mean to be saved?" Paul usually composed his epistles to congregations that he had established, the letter to the church in Rome is an exception. Paul had three purposes in his writing of the letter. He had a practical, strategic, and theological purpose. Practically, Paul had already evangelized many of the Roman provinces and was getting ready to visit Spain. Therefore, he hoped that the Roman Christian would provide a base of support for him in much the same way that Antioch had done during the early evangelization of the East. Strategically, if the Roman Church was to provide a solid base, its Gentile and Jewish factions had to put it all together. You will notice that Paul dedicates a lot of time to trying to bring peace between Jews and Gentiles. His theological purpose was that he felt he needed to establish his theological credentials. Therefore, he wrote a letter that set forth his view of the logic of the gospel.[58]

Since Paul had not established the church of Rome, he starts his letter by introducing himself and by explaining why he had not yet visited Rome. Then, not wasting any time, he summarizes the gospel, "For I am not ashamed of the gospel of Christ, for it is the power of God to salvation for everyone who believes, for the Jew first and also for the Greek. For in it the righteousness of God is revealed from faith to faith; as it is written, "The just shall live by faith" (Romans 1:16–17). Then in verse 18, he starts his main argument, namely, "Why do men need the gospel?" Why? Because we all have a common disease, if you will, that is, sin! Sin brings about the wrath of

---

[58] George R. Knight, *Exploring Romans: A Devotional Commentary* (Hagerstown, MD: Review and Herald Publishing Association, 2010), 16–19.

God because "they are 'without excuse' since 'from the creation of the world' His 'eternal power and divine nature' have been evident to all people (v. 20). That is, even people who don't have the Bible have some word from God, some knowledge of who He is and what He stands for."[59]

So from verses 21–32, Paul describes the results of sin, and these go from bad to worst. "When the heathen (Gentiles) willfully turned away from God and shut them out of their minds and hearts, God left them to walk in their own ways of self-destruction."[60] The phrase "God gave them up" is mentioned three times in these passages. God does not hold a gun to our head to make us do what He wants. After doing all that He could to show the Gentiles who He was and what He required, since they did not want to hear it, He let them have what they wanted.

God delivered sinful humanity over to its own desires. In a move that our contemporary world would say is the most terrifying thing God could do, God punishes sin by letting us have control over our own destinies. God's wrath, therefore, does not mean some divine restraint imposed as punishment on humanity. Rather, the wrath gives us a free hand to do whatever our desires incline us to do. The way God in His wrath delivers humanity over to the just punishment of sin is to become permissive. He withdraws the gracious power of His absolute Lordship and allows other lordships to prevail.[61]

The same is true today. Someone once told me, "Be careful what you want because you might just get it." Sin gives birth to sin, and before you know it, you come to view evil as normal. So

> In response to the evil lusts of their hearts, God abandoned them to heterosexual uncleanliness—adultery, fornication, lewdness, prostitu-

---

[59] Ibid., 51.
[60] "Gave Them Up" [Romans 1:24], *Seventh-day Adventist Bible Commentary (SDABC)*, rev. ed., ed. Francis D. Nichol (Washington, DC: Review & Herald, 1976–1980), 6:480.
[61] Paul J. Achtemeir, *Romans: Interpretation: A Bible Commentary for Teaching and Preaching* (Louisville, KY: John Knox Press, 1985), 39.

tion, harlotry, and more. Life became for them a round of sex orgies in which to dishonor their bodies among themselves (vs. 24). This abandonment by God was because they first abandoned truth about him for the lie of idolatry. An idol is a lie, a false representation of God. An idolater worships the image of the creature, and thus insults and dishonors the Creator, who is eternally worthy of honor and glory, not of insult. (vs.25) For the same reason God gave people up to erotic activity with members of their own sex. Women became lesbians, practicing unnatural sex and knowing no shame (vs. 26). Men became sodomites, in total perversion of their natural function. Turning away from the marriage relationship ordained by God, they burned with lust for other men and practice homosexuality (vs. 27).[62]

Understanding the nature of sin and how Satan works is very important, and as already mentioned, sin gets worse with every step you take. No one who reads these passages objectively can ignore the fact that same-sex relationships are presented as immoral, the result of lust, vile passions, and debased minds. It is interesting that, like Jesus, Paul goes back to creation as the foundation of his argument: "For since the *creation of the world* His invisible attributes are clearly seen, being understood by *the things that are made*, even His eternal power and Godhead, so that they are without excuse" (Romans 1:20, emphasis supplied). God created humanity male and female, and the sexual union is to take place only between male and female. Any deviation from God's blueprint is rebellion against God, no matter how people will try to justify it. And they do try to justify it.

For example, Robert A. J. Gagnon quotes John R. Jones, a Seventh-day Adventist New Testament scholar who says that "Paul's

---

[62] Macdonald, *Believer's Bible Commentary*, 1670.

views in Romans 1:24–27 can be discounted because Paul, as a child of his historical environment, simply could not have conceived of an innate homosexual orientation or a committed same-sex sexual relationship… Paul operated with his culture's misguided notions about homosexual sin."[63] If one can ignore a portion of scripture by arguing that the author was not as well informed as we are today, then we can ignore any portion of scripture using the same argument.

Let us again look at verses 26–27:

> For this reason God gave them up to vile passions. For even their women exchanged the natural use for what is against nature. Likewise also the men, leaving the natural use of the woman, burned in their lust for one another, men with men committing what is shameful, and receiving in themselves the penalty of their error which was due.

For what reason did God give them up to vile passions? Because they "exchanged the truth of God for the lie" (v. 25). To exchange, the Greek word *metallassó* means to give or take something in return for something else. So they exchanged the truth of God and of the things He made since the creation of the world (v. 20) for the lie that men and women can engage in sexual relationships against nature or according to things that are unnatural. Thus, doing things against nature goes against the things that God has shown since the creation of the world by the things that are made. While God made many things during the creation, He also made humanity male and female.

Yet Alicia Johnston argues,

> Paul's point is not that homoeroticism is wrong for straight people because it's unnatural for them, but it would be natural for gay and

---

[63] Robert A. J. Gagnone, "The Scriptural Case for a Male-Female Prerequisite for Sexual Relations," 92.

bisexual people. That kind of reading is out of step with Paul's culture. That's what the words might have meant in our culture, but natural and unnatural had a different meaning in Paul's day. That's because Paul's culture didn't conceptualize sexual orientation the way we do. They didn't believe some people would naturally fall in love with their same gender and be suited best for partnership with their same gender. If Paul spoke to a culture like ours, and to people in the heterosexual and LGBTQ communities today, we might imagine that he intended for his words to apply to straight people for whom same sex is unnatural.[64]

The fact, however, is that

> Expressions such as "uncleanness," "dishonor" and "dishonoring," "contrary to nature," and "shame, shamefull (ness), and indecency" are all terms that Hellenistic Jewish literature uses to refer to sinful behavior... The nature argument in Romans 1:24–27 is...an extension of the Creation argument in 1:18–23. For some basic matters, what God intends for us should be readily transparent "by means of the things made" ever since "the creation of the world" (1:20). This is what "contrary to nature" means in Romans 1:26—acting in such a manner that one suppresses the transparent evidence in the material structures of Creation regarding God's will for one's life.[65]

---

[64] Johnston, 253.
[65] Gagnone, 98–99.

What is sad about this is that LGBTQ+ activists argue that their beliefs do not affect anybody but themselves. Yet they endlessly promote this through the many avenues of media. As already discussed, one just has to type transgender on YouTube, and the results will show a plethora of videos promoting the lifestyle and encouraging others to participate in such a lifestyle.

Paul ends chapter 1 by saying, "Who, knowing the righteous judgment of God, that those who practice such things are deserving of death, not only do the same but also approve of those who practice them" (v. 32).

> It may strike us as odd that Paul in verse 32 seems to think approving such acts is worse than doing them, but what he is pointing to is the fact that those who do things not only do them in their own lives but make them a matter of public encouragement for others to follow. Not content to let wrath take its course in their lives, such people, Paul says, seek to make the measure of their sinful conduct the norm for the conduct of others. It is a desire to make their private sin the measure of public conduct that Paul is condemning here.[66]

This seems to describe the world we are living in today. We live in a time where what was wrong is right and what was right is now wrong. There was a time when there were no arguments against the clear statements of scripture, but that time is long gone. Today, even so-called Christian scholars are defending political correctness in the name of scripture, and unfortunately, this is also happening in the Adventist Church.

> We live in a society that approves and applauds a great deal of evil... Modern society

---

[66] Paul J. Achtemeir, 41–42.

really hasn't moved beyond the ancient world in such matters. It is true, of course, that we no longer feed people to lions or let gladiators battle to the death. No, we are much more sophisticated in the sense that we do the same things in virtual reality through our media… And it reveals much about Christian confusion on this topic.[67]

LGBTQ+ ideology is being presented today either as a sickness (mental health problems) or as a legitimate alternative lifestyle. Either way, it leads to confusion. As Christians, we must be careful not to accept the world's moral judgments or to take the word of so-called scientists and mental health professionals as if it were the gospel. Furthermore, we must be careful about affirming people's "emotions" and "feelings" as a way to discover truth. We must be guided by God's word and maintain a biblical worldview.

1 Corinthians 6:9–11

> Do you not know that the unrighteous will not inherit the kingdom of God? Do not be deceived. Neither fornicators, nor idolaters, nor adulterers, *nor homosexuals, nor sodomites,* nor thieves, nor covetous, nor drunkards, nor revilers, nor extortioners will inherit the kingdom of God. *And such were some of you.* But you were washed, but you were sanctified, but you were justified in the name of the Lord Jesus and by the Spirit of our God. (emphasis supplied)

---

[67] Knight, 56.

Understanding the background purpose for the epistle will help better comprehend the words of these passages.

> Ancient Corinth was (and is) in southern Greece, west of Athens, strategically situated on the trade routes in Paul's day. It became a great center for international commerce, and immense quantities of traffic came to the city. Because of the depraved religion of the people, it soon became the center also for the grossest forms of immorality, so that the name Corinth was a byword for all that was impure and sensual.[68]

> The main burden of this epistle is twofold: first, reproof for the backsliding, which had resulted in the introduction into the Church of practices that corrupted the teachings of the gospel; and second, instruction or explanation, regarding the points of belief and practice concerning which the believers had sought for clarification.[69]

In chapter 6, Paul starts by admonishing believers against having lawsuits against each other. His argument is that believers (the church) should be able to resolve these matters among themselves, instead of bringing outsiders to handle them and, in so doing, bringing disrepute to the cause of God.

> Now therefore, it is already an utter failure for you that you go to law against one another. Why do you not rather accept wrong? Why do you not rather let yourselves be cheated? No, you

---

[68] Macdonald, *Believer's Bible Commentary*, 1750.
[69] "Theme" [1 Corinthians], *Seventh-day Adventist Bible Commentary (SDABC)*, rev. ed., ed. Francis D. Nichol (Washington, DC: Review & Herald, 1976–1980), 6:657.

yourselves do wrong and cheat, and you do these things to your brethren! (v. 7–8)

The believers in Corinth should have known better, which is why Paul continues in verses 9–10 by listing a series of behaviors that, like what was happening in the church as a result of the lawsuits against one another, are inconsistent with the Christian lifestyle. Nobody disagrees that idolatry, drunkenness, fornication, and adultery have no place among Christians. Although these behaviors do exist in the Christian Church, "for all have sinned and fall short of the glory of God," no one is trying to find scriptural reasons the church should affirm these behaviors. In fact, Paul says, "Do not be deceived," those who behave in such a matter and continue in them without repenting will not inherit the kingdom of God (v. 10). The issue changes when it comes to "homosexuals."

The Greek word used here for *homosexual* is the adjective *malakos*, which happens to be in the nominative masculine plural. The nominative in Greek grammar is used to indicate the subject of a sentence. Thus, the subject in the sentence is masculine in gender behaving soft, delicate, or effeminate.[70]

> When used in connection with terms expressive of sensual vice as those found in vs. 9, it designates homosexuals, more particularly those who yield themselves to be used for such immoral purposes... The list of sins found in vs. 9, 10 includes most of the common sins of the flesh. If a man persists in cherishing any of these evil habits, he will be excluded from the kingdom of God.[71]

---

[70] "3120, malakos," Bible Hub https://biblehub.com/greek/3120.htm.
[71] "Effeminate" [1 Corinthians 6:9], *Seventh-day Adventist Bible Commentary (SDABC)*, rev. ed., ed. Francis D. Nichol (Washington, DC: Review & Herald, 1976–1980), 6:699.

It is interesting that in verse 9, with the exception of idolatry, Paul mentions sexual sins. The reason idolatry is mentioned may be that among heathen people, licentiousness was usually connected with idol worship. Another reason for including idolatry is that licentiousness centers on the sexual abuse of the human body, and those who practice it may be said to make an idol of the means by which their lust is gratified.[72] Paul seems to place *malakos* under the umbrella of sexual immorality or *pornoi* in the Greek. Thus, sexual immorality can cover a number of behaviors; fornication, which would be the act of having sex with someone one is not married to; adultery, which is when a married person has a sexual relationship with someone not his/her spouse; homosexuality, which describes a person who is romantically and/or sexually attracted to people of their own sex; and sodomites, from the Greek *arsenokoites*, which is defined as "a male engaging in same-gender sexual activity."[73] Although Paul does not mention bisexuals, transgenders, queers, etc., we must also include them here because such behaviors, as already seen, go contrary to God's blueprint established at creation. They would all fall under the umbrella of sexual immorality.

"Malakos" and "Arsenokoites"

The above two words translated as homosexuals are the subject of some controversy. Some scholars believe that when Paul uses the word *arsenokoites*, he is quoting from the Old Testament, particularly Leviticus 18:22 and 20:13. Let us look. "You shall not lie with a male as with a woman. It is an abomination," and "If a man lies with a male as he lies with a woman, both of them have committed an abomination. They shall surely be put to death. Their blood shall be upon them." Of course, Paul would be using the Septuagint (the Greek translation of the Old Testament), thus, "you shall not lie

---

[72] Ibid., "Idolaters."
[73] "733, arsenokoites," Bible Hub https://biblehub.com/greek/733.htm.

[koite] with a man [arsenos] as with a woman."[74] Since *arsenokoites* is only mentioned twice in the New Testament (1 Corinthians 6:9 and 1 Timothy 1:10) and both used by the apostle Paul, it is difficult to determine how else this word was used elsewhere. Yet this does not stop Johnston from speculating what *arsenokoites* could mean.

> In Rome, financial exploitation (and other controlling behavior) was frequently referred to in sexual terms. It's similar to slang and expletives common in every language today, like "he screwed me over." Considering the latter usage of "arsenokoites" refer to financial exploitation, it's feasible that this word could have described people who cheat or otherwise exploit others. Or it could more directly referred to someone who trades in catamites (a young boy enslaved and raped), possibly kidnapping and enslaving young boys, a definition that might fit well with 1 Timothy 1:10.[75]

While acknowledging that she is speculating, notice how she eliminates *arsenokoites* from the umbrella of sexual immoral behaviors listed by Paul in 1 Corinthians 6:9. She does the same with the word *malakos* or *malakoi*. She says,

> When Paul used the word "malakoi" he was using a word in Greek that was the opposite of "virtus." "Malakoi were feminine, soft, and morally weak. They had no self-determination. They were dishonest, conniving, lacking control. They were mush, filling their lives with luxury and avoiding hardship. They love makeup and fine clothing. They ate before they were hungry. They slept before they were tired. They were afraid

---

[74] Johnston, 232.
[75] Ibid., 233.

of a fight... A "malakos" was not necessarily a man who had sex with other men... "Malakoi" are those people who cannot put up with hard work... It should be clear that "malakoi" was not a sexual term. It referred to men who were effeminate. Indeed, nearly every translation before the twentieth century used some version of the word effeminate. Men penetrated by other men would be "melakoi," but that was neither the most common nor the most morally salient understanding of the word.[76]

Again, one cannot ignore the connection of both these words *malakos* and *arsenokoites* with sexual offenses. We see the same thing in 1 Timothy 1:8–10:

> But we know that the law is good if one uses it lawfully, knowing this: that the law is not made for a righteous person, but for the lawless and insubordinate, for the ungodly and for sinners, for the unholy and profane, for murderers of fathers and murderers of mothers, for manslayers, *for fornicators, for sodomites,* for kidnappers, for liars, for perjurers, and if there is any other thing that is contrary to sound doctrine. (emphasis supplied)

Once again, Paul ties sodomites "arsenokoites" with the sexually immoral "pornois." These are part of the ungodly and sinners. Sexual immorality (porneia) of any kind is part of the works of the flesh (Galatians 5:19) and those practicing these will not inherit the kingdom of God. To attribute any other meaning to these words is simply "grasping at straws."

---

[76] Ibid., 235–237.

It is important to clarify that saying that those who practice any kind of behavior under the sexual immorality umbrella (LGBTQ+ ideology and lifestyle) will not inherit the kingdom of God is not an automatic sentence. As Paul said in Romans 1:16, "For I am not ashamed of the gospel of Christ, for it is *the power of God to salvation for everyone who believes…*" The gospel provides the power to change, but he who desires a transformation must realize his need for it. We will address this in chapter 4.

As we have seen, addressing transgenderism from a Christian perspective is not an easy task for many Christians have drunk the proverbial "Kool-Aid" and have bought into a politically correct ideology attempting to justify it using the Bible. While in some cases their explanations seem eloquent and meaningful, what we have seen is that they are "grasping at straws" and taking huge leaps of logic. The premise of this book is that affirming the LGBTQ+ lifestyle and ideology will damage our witness and the proclamation of the Present Truth for this time. We will explore this in the next chapter.

CHAPTER 3

A Dangerous Compromise

In my book *The Present Truth and the Three Angels' Messages*, I present the subject of Creation as part of the Three Angels' Messages of Revelation 14 and, thus, part of the Present Truth for today.

Why does God include the doctrine of Creation as part of the present truth? It would seem obvious, but we live in a time when belief in Creation is often ridiculed. In fact, a Gallup poll published in July 2019 revealed that forty percent of U.S. adults ascribe to a strictly creationist view of human origins, believing that God created them in their present form within roughly the past 10,000 years. However, more Americans continue to think that humans evolved over millions of years—either with God's guidance (33%) or, increasingly, without God's involvement at all (22%). Thus, most Americans do not accept the story of Creation as presented in Genesis 1 and 2… While 40 percent of Americans support creationism, as stated above, evolution has crept into Christianity as well in the form of theistic evolution. What is theistic evolution? The theistic evolutionist holds a position somewhat between that of the absolute evolutionist and the creationist. He believes that God created the materials of our universe and then guided and superintended the process by which all life has evolved from the very simplest one-celled form on up to the sophisticated forms which we know today.[1]

So it seems that with respect to the story of Creation many Christians have compromised. Compromise! If you looked up the definition of the word, you would read that it is an agreement or a settlement of a dispute that is reached by each side making concessions.[2] I have often been a critic of political parties in the United States because it seems that no matter what the state of our country is, nobody is willing to be the bigger person. Everybody sticks to their guns, so to speak, and nobody is willing to compromise. I think that our country would be a lot better if our leaders compromised a little, don't you?

So to compromise may seem like the right thing to do, at least in the secular world. But is it safe to compromise in the spiritual realm? Someone once said that compromise is simply changing the question to fit the answer. Notice that in the definition, each side must make concessions. Is it safe for us to make concessions in our spiritual lives? Is it possible to compromise with Satan? I am reminded of a true story I read some time ago:

> Neville Chamberlain was known for his policy of appeasement. As the prime minister of Britain before World War II, he knew that the country was still weary from the first World War and wanted to avoid a European war at all costs. The problem was that at the same time Hitler was planning to overrun Europe, including Britain. Chamberlain did not want Britain to have to confront Hitler and his army, so in September of 1938 he reached an agreement with Hitler that resulted in the Munich Pact. Italy and France

---

[1] Nelson Mercado, *The Present Truth and the Three Angels' Messages* (Nampa, ID: Pacific Press Publishing Association, 2021), 66.
[2] "Compromise," *Merriam-Webster*, accessed September 18, 2023, https://www.merriam-webster.com/dictionary/compromise.

joined Britain in agreeing to surrender parts of Czechoslovakia to Germany in return for Hitler's agreement not to invade any other European countries. Chamberlain confidently came home proclaiming, "Peace in our time." They really believed that by giving into Hitler's demands he would stop, or limit, his aggression. And, at that point, America was standing back hoping the whole thing would go away. But Hitler arrogantly ignored the pact, taking most of Czechoslovakia and invading Poland. It became obvious that France and Britain were in his sights as well. The Munich Pact is now a universal symbol of the failure of the policy of appeasement.[3]

We cannot compromise with sin and think it will turn out okay. However, there are those who view a compromise about creationism as unimportant. That is, many believe that we can still be "good card-carrying" Seventh-day Adventists and no longer believe in creation because none of our other beliefs will be affected. Thus, I shared *seven reasons it matters what we believe about creation*:

1. Scripture has a position.
2. Jesus took a position.
3. Relationship to the plan of salvation.
4. Foreshadows the new earth.
5. Implications for the character of God.
6. Implications for the worth of human beings.
7. Implications for the Sabbath.[4]

The conclusion was that rejecting a literal six-day creation cannot be isolated from the rest of our beliefs, believing they will not be

---

[3] Rodney Buchanan, "Evil Will Not Compromise," *Sermon Central*, accessed September 18, 2023, https://www.sermoncentral.com/sermon-illustrations/9703/evil-will-not-compromise-by-sermon-central.

[4] Mercado, 68–70.

affected. Like a row of dominos standing one in front of the other, when one falls, it brings down all the others.[5] However, there are those who believe that affirming the LGBTQ+ ideology and lifestyle will not affect the pillars of our faith. Former Seventh-day Adventist pastor Alicia Johnston says it this way:

> The Adventist church opposes same gender marriage and transgender identity, but that teaching is not part of the core belief systems of the church. If we change that one belief, as I advocate, there's no need to change any other belief. Opposition to same-sex marriage and transgender identity is not part of the baptismal vows. It's not integral to the structure of the belief system. Opposition is a second-tier theological conclusion, not a foundational assumption… Advocating for affirming same-gender marriage and transgender identity within a framework that is distinctly Adventist is entirely consistent.[6]

What does Johnston want the church to do? Compromise. "It will be all right if we simply compromise on this small issue of LGBTQ+ ideology." How has society compromised on this issue? By saturating everything with the LGBTQ+ ideology. We hear about it in the news, sitcoms, cartoons, movies, social media, you name it. Little by little, opinions on the issue change, one person at a time, until, "Voila!" the authorities establish laws that, while protecting the rights of members of the LGBTQ+ community (I am all for that), diminish the rights of those who want to maintain a biblical worl-

---

[5] Ibid.,70.
[6] Alicia Johnston, *The Bible and LGBTQ Adventists: A Theological Conversation about Same-Sex Mariage, Gender, and Identity,* (Affirmative Collective, 2022), 10.

dview. Make no mistake, Satan is using the same strategy inside the church. Notice,

> The Adventist church is organized from the ground up. We've forgotten this. Too many layers of administration make it seem that only administrators make decisions. But that isn't true. The Adventist church is a representative organization. Church members elect the people who run the church. Power ultimately comes from members who change rules and change officers in their conference constituency meetings. They select the Executive Committee that is ultimately responsible for all significant decisions outside of those meetings. That means members, and only members, empower administrators to make changes. *That's why this book exists (The Bible & LGBTQ Adventists). Members need tools. We need theological teaching that doesn't come from the institution because the institution's resistance to change means many new ideas are suppressed.*[7] (emphasis supplied)

I am thankful for the organization of the Seventh-day Adventist Church. I believe it is God ordained. Indeed, if administrators are making decisions that run contrary to a "Thus saith the Lord," the church members should take the steps necessary to remove such administrators from their leadership positions. But notice that Satan's strategy is very similar. Between the lines, Johnston is saying that we should stop reading books written by church authors because they reflect the resistance of the church to "new ideas." The solution, in her mind, seems to be that people read books from outside the church that promote these "new ideas."

---

[7] Ibid., 330.

Now I am not saying that we should only read books that are written by Adventist authors. I, for one, read a variety of books written by non-Adventist authors as well, and I have learned and been blessed by many. But she seems to be saying, "Throw away the Adventist books because they are part of the resistance." Her strategy is no different from what we see Satan using in society today. If he were to saturate the members of the church with the LGBTQ+ ideology and convince them that it is biblical and God ordained, he could ensure that the church leaders make changes and affirm this ideology. We must be careful because for every truth of God, Satan has a counterfeit. This does not mean that we sweep this topic under the rug so as not to see it. In part, the premise of this book is that it is time we have conversations with those in the LGBTQ+ community. We also need to teach and preach on this subject but from a biblical perspective and without compromising.

Speaking of the church, Johnston continues by saying, "The institution is the problem. It constrains members' compassion. If Adventist individuals felt the moral responsibility to make their own decisions, everything would be different. In this instance, Adventist people are better than their institution. Adventist people would suffer longer and study deeper if the decisions rested on them alone. This is a problem."[8] The implication, then, would be to have a church without guidelines and perhaps without baptismal vows. Everyone can believe what they want. Do you see how dangerous this ideology can be?

Johnston, obviously, is not the only one who disagrees with the Adventist Church's stance on LGBTQ+ ideology. For example,

> The pastor of Andover Seventh-day Adventist Church, Adam Breiner, announced his decision to step down from his role this summer, citing differences with the church's structure in relation to ministering to the LGBTQ community. During a heartfelt sermon, Pastor Breiner expressed that he believed the current structure of

---

[8] Ibid., 329.

the Seventh-day Adventist Church does not adequately allow for outreach to gay and transgender individuals, stating that the church environment sometimes encourages members to act on biases, misunderstandings of Scripture, and fears. He mentioned that this interpretation of the church's teachings often makes the LGBTQ community members feel marginalized and unable to experience God's love authentically.[9]

Bryan Ness, a biology professor at Pacific Union College, wrote an article titled "There Is More to Human Sexuality than XX and XY." In it, he defends consensual homosexual relationships as part of God's will for mankind. He ends his article by saying,

> I am convinced that a large part of the reason the church persists in prohibiting same-sex marriage is due to misguided purity concerns, driven by disgust of same-sex sexual behavior. People often overcome these biases when a family member or close friend comes out as gay or transgender, and it enables them to normalize their conception of what LGBTQ+ people are like. Once the church begins to see LGBTQ+ people as a normal part of the spectrum of human variation in sexuality and gender, it should enable us to see the moral rightness of same-sex marriage. A number of Christian denominations have been able to come to this conclusion, and it is my hope that the Seventh-day Adventist Church will reach this point soon as well.[10]

---

[9] "Pastor Leaves Andover SDA Church over LGBTQ Inclusivity," *Adventist Today.org* (August 2023), accessed September 19, 2023, https://atoday.org/pastor-leaves-andover-sda-church-over-lgbtq-inclusivity-concerns-in-sda-structure.

[10] Bryan Ness, "There Is More to Human Sexuality than XX and XY," *Spectrum Magazine* (February 2020), accessed September 19, 2023, https://

Back in 2017, NBC News published an article titled "Conservative Pastor Overcomes Struggles to Accept Transgender Daughter." In the article, Pastor Kris Widmer describes how his son Timothy came "out of the closet" as a transgender and called himself Teagan. My hat off to the Widmer family for sharing their story, as I have seen their video on the "Outspoken" video Series published by SDA Kinship International, an organization that provides support for Seventh-day Adventist members who are LGBTQ+. As a Seventh-day pastor myself, I imagine this must have been a terrible ordeal. The article, unfortunately, ended with this statement attributed to Debbie Widmer, Pastor Widmer's wife, although stated by Kris on the video: "We would like the church to continue to grow and change and to become the community of Christ, where love is more important than law and people are more important than policy,"[11] Notice that the desire is that the church changes its position. What is the church's position? In 2017, the church published the following statement:

> The increasing awareness of the needs and challenges that transgender men and women experience and the rise of transgender issues to social prominence worldwide raise important questions not only for those affected by the transgender phenomenon but also for the Seventh-day Adventist Church. While the struggles and challenges of those identifying as transgender people have some elements in common with the struggles of all human beings, we recognize the uniqueness of their situation and the limitation of our knowledge in specific instances. Yet, we believe that Scripture provides principles

---

spectrummagazine.org/news/2020/there-more-human-sexuality-xx-and-xy.

[11] John Paul Bramme, "Conservative Pastor Overcomes Struggles to Accept Transgender Daughter," *NBC News* (May 2017), accessed September 19, 2023, https://www.nbcnews.com/feature/nbc-out/conservative-pastor-overcomes-struggles-accept-transgender-daughter-n757066.

> for guidance and counsel to transgender people and the Church, transcending human conventions and culture… Due to contemporary trends to reject the biblical gender binary (male and female) and replace it with a growing spectrum of gender types, certain choices triggered by the transgender condition have come to be regarded as normal and accepted in contemporary culture. However, the desire to change or live as a person of another gender may result in biblically inappropriate lifestyle choices.[12]

Yes, there are complexities in the LGBTQ+ ideology and lifestyle that are hard to understand. However, when we look at the world through biblical lenses, we will better understand the "Great Controversy" and see that the Bible provides enough information for the church to take a stand against this ideology. This does not mean that the church rejects members of the LGBTQ+ community. The statement on transgenderism quoted above also provides principles for dealing with this issue (we will look at these later). LGBTQ+ people are welcomed, but welcoming them does not mean that the lifestyle and ideology must be affirmed. Therein lies the controversy because the desire of many is for the church to change. With all due respect to the Widmer's, and all who struggle with gender identity in the church, if the church is following scripture (and it is on this issue), when it comes to sin and morality, it is us that must change, not the church. And even if the church compromised on this issue and did change, God does not change (Malachi 3:6, Hebrews 13:8, and Psalm 33:11).

Unfortunately, some individual churches have compromised on the issue, although the church at large has not. Many by now have heard that the Hollywood Seventh-day Adventist Church has

---

[12] "Statement on Transgenderism," *Seventh-day Adventist Church* (April 2017), accessed September 19, 2023, https://www.adventist.org/official-statements/statement-on-transgenderism.

ordained a transgender woman as an elder in their church. The story (Rhonda's) is also included in the "Outspoken" video series. Unfortunately, there are some trends that are worrisome.

On the webpage of Union College, another one of the Seventh-day Adventist Educational Institutions, they wrote "LGBTQ+ Community at Union." It says,

> Live in Iris House with other LGBTQ+ students. Join the Union Pride club. Take part in annual events such as the Pride fest during Pride Week in the Spring term. Find support related to coming out or being out from designated members of the campus community who have trained to be Allies. Feel free to be yourself and express your sexual orientation and gender identity, no matter what form it takes. Union is committed to fostering and maintaining an environment that is welcoming and safe for all students and employees. We offer an array of resources to help members of the LGBTQ+ community fit in, grow and thrive; to end discrimination and bias; and to promote awareness, understanding, and acceptance of gender variations.[13]

Again, there is no room for discrimination against anyone. However, it seems that more and more Adventists are siding with political correctness and compromising their beliefs. This has led the church to publish an additional statement clarifying where it stands:

> The Seventh-day Adventist Church has published clear statements regarding human sexuality, homosexuality, and transgenderism. All these statements were published after a careful study of

---

[13] "LGBTQ+ Community at Union," *Union College*, accessed September 19, 2023, https://www.union.edu/intercultural-affairs/lgbtq-union.

God's Word found in the Holy Scriptures, as it provides the authoritative basis to appropriately understand His will on all issues facing humankind including that of human sexuality. From our study of God's Word, joined with reading the Spirit of Prophecy, we find human sexuality portrayed as a heaven-ordained institution of marriage between one man and one woman. In expressing our understanding of God's will on human sexuality, we have done so with Christ-like love and compassion knowing that all have sinned and fall short of His glorious standard for living (Romans 3:23). As a church family, we are to be an extension of God's love for all humanity and be intentional in supporting those who struggle with sin in all its forms while nurturing a lifestyle that is in harmony with God's Word. We believe that all sinful humankind can be new creations in Christ as II Corinthians 5:17 indicates: "Therefore, if anyone is in Christ, he is a new creation; old things have passed away; behold, all things have become new."

In recent weeks, some local individuals or sometimes local church organizations in their local settings have sought to provide support for those living alternative human sexuality lifestyles that are inconsistent with our biblical understanding of this issue and published voted statements of the Seventh-day Adventist Church. For some in their local settings, there have even been deliberate efforts to advance the cause of alternative human sexuality lifestyles without regard for the authority of God's Word and the counsels provided in the Spirit of Prophecy. Although these activities have been locally-sponsored, through social media they have been announced far and wide creating confusion and concern among church members who have been asking for a clear yet kind position on the matter from church leaders at various levels.

The General Conference affirms the voted statements on human sexuality, homosexuality, and transgenderism published by the Seventh-day Adventist Church and does not support, endorse, or condone activities that seek to promote human sexuality behaviors not in accordance with God's Word. Under the guidance of the Holy Spirit, the General Conference and its divisions will continue to work with the various levels of our church structure to resolve the issues emerging from these locally sponsored activities while maintaining Christ-like love and compassion for all people. The General Conference and other church entities will work diligently, according to the precepts and instructions of the Holy Word of God, to bring clarification and resolution to challenges that are faced. Every member of the church worldwide should stay close to the Word of God in daily living and through earnest prayer ask for God's direct intervention in situations where there is a departure from His divine instructions in the Bible and the Spirit of Prophecy. Undoubtedly, there will be more attempts by various groups to undermine the plain instructions from the Word of God and the voted statements of the world church on these matters. When individuals wish to share concerns, work closely with local church, conference, union, or institutional leaders in Christ-like love and compassion to address locally sponsored activities that are not in harmony with God's Word.

> Let us hold fast to God's precious Holy Word, the Bible, accepting Christ's justifying and sanctifying righteousness as we look forward to His soon second coming.[14]

I applaud the church leadership for taking a stand on this sensitive yet controversial issue. It is not a popular stand. In fact, it is one that has been very heavily criticized. Ellen White wrote a powerful statement found in the book *Education*, page 57:

> The greatest want of the world is the want of men—men who will not be bought or sold, men who in their inmost souls are true and honest, men who do not fear to call sin by its right name, men whose conscience is as true to duty as the needle to the pole, men who will stand for the right though the heavens fall.[15]

A Danger to the Present Truth

As seen above, Johnston and perhaps others do not believe that affirming LGBTQ+ ideology and lifestyle will affect any of the other beliefs we hold as Seventh-day Adventists. I firmly disagree. In the previous chapter, I mentioned how Johnston interprets the creation account. Here it is again:

> God separated the light of day from the darkness of night (Gen. 1:4,5). But we know

---

[14] 'Statement of the General Conference Regarding Locally Sponsored Activities Promoting or Supporting Nonbiblical Human Sexuality Lifestyles," *ANN* (June 2023), accessed September 19, 2023, https://adventist.news/news/statement-of-the-general-conference-regarding-locally-sponsored-activities-promoting-or-supporting-non-biblical-human-sexuality.

[15] Ellen G. White, "True and Honest Men," *Education*, accessed September 19, 2023, https://egwwritings.org/read?panels=p29.242&index=0.

that there is also an in-between time of twilight when the sun sets and rises. These emerge from the spaces of overlap, when one aspect of God's creation touches another. Does that mean sunsets and sunrises are outside of God's will? Of course not. These words were not intended to exclude sunsets from God's creative intent simply because they aren't day or night. Neither are sunsets in accident. The author simply did not include every possibility. Day and night are excellent examples of God's creation, not the only options... Many use Genesis 1:27 to indicate that "male and female" is all God created. This interpretation ignores the possibility of a Hebrew merism and is inconsistent with the rest of the creation narrative. The creation categories simply are not intended to explain all that can be, all that should be, or all that can morally and ethically be considered good.[16]

It is the same argument made by Linda Tatro Herzer:

Genesis 1 is such a poetic articulation of creation that I believe the author of Genesis was not trying to write a scientific explanation of the creation of all things... Consequently, when interpreting the verses in this chapter, we must be very careful about arguing from silence, that is, we should be cautious of our drawing a logical conclusion based on what the text does not state. This means that, just because Genesis 1 does not make a statement about a particular aspect of creation, this does not mean that reality does not

---

[16] Johnston, 61–63.

exist in creation, nor that it is not part of God's good creation.[17]

She then quotes Genesis 1:3–5, "Then God said, 'Let there be light'; and there was light. And God saw the light, that it was good; and God divided the light from the darkness. God called the light Day, and the darkness He called Night. So the evening and the morning were the first day." Then she argues, "Taking this poetic passage literally and believing that it explained all the realities that God created regarding a twenty-four-hour period would result in us believing that there is nothing other than night or day. Of course, we know from experience that there is also dusk and dawn, those times of day when it is not totally daily, but it is not totally night either."[18] She makes the same argument with Genesis 1:27, "So God created man in His own image; in the image of God He created him; male and female He created them," and concludes, "Some say this mean God has created only male and female. But might there be a dawn and a dusk, a shoreline and a marshland, another classification Kingdom in the realm of male and female? The reports of modern medicine answer this question with a resounding 'Yes!'"[19]

As I listen to these arguments, I am reminded of a similar one made by someone in Genesis 3:1: "Has God indeed said, 'You shall not eat of every tree of the garden'?" In essence, Satan was bringing in doubts about the clear word of God: "Did God really say that?" "Are you sure?" "Maybe you misunderstood Him," or "Maybe you do not need to take His word so literally. After all, His words seem more poetic than literal." You see, once you begin to doubt the clear word of God and try to explain it away, you are in very dangerous territory because you can make the word of God mean anything you want.

What if I made the same argument concerning the Sabbath? "Genesis is written in poetic form. God did not literally say we must keep the seventh day but that we must dedicate one day in seven to

---

[17] Linda Tatro Herzer, *The Bible and the Transgender Experience: How Scripture Supports Gender Variance* (Cleveland, OH: The Pilgrim Press, 2016), 52.
[18] Ibid.
[19] Ibid., 54.

Him." While Herzer is not a Seventh-day Adventist, Johnston still claims to be and still believes in the Sabbath, although she no longer attends a Seventh-day Adventist Church.[20] If the Seventh-day Adventist Church were to change its stance on the LGBTQ+ ideology and lifestyle, it would do so believing that scripture defends the lifestyle as normal and God ordained. LGBTQ+ supporters would shout, "Hooray, it's about time." But we cannot ignore the implications of such a move.

If the church were to start making the same arguments that Johnston and Herzer made, then this would endanger our belief in creationism. The Bible says that God created the world in six literal days and rested on the seventh. If you use the poetic argument or the one about "Hebrew Merisms," then an argument could be made against a literal six-day creation. "Maybe the writer of Genesis poetically said that God created in six days, but the reality is that each day was an undetermined period of time. Thus, creation could have taken millions, if not billions, of years." Is not this the argument made by those who believe in evolution or the compromised version of it, "theistic evolution?"

So if the church affirms LGBTQ+ ideology, the belief in a literal six-day creation story goes by the wayside. Please remember that a literal six-day creation is part of the Present Truth as I argue in the book *The Present Truth and the Three Angels' Messages*. Notice that I am not saying that the church would publicly proclaim that it no longer believes in a literal six-day creation story but becoming an "affirming" church will begin to cast doubts on everything else we believe. Again, this was Satan's strategy from the very beginning: "Did God really say that...?" Hey, if Genesis is written in poetic form, maybe Satan does not even exist, and maybe the serpent is just an impersonation of evil. Can you see how far this can go?

Let us continue. By casting doubt on a literal six-day creation story, we cast doubt on the reliability of the Bible. After all, biblical writers believed in a literal six-day creation account. "By the word of the Lord the heavens were made, And all the host of them by the

---

[20] Johnston, 336.

breath of His mouth" (Psalm 33:6). "For in six days the Lord made the heavens and the earth, the sea, and all that is in them, and rested the seventh day. Therefore the Lord blessed the Sabbath day and hallowed it" (Exodus 20:11).

We also cast doubts on Jesus. As we have already seen, Jesus went back to the story of creation in Matthew 19:4 when answering the question about divorce. "Have you not read that He who made them at the beginning 'made them male and female'?" If Jesus was mistaken about creation, can He be the perfect Messiah? It is a valid question.

The most obvious implication is what compromising with this ideology will do to our belief on the seventh-day Sabbath. By casting doubts on a literal reading of Genesis, as already mentioned, the Sabbath, too, can be interpreted in a poetic symbolic form. And if we were to defend the Sabbath by saying, "Oh no, this part of Genesis is literal," we would lose credibility, and rightly so. The fact is that the fourth commandment gives us the reason we are to remember to keep the Sabbath holy: "For in six days the Lord made the heavens and the earth, the sea, and all that is in them, and rested the seventh day. Therefore the Lord blessed the Sabbath day and hallowed it" (Exodus 20:11). But if God did not really make the heavens and the earth in six days, then we have no reason for keeping the weekly Sabbath. Or at the very least, we have lost our credibility in trying to defend it.

Let us continue. As mentioned above, the fourth commandment presents the Sabbath as connected to a literal six-day creation. If that is wrong, then this calls into question all of them. At the very least, it would justify the ideology of "just nine of them."

The first angel's message of Revelation 14 says,

> Then I saw another angel flying in the midst of heaven, having the everlasting gospel to preach to those who dwell on the earth—to every nation, tribe, tongue, and people—saying with a loud voice, "Fear God and give glory to Him, for the hour of His judgment has come; and worship

Him who made heaven and earth, the sea and springs of water." (vv. 6–7)

Affirming the LGBTQ+ ideology does away with our belief in creation, the law, and the Sabbath.

The message of the second angel reads, "Babylon is fallen, is fallen, that great city, because she has made all nations drink of the wine of the wrath of her fornication" (Revelation 14:8). In *The Present Truth and the Three Angels' Messages*, I define *Babylon* as "a religious-political system that defies God, confuses the world, and oppresses God's people; therefore, it is the enemy of both God and His people."[21] I also showed that the early church referred to Rome as Babylon, so we can safely assume the apostle John did so as well. Furthermore, in Revelation 17:1–5, John describes Babylon as an impure woman, which represents an impure, apostate church. Then I ask the question, "Does history provide us with a religious-political power that, in turn, is also a church and has its base in Rome?"[22] Well, yes it does. It is here that we embarked on the study of Daniel 7 and the "Little Horn." We identified the little horn (antichrist power) by the eight characteristics given in Daniel 7. One of those characteristics is found in Daniel 7:25: "And shall intend to change times and law."

For the most part, Seventh-day Adventists interpret Bible prophecy through historicism.

> The historicist method understands the prophecies of Daniel and Revelation to meet their fulfillments in historical time through a sequence of events running from the prophet's time down to the establishment of God's Kingdom at the end of the world. This method

---

[21] Mercado, 96.
[22] Ibid.

has been the cornerstone in Adventist interpretation of apocalyptic.[23]

As such, we understand that Babylon represents papal Rome (Roman Catholicism), who was the one responsible for transferring the solemnity of the seventh-day Sabbath to Sunday. Thus, papal Rome intended to "change times and law."

However, as we have already seen, becoming an "affirming" church with respect to LGBTQ+ ideology and lifestyle leads to throwing out our belief in creation, the law, and the Sabbath. If the Sabbath is just a poetic symbol (which is the only logical conclusion if we were to accept the arguments made by LGBTQ+ activists), then we have no biblical reason for keeping it; being this the case, papal Rome did not do anything wrong in adopting Sunday as the day of rest. After all, the implication would be that since Genesis is not to be interpreted literally, the account of the seventh-day Sabbath in Genesis 2 just meant that we needed to dedicate one day in seven to God. Thus, any day would do.

The second angel of Revelation 14:8 says that Babylon is judged (has fallen) "because she has made all nations drink of the wine of the wrath of her fornication." This wine of her fornication represents the doctrines established by Babylon (papal Rome) that have confused Christianity.[24] One of such doctrines is Sunday as the day of rest. Since the only logical conclusion is that Adventists are wrong about the Sabbath (we are assuming this to be the case if we affirm LGBTQ+ ideology), then perhaps our view of Babylon and papal Rome is also mistaken.

Another doctrine that has confused Christianity and the world is that papal Rome is responsible for the belief in the immortality of the soul. Therefore, Ellen White advises, "Through the two great errors, then immortality of the soul and Sunday sacredness, Satan will bring the people under his deceptions. While the former lays

---

[23] Tom Shepherd, "Interpretations of Biblical Types, Allegories, and Parables," in *Understanding Scripture: An Adventist Approach*, ed. George W. Reid (Silver Spring, MD: Biblical Research Institute, 2005), 249.

[24] Mercado, 114.

the foundation of spiritualism, the latter creates a bond of sympathy with Rome."[25] Since we have concluded that Adventists are wrong about the Sabbath and papal Rome (by affirming LGBTQ+ ideology), then Ellen White was wrong on at least part of this statement. Considering everything the Spirit of Prophecy says about the Sabbath and the end-time role of papal Rome, we must also reconsider our view of Ellen G. White as having the gift of prophecy. Perhaps she is a false prophet, like many of her critics say.

Finally, the message of the third angel of Revelation 14 warns,

> If anyone worships the beast and his image, and receives his mark on his forehead or on his hand, he himself shall also drink of the wine of the wrath of God, which is poured out full strength into the cup of His indignation. He shall be tormented with fire and brimstone in the presence of the holy angels and in the presence of the Lamb. And the smoke of their torment ascends forever and ever; and they have no rest day or night, who worship the beast and his image, and whoever receives the mark of his name. (vv. 9–11)

Seventh-day Adventists understand the beast of Revelation 13 to be the same entity as the little horn of Daniel 7, that is, papal Rome. Furthermore, they understand the mark of the beast to be Sunday worship when it is mandated by the governing authorities. However, by affirming the LGBTQ+ ideology and lifestyle, the church would have to agree with the biblical interpretation of its activists. Therefore, as we have seen, Adventists would be wrong about creation, the law, the Sabbath, the role of Babylon, the little horn, the Spirit of Prophecy, and Ellen G. White; and by extension, they must be wrong about the mark of the beast. Considering that it

---

[25] Ellen G. White, *The Great Controversy Between Christ and Satan* (Nampa, ID: Pacific Press Publishing Association, 2005), 588.

would mean that the Adventist method of biblical interpretation is suspect, then our view of the sanctuary is wrong as well. This would also affect the proclamation of the everlasting gospel, which is part of the message of the first angel (Revelation 14:6–7). Not to mention the doctrine of the Investigative Judgment that started in 1844, a doctrine that is closely tied to the Adventist understanding of the sanctuary.

One more thing, in the book of Revelation, God's people are described this way: "And the dragon was enraged with the woman, and he went to make war with the rest of her offspring, who *keep the commandments of God and have the testimony of Jesus Christ*" (12:17, emphasis supplied). "Here is the patience of the saints; here are those who *keep the commandments of God and the faith of Jesus*" (14:12, emphasis supplied). The Adventist understanding of its role as God's end-time remnant is tied to these passages. Our argument has always been that, contrary to the majority of Christianity, Adventists really keep the commandments (all ten) because we have understood the importance of the seventh-day Sabbath, and as a love response to Jesus, we keep it holy. However, we have already concluded that Adventists will be found wrong on the Sabbath issue if they affirm the LGBTQ+ ideology and lifestyle. Being this the case, we cannot be God's end-time remnant people.

The Seventh-day Adventist Church has twenty-eight fundamental beliefs, and it is important to notice that if the church were to compromise and affirm the LGBTQ+ ideology and lifestyle, it would have to revise or do away with at least the following fundamental beliefs:

- Fundamental belief 6: creation, for the reasons mentioned above
- Fundamental belief 10: the experience of salvation, as this is tied to our understanding of the sanctuary, for the reasons mentioned above
- Fundamental belief 13: the Remnant and its Mission, for the reasons mentioned above

- Fundamental belief 15: baptism, for we would have agreed to baptize people in their sins
- Fundamental belief 18: the gift of prophecy, for the reasons mentioned above
- Fundamental belief 19: The Law of God, for the reasons mentioned above
- Fundamental belief 20: The Sabbath, for the reasons mentioned above
- Fundamental belief 22: Christian behavior, for we would ignore the concept of holiness and, instead of being set apart and different, we would be acting like the rest of the world
- Fundamental belief 23: The marriage and the family, for we believe that marriage is to be only between a male and a female, and this is the foundation of a family
- Fundamental belief 24: Christ's ministry in the heavenly sanctuary, for the reasons mentioned above

Not to mention our baptismal vows would also need a major revision. Let me quote Alicia Johnston once again, "The Adventist church opposes same gender marriage and transgender identity, but that teaching is not part of the core belief system of the church. If we change that one belief…there is no need to change any other belief."[26] With all due respect, I don't think so! Like a row of dominos, when one falls, the rest follow along. This is why affirming the transgender (or LGBTQ+) movement is so dangerous to the Present Truth.

Itching Ears

The apostle Paul counseled young Timothy to "preach the word! Be ready in season and out of season. Convince, rebuke, exhort, with

---

[26] Johnston, 10.

all longsuffering and teaching" (2 Timothy 4:2). Why did Paul tell this to Timothy?

> For the time will come when they will *not endure sound doctrine*, but according to their own desires, because *they have itching ears*, they will heap up for themselves teachers; and they *will turn their ears away from the truth and be turned aside to fables*. But you be watchful in all things, endure afflictions, do the work of an evangelist, fulfill your ministry. (vv. 3–5, emphasis supplied)

The term "itching ears" is a term used to describe people who seek out messages and doctrines that support their own lifestyle.

> Not of the teachers, but of those who "will not endure sound doctrine," as the Greek makes clear. Because of their perverted "lust" these shallow minded hearers "itch" for fanciful interpretations of Scripture with which to gratify their curiosity and personal "desires." They are interested only in those portions of Scripture they can construe as promising them peace and security. They neglect the stern demands of "sound doctrine" which cut deep into a man's soul. They have a superficial desire for religion, but only for so much of it as will not disturb the routine of their perverted lives.[27]

I truly do not mean to be disrespectful, but some of the "itching ears" interpretations of scripture given by LGBTQ+ activists could be comical if they were not so dangerous. They begin to see gender

---

[27] "Itching Ears" [2 Timothy 4:3], *Seventh-day Adventist Bible Commentary (SDABC)*, rev. ed., ed. Francis D. Nichol (Washington, DC: Review & Herald, 1976–1980), 7:348.

issues in everything. I am reminded of this statement I heard on the radio that has been attributed to psychologist Abraham Maslow: "If the only tool you have is a hammer, you tend to see every problem as a nail." Let me give you a few examples from the book *The Bible and the Transgender Experience* that I have already quoted. Herzer, highlighting the differences between Esau and Jacob, quotes Genesis 25:27–28, "So the boys grew. And Esau was a skillful hunter, a man of the field; but Jacob was a mild man, dwelling in tents. And Isaac loved Esau because he ate of his game, but Rebekah loved Jacob." She then quotes Genesis 27:11, where Jacob tells his mother, "Look, Esau my brother is a hairy man, *and I am a smooth-skinned man.*" (emphasis supplied). Notice her conclusion:

> Does all this mean that Jacob was effeminate, or gay, or some form of transgender? We cannot know for sure, because along with not using the twenty-first century words we find under the transgender umbrella, the Bible, as it was originally written, also did not use historically modern words like gay, lesbian, or homosexual. Consequently, while we cannot conclusively determine the Patriarch Jacob's gender identity or sexual orientation from the biblical accounts, I think it is accurate to say that, given his preference for women's work and for spending his days among the women of his tribe, *he was definitely gender variant*; Jacob did not conform to the cultural expectations of the men of his day.[28] (emphasis supplied)

Notice that part of the problem with this gender identity confusion is the issue of gender roles. That is, if a person does not behave in a way a male is expected to behave, for example, or likes something that a male is expected to like, that person must be gender variant

---

[28] Herzer, 84.

and believe he is a female. Or if a female does not like things females are expected to like or behaves differently from a typical female, she is truly a male. Thus, steps must be taken to correct the mistake made by God!

Here is another example. Herzer comments on Joseph, Jacob's son. As we know, Jacob gave Joseph a tunic of many colors. The NIV translates this tunic as an "ornate robe." Apparently, according to Herzer, this "ornate robe" was a garment worn only by the virgin daughters of kings, (see 2 Samuel 13:18–19). Then she adds,

> Now why would a father who loves his son very much give him the kind of garment worn by the virgin daughters of kings? Wouldn't Jacob have known that wearing girls' clothing would make his beloved son at target of ridicule and bullying? And why would Joseph wear such a thing out in public? Wouldn't he be embarrassed to be seen wearing a girl's garment? ... One possible interpretation is that Jacob was sympathetic to a boy who felt drawn to female activities and clothing. So out of his great love for his son Joseph, *Jacob gave him an ornate robe that affirmed Joseph's gender nonconformity.* Jacob knowingly and lovingly gave Joseph the kind of garment worn by the virgin daughters of the king. And *Joseph wore this girly garment gladly.*[29] (emphasis supplied)

So, as it turns out, if we follow Herzer's argument, Joseph was transgender. Here is one more example, Deborah. Deborah, according to Herzer, performed functions and activities expected of a man. "Deborah served as a judge in Israel, this account is nothing short of a *gender variant* miracle story"[30] (emphasis supplied)! If you are like me, you probably laughed as you read these interpretations. These

---

[29] Ibid., 89.
[30] Ibid., 92.

are clear examples of having "itching ears," "turn their ears away from the truth, and be turned aside to fables." I suppose the argument can be made that the LGBTQ+ movement and their desire to be affirmed in the church by looking for biblical reasons are a prophetic fulfillment of the word of God. However, affirming the LGBTQ+ ideology and lifestyle would be a very dangerous compromise.

CHAPTER 4

Grasping at Straws

BY NOW, YOU HAVE NOTICED that I have spent a lot of time commenting on arguments made by Alicia Johnston, a former Seventh-day Adventist pastor who came out as bisexual in 2017 while pastoring the Arizona Foothills Community SDA Church. Her resignation after coming out made national news. In a video, Johnston said, "I don't know how to minister anymore without being honest about that," shortly before saying, "I, myself, am bisexual… I want to break the deadly silence that exists in churches that don't affirm LGBT people for who they are. That silence has to be broken to reach queer people who feel today like I used to feel; ashamed, unwanted and inconvenient."[1]

Let me say that in spite of my disagreements with Johnston, I have the utmost respect for her and for those like her who have come out in spite of the repercussions. I can only imagine the battle in her mind as she contemplated what she had to do, which she eventually did do. Her book—which I have quoted many times and will quote many times more—is one of the best books I have read on the LGBTQ+ ideology. Perhaps it is because in some ways I can relate to her and I know what it takes to be a Seventh-day Adventist pastor. She is very clear and compassionate in her writing.

However, as I have already alluded to, I think she takes huge leaps in logic and makes certain assumptions that are not correct. Thus, I would like to dedicate this chapter to presenting some of these leaps and assumptions so as to clarify any misunderstandings.

---

[1] John Paul Brammer, "Adventist Pastor Resigns after Coming Out as Bisexual," *NBC News* (May 2017), accessed September 19, 2023, https://www.nbcnews.com/feature/nbc-out/adventist-pastor-resigns-after-coming-out-bisexual-n753391.

Marriage and the Sabbath

As I have already pointed out, affirming the LGBTQ+ ideology and lifestyle will impact the belief in the seventh-day Sabbath. Primarily, this occurs because of the leaps in logic the LGBTQ+ activists make with Genesis 1–2 to justify the possibility of the existence of more than the two genders (male and female). Johnston places a lot of emphasis on marriage, that is, she wants to have the same privileges that heterosexuals do and be able to marry and be recognized as such by the church.

Johnston does not believe that allowing for same-sex marriage will affect the Sabbath in any way. She explains,

> Marriage and the Sabbath are institutions in different ways. The Sabbath is an institution for everyone, for all of God's creation to participate indirectly. Even cattle ought to be part of the Sabbath rest (Exodus 20:8–11). Even non-Israelites are to keep the Sabbath (Isaiah 56:3). On the other hand, marriage is only an institution for some. Other parts of scripture encourage avoiding the institution of marriage. (Matthew 19:10–12; 1 Corinthians 7:8, 32–35). There are certainly no such texts about avoiding the Sabbath.[2]

It is true that the Sabbath was created for all humanity (Mark 2:27) and that not all people marry or choose to marry. However, because of sin, not everyone keeps the Sabbath, even though it

---

[2] Alicia Johnston, *The Bible and LGBTQ Adventists: A Theological Conversation about Same-Sex Mariage, Gender, and Identity,* (Affirmative Collective, 2022), 41.

was created for everyone. Could the same be said about marriage? Speaking of this, Ellen G. White seems to say that this is possible.

> When the Pharisees afterward questioned Him concerning the lawfulness of divorce, Jesus pointed His hearers back to the marriage institution as ordained at creation. "Because of the hardness of your hearts," He said, Moses "suffered you to put away your wives: but from the beginning it was not so." Matthew 19:8. He referred them to the blessed days of Eden, when God pronounced all things "very good." Then *marriage and the Sabbath had their origin, twin institutions for the glory of God in the benefit of humanity.* Then, as the Creator joined the hands of the holy pair in wedlock, saying, A man shall "leave his father and his mother, and shall cleave unto his wife: and they shall be one" (Genesis 2:24), *He enunciated the law of marriage for all the children of Adam to the close of time.* That which the Eternal Father Himself had pronounced good was the law of highest blessing and development for man. Like every other one of God's good gifts entrusted to the keeping of humanity, marriage has been perverted by sin; but it is the purpose of the gospel to restore its purity and beauty. In both the Old and the New Testament, *the marriage relation is employed to represent the tender and sacred union that exists between Christ and His people,* the redeemed ones whom He has purchased at the cost of Calvary.[3] (emphasis supplied)

---

[3] Ellen G. White, "Is It Lawful for a Man to Put Away His Wife?"—Matthew 19:3," *Thoughts from the Mount of Blessing,* 63, accessed September 20, 2023, https://egwwritings.org/read?panels=p150.328(150.332)&index=0.

I realize that I am making an assumption on whether everyone was to be married if sin had not entered the world; but the fact that she says that, like the Sabbath, it was to be a benefit for humanity seems to lead us in that direction. I also want to point out that "the law of marriage was for all the children of Adam until the close of time. What law? The only law clearly implied in the story of creation in connection to marriage is, "Therefore a man shall leave his father and mother and be joined to his wife, and they shall become one flesh" (Genesis 2:24). Genesis 2:24 speaks of the pattern in which marriage is to occur, between a man and his wife (male and female). This, according to Mrs. White, was intended until the end of time.

What changed? Well, sin put a "monkey wrench" into the whole thing. Thus, not everyone keeps the Sabbath (as God intended), and not everyone gets married, or as is unfortunately happening today, some people marry contrary to God's blueprint. Now someone reading this might argue, "Hold on, Pastor, if a person does not keep the Sabbath, it is a sin, so does that mean if a person does not marry, it is also a sin?" Obviously not, the Bible speaks of many God-fearing people who were not married; Jesus Himself was not married. The difference is that the Sabbath is part of God's moral law, while marriage, although protected in the Ten Commandments ("Thou shall not commit adultery"), is not commanded.

We know that the Sabbath will be kept in heaven for all eternity, "And it shall come to pass that from one New Moon to another, and from one Sabbath to another, all flesh shall come to worship before Me," says the Lord (Isaiah 66:23). However, Jesus said that marriage will not take place in heaven: "For in the resurrection they neither marry nor are given in marriage, but are like angels of God in heaven" (Matthew 22:30). While Ellen White says that the Sabbath originated in Eden,[4] one can safely assume that even before the creation of our world, God also had a special day where all His creation worshiped Him. Thus, there was always a Sabbath, and when God

---

[4] Ellen G. White, "Satan's Enmity against the Law," *Patriarchs and Prophets*, 336, accessed September 19, 2023, https://egwwritings.org/read?panels=p84.1507&index=0.

created Earth, He just simply worked it into creation. While marriage clearly was not part of heaven, because the angels do not marry, and when we get there, we will be like them, so we will not marry.

Clearly, there are differences between marriage and the Sabbath, but it is a stretch to twist those differences to say, as a Seventh-day Adventist would if they affirmed the LGBTQ+ ideology and lifestyle, that "Yes, we should keep the Sabbath as God says because He established it at creation (Exodus 20:8–11), but the pattern of marriage can be tweaked to include members of the same sex." Here is an example: Johnston argues that, while the Sabbath was made holy at creation, marriage was not made or called holy.[5] Perhaps she believes that because marriage is not holy, we can do with it as we please. As we already discussed, the term *holy*, in both the Hebrew and the Greek simply means "set part." God set apart the seventh day from the other six. Perhaps He did not think it necessary to set apart Adam and Eve's marriage, because at the time, it as just them.

Here is another leap in logic Johnston makes.

> According to the Bible, the seventh-day Sabbath is not the only holy day. The Sabbath is the first and most enduring holy day, but not the only one. There are many holy days. When the Israelites were reminded of the seventh-day Sabbath on Mount Sinai, there were also given other days and years to keep holy (Exodus 23:10–17; Leviticus 16, 23, 25). These holy days were also called sabbaths.

Johnston is absolutely correct. However, although she alludes to this, these additional sabbaths were part of the ceremonial law, the law that became a necessity when humanity sinned. The annual sabbaths pointed to the work of Jesus and were "nailed to the Cross" once Jesus died. The weekly Sabbath is different. It is holy for a whole different reason (a memorial of creation) and existed before sin came

---

[5] Johnston, 41.

into the world. It was not abolished after the death of Jesus. But here is the huge leap:

> Since the creation of the seventh-day didn't exclude other sabbaths, why does the relationship between Adam and Eve exclude other marriages or lifelong commitments? What about celibate communities? What about other formations of extended family? *What about same-sex marriage?* The key is not whether new ways of doing things arise, but whether these new things abolish and replace what was established at creation, and ultimately whether these new things are moral and good in their own right.[6] (emphasis supplied)

So her assumption here is that since there were other sabbaths besides the seventh-day that were kept holy, there must be other forms of marriage as well. Talk about an acrobatic leap in logic. Again, it is clear that there are some differences between marriage and the Sabbath, but what we see in Genesis is that they were both a pattern for humanity to follow.

Let me point out one more thing: Ellen White's statement quoted above says, "In both the Old and the New Testaments, the marriage relation is employed to represent the tender and sacred union that exists between Christ and His people." There is an important symbol in marriage. That is, the marriage of Christ to His church. The parable of the foolish virgins is a good example: Jesus is the Bridegroom (Matthew 25:1, 6), and the bride would clearly be the church, whom He is coming for (v. 13). In Ephesians 5:25–32, the apostle Paul explains how husbands should treat their wives and uses an illustration saying that they (husbands) should love their wives as Christ (Bridegroom) loved the church (bride).

In Revelation 19, the apostle John poetically describes the coming of Jesus: "Let us be glad and rejoice and give Him glory, for *the*

---

[6] Ibid., 45.

marriage of the Lamb has come, and *His wife* has made herself ready" (v. 7, emphasis supplied). In chapter 21, John describes the New Jerusalem, "Then I, John, saw the holy city, New Jerusalem, coming down out of heaven from God, prepared *as a bride* adorned for *her husband*" (v. 2, emphasis supplied). Not to mention the fact that in Bible prophecy, a woman represents the church, that is, it represents us. Thus, we are the bride, and Jesus is the Bridegroom.

> The Old Testament prophets found in marriage an appropriate vehicle for telling the story of Yahweh's faithfulness in the face of Israel's idolatry. The New Testament authors drew from this Old Testament imagery (e.g., Rom. 9:25; 1 Peter 2:9–10). They spoke of marriage as a picture of the great mystery of salvation—the union of Christ and the church. Marriage illustrates Christ's self-sacrifice for the church as well as the submission to Christ. (Eph. 5:21–33) of a people who anticipate the future coming of their Lord (Matt. 25:1–13; Rev. 19:7; 21:2; 21:9–10). In this manner, marriage provides a picture of the exclusive nature of our relationship to God in Christ. Just as marriage is to be an exclusive, inviolate, and hence holy bond, so also our relationship to God must be exclusive and holy, for as God's covenant people we can serve no other gods but the one God (Ex. 20:3).[7]

Symbols are important to God, which is why, for example, Adventists, following the Bible, baptize by immersion. The sprinkling of water won't cut it. Why? Because baptism represents the death, burial, and resurrection of Christ and the believer. The symbol represents an important fact. This is why marriage between a

---

[7] Stanley J. Grenz, *Welcoming but Not Affirming* (Louisville, KY: Westminster John Knox Press, 1998), 106.

man and a woman represents the intimate relationship that God (the Bridegroom) wants to have with us, the church (His bride). Same-sex marriage does not follow the symbol, no matter how some want to twist it.

Modification of the Law

In Numbers 27, we read an interesting story concerning inheritance laws. This story is presented by Johnston to make her point. Israel was a patriarchal society. In those days, women did not have many rights. Thus, if the patriarch of the family died and he did not have any children or at least a male child, the inheritance would pass to his closest family member, but it would not stay in the immediate family. The daughters of Zelophehad had a problem with that.

> And they stood before Moses, before Eleazar the priest, and before the leaders and all the congregation, by the doorway of the tabernacle of meeting, saying: "Our father died in the wilderness; but he was not in the company of those who gathered together against the Lord, in company with Korah, but he died in his own sin; and he had no sons. Why should the name of our father be removed from among his family because he had no son? Give us a possession among our father's brothers." (Numbers 27:2–4)

Moses did not know what to do about this, so, as any good leader would do, he asked God. God answered,

> The daughters of Zelophehad speak what is right; you shall surely give them a possession of inheritance among their father's brothers, and cause the inheritance of their father to pass to them. And you shall speak to the children

of Israel, saying: "If a man dies and has no son, then you shall cause his inheritance to pass to his daughter." (vv. 7–8)

Then God tweaked the law to make allowances for daughters who were in the same position in the future. So God modified His law to meet a need.

Johnston quotes Roy Gane from his book *Old Testament Law for Christians* as saying,

> How could the Old Testament law be normative if they were not comprehensive and if they can be flexibly applied to individual cases? First, the laws are paradigmatic examples that give positive behaviors, and when problems arise, the laws are to serve as starting points for deliberation of cases that are related but present variables. Second…while the letter of the law was important, it was to be sensitively and contextually applied in light of the spirit of the law as a whole, recognizing that no law code can explicitly account for all the complexities of human life.[8]

Johnston states, "There we have it. The laws are not to be applied inflexibly but flexibly."[9] Then, as if in some way acknowledging that the Bible speaks against the transgender lifestyle, she says,

> Even if the plain meaning of the text forbids gender transition, deliberation leads us to different conclusions. For the sake of justice and love, it shouldn't be applied that way to transgender people… Sometimes circumstances mean going against the surface meaning. The intent

---

[8] Johnston, 146.
[9] Ibid.

is always more important. From day one of the law, this has consistently been recognized, especially within the text itself. It's difficult to become a serious student of the Hebrew Torah without seeing this reality... All I need to do to arrive at affirming same-sex marriage and transgender identity is apply these principles.[10]

Now let us think about this carefully and recognize the danger. If we are convinced to use this argument because biblical laws are meant to be flexible, we can apply that to just about anything the Bible says. Yes, there were times, like in the story of the daughters of Zelophehad, when the law was tweaked to fit the need. However, that situation did not involve a moral issue. With all due respect to Johnston, we cannot and should not ever tweak what the Bible says to help people feel comfortable with their sins.

While the desire for the church as a whole to change its theology on LGBTQ+ issues is something that other denominations are dealing with, as we saw in the previous chapter, those who identify as LGBTQ+ and in some cases their family members want the Seventh-day Adventist Church to change their theology. Johnston mentions the story of Peter and Cornelius found in Acts 10. Luke tells us that, while Peter was lodging at the house of Simon the Tanner, he received a vision around noon. It was lunchtime, Peter was hungry, and God took advantage of this by sending a vision having to do with animals. Peter "saw heaven opened and an object like a great sheet bound at the four corners, descending to him and let down to the earth. In it were all kinds of four-footed animals of the earth, wild beasts, creeping things, and birds of the air. And a voice came to him, "Rise, Peter; kill and eat." But Peter said, "Not so, Lord! For I have never eaten anything common or unclean" (Acts 10:11–14). This was repeated three times, but at that time, Peter did not understand the vision as he thought it had to do with food. What Peter did not know was how God was working behind the scenes. God had also sent a vision

---

[10] Ibid., 146–147.

to Cornelius, a Roman Centurion, and thus, a Gentile. However, Cornelius was a God-fearing man, so God wanted to reveal the gospel to him. Through the vision, He gave him instructions on how and where to find Peter. Long story short, Cornelius found Peter, and it was at this time that Peter comprehended what God wanted him to understand through the vision of the animals. The vision was not about eating unclean animals but about God's desire for the Gentiles to be saved, a thought that Peter (a Jew) would have never thought of because Gentiles were "unclean" in the mind of a Jew.

Notice the words of Peter in verse 28, "You know how unlawful it is for a Jewish man to keep company with or go to one of another nation. But God has shown me that I should not call any man common or unclean." God was correcting Peter's prejudice. This story, among others, shows us that salvation is available to anyone who wants it: "There is neither Jew nor Greek, there is neither slave nor free, there is neither male nor female; for you are all one in Christ Jesus" (Galatians 3:28).

However, Johnston takes the lesson of this story a bit further.

> Sometimes the theological question that seems so pertinent is only the surface. In this case, the real issue was one of *preconceived ideas*. What Peter knew to be unclean, what seemed vile and unholy to Peter's understanding, could be made holy by God. Equally important, *the inclusion* of Gentiles meant *theology had changed*. This doesn't mean the Bible had to change. Theology is merely our understanding of the Bible, and sometimes we get it wrong. We are fallible... They baptized people who, moments ago, were considered unclean. They baptized them in the name of Jesus without circumcision. A barrier to church membership was set aside at the leading of the Holy Spirit. What if Peter had instead said, "I love the Gentiles, but I disapprove of their lifestyle. They have to be circumcised and keep the

law." Would that have been genuinely loving? Would that have opened the door for Gentiles interested in learning about Jesus? Or would he have prevented Gentile *inclusion*?[11]

Notice Johnston's subtlety. Her implication is that the church's stance on gender and LGBTQ+ issues is a "preconceived idea." The solution to this is for our theology to change. Notice how carefully she wants to clarify that it is not changing the Bible but our understanding of what the Bible says on the issue.

You know, as a pastor, part of my job is to teach and preach. In doing this, I often like to anticipate people's questions and thought processes. If I were to agree with Johnston and say that the church's stance on gender issues is a "preconceived idea" and that it should change its theology, the reality is that we could say this just about everything we stand for and I am sure somebody would be thinking the same thing. There are statements that I have heard that for some reason stick with me even when many years have gone by. I remember reading that when it comes to understanding the Bible, "we have to let the obvious explain what is not obvious." There are issues that may not seem so clear to us, so as good Bible students, we have to search for other passages that will help clarify these issues. In my opinion (you may take this with a grain of salt), the gender issue is very clear in scripture. However, we have a natural tendency, due to our sinful nature, to try to justify our desires and behaviors in order to feel better about them. When this happens, as it relates to the Bible, we begin to see things that are not there. This seems to be the case with this story as to how Johnston views it.

In Acts 11, the story continues as Peter had to explain to the church why he had visited the house of a Gentile. Please understand

---

[11] Ibid., 186.

that this was a big deal in the primitive church. So Peter explains himself and shows how God was involved in the whole thing.

> On hearing this account, the brethren were silenced. Convinced that Peter's course was in direct fulfillment of the plan of God, and that their prejudices and exclusiveness were utterly contrary to the spirit of the gospel, they glorified God, saying, "Then hath God also to the Gentiles granted repentance unto life." Thus, without controversy, prejudice was broken down, the exclusiveness established by the custom of ages was abandoned, and the way was opened for the gospel to be proclaimed to the Gentiles.[12]

There is a twofold issue here, one that we see throughout the New Testament, especially in the writings of Paul. Can Gentiles be saved, and do they have to be circumcised? Yes, Gentiles can be saved—God wanted to save them, through the same method He made salvation available for all humanity, Jesus. The answer to the second part is no, they do not have to be circumcised. You see the issue of circumcision was very important to the Jews, but one must remember that the Jews had filled their religion with all sorts of burdens, circumcision being one of them. To them, it was a salvation by works issue. However, we know that salvation is a gift: "For by grace you have been saved through faith, and that not of yourselves; it is the gift of God, not of works, lest anyone should boast" (Ephesians 2:8–9).

Johnston correctly says that "circumcision was a burden to lift. God makes no distinctions. All people are equal."[13] However, she seems to be equating circumcision, which was a "salvation by works" issue, with the fact that the church does not condone LGBTQ+

---

[12] Ellen G. White, *Acts of the Apostles* (Nampa, ID: Pacific Press Publishing Association, 2005), 142.
[13] Johnston, 188.

ideology and lifestyle. In her mind, this is a burden that must be lifted from them because, you see, for the most part, a person who is actively engaged in the LGBTQ+ lifestyle is not accepted as a member of the church or baptized, and rightly so. This has nothing to do with the church not wanting to be inclusive; it has to do with accepting sin as normal.

Let me give you an example. Let's just say that I am conducting an evangelistic meeting. There is a gentleman who has been coming to all the meetings; has been responding to my appeals; and, at the end of the topic on baptism, wants to be baptized. Well, we usually talk to those wanting this and make the arrangements. Part of the conversation involves getting to know this person better. So let's just say that in this conversation, I found out that he is not married but is living with his girlfriend and they have a sexual relationship. Should I baptize this person? Well, not yet. Why? Because he is actively living in sexual immorality, that is, he is living in sin. If he wants to get baptized, he must do something about his situation, whether it is changing his living arrangements with his girlfriend or getting married. This situation is very common in some of the Hispanic churches, and I have married couples who are living together before they get baptized.

Should we change this procedure in an effort to be inclusive? I am sure Johnston would say no, or at least I hope she would. But she would say that this is different because living in sexual immorality is a sin. I would agree with her, but so is the LGBTQ+ lifestyle, and the church believes this, even though some church leaders, to their demise, have compromised on this in an effort to be politically correct.

Criticizing the church's rules about how and when it accepts new members, she says,

> Agreement with the church's sexual ethics is a required part of membership, especially leadership. This applies to everyone. LGBTQ People are no exception. We love the people we forbid the lifestyle. We love the sinner; we hate the sin.

Most of us who are gay, bisexual, and transgender push back against this thinking. We have questions. Can we always separate the person from the behavior? Or are there some situations in which restricting a particular behavior also excludes a whole class of people?

My answer involves asking a question, and that is, what is the alternative? The alternative would be to throw away all the rules and just baptize and receive into membership anyone who wants to join, no questions asked. We are to make no requirements before or after baptism. Well, perhaps this is what modifying the law and changing our theology looks like. But I do not think this is what Peter had in mind when he said, "But you are a chosen generation, a royal priesthood, *a holy nation*, His own special people, that you may proclaim the praises of Him who *called you out of darkness* into His marvelous light" (1 Peter 2:9, emphasis supplied). Or what Paul meant when he told young Timothy, "I write so that you may know *how you ought to conduct yourself in the house of God*, which is the church of the living God, *the pillar and ground of the truth*" (1 Timothy 3:15, emphasis supplied). The church is to be holy (set apart, different), there is a certain way we ought to conduct ourselves in God's house, and there is an expectation to hear the truth in God's church and to see people living that truth. To change—in order to be more like those who "see the light" on gender issues and to be more "inclusive" of people who do not want to change—is to compromise. However, when we compromise with the enemy, we always end up on the losing side.

Love Requires Approval

Her name was Kathy (or so I thought), and she was new at our church. Since at the time I pastored three churches, I was not with this congregation every Sabbath. I introduced myself, thanked her for visiting our church, and talked about other pleasantries. However, it wasn't long before controversy arose. You see, Kathy wasn't really

Kathy. Kathy was Kevin. Kevin was a man with several health issues for which he sought medical treatment in town. As it turned out, some of the church's members were nurses and were familiar with Kevin, known in the church as Kathy. This would not necessarily be an issue except for the fact that Kevin (now Kathy) was using the women's bathroom. Some of the ladies felt uncomfortable, and rightly so. They were concerned for their little daughters. As a pastor, I have to be aware of issues that could lead to legal liabilities, but I have not experienced a situation like this before. Being a relatively new pastor, I sought advice from the conference's ministerial director. It is his job to be the pastor of pastors and to counsel and advise us when we are facing difficult situations. I chuckle now thinking of his response, "Nelson, I have been a pastor for more than twenty years and I have never been in a situation like this or heard of anyone who has had to handle a similar situation. I don't know what to do." Mind you, this took place around 2015 or so if I remember correctly.

In situations like these, where there are potential legal liabilities, the conference refers us to its lawyers to seek advice. Sometimes, it is helpful; sometimes, it is not. In this case, our church had a bathroom in the fellowship hall that was away from the foyer, and it provided the privacy Kathy needed. Following the legal advice, we asked Kathy to use this bathroom. I remember my head elder, and I visited Kathy in her home. After the pleasantries, we got to the meat of the situation. We talked about her transition, as Kevin dressed as a woman and looked like a woman. Kathy told us about her history and how she viewed the issue of being transgender. We were cordial and friendly with her, so we seemed to hit it off.

At one point, Kathy asked permission to address the church and give a class to educate the church on gender variant issues so that hopefully the church would embrace her and accept her as normal, which was the way she viewed herself. My head elder and I shared with her what the Bible teaches and where the church stood on the issue. We talked about this with her several times, and I even gave her a book on the issue. Well, we had to agree to disagree as Kathy did not agree with the way we interpreted the Bible. Still, Kathy was gracious to us. She accepted the arrangements to use a separate bathroom, although told us that she knew people who would have taken the church to court if they were in her situation. Anyway, although we as a church did not approve of Kathy's ideology and lifestyle and made that clear to her, we loved her and made her feel welcomed, valued, and appreciated. Obviously, Kathy was never baptized, but she continued attending our church Sabbath after Sabbath for close to two years until she succumbed to her health problems. Love makes all the difference.

Love is a word that, at least in English, we throw around all the time. I love chocolate (hint hint), I love the Philadelphia Eagles, I love my wife's bean soup, I love my dog Bailey, and I love my wife and children. Of course, as Christians, we recognize that we must love one another. Jesus said it this way, "A new commandment I give to you, that you love one another; as I have loved you, that you also love one another. By this all will know that you are My disciples, if you have love for one another" (John 13:34–35). But let's face it, how do we love one another? Can we love others whom we don't agree with? If so, how do we show that love? We could write a book on that alone, and many have. And it is here where the rubber meets the road. The LGBTQ+ community wants to feel loved. I mean, don't we all? This is important.

Should we love those of the LGBTQ+ community? You say, "Well, of course, we should." But how do we show that love to them and how will our efforts be received? Let me share a few important points about love in the context of this book.

Love promotes dignity

> We need to understand who our neighbors are: people made in God's image... The truth that man and woman are made in God's image is the foundation for human dignity—the concept that individuals possess an inviolable worth deserving of honor and respect... A transgender person (LGBTQ+) is made in God's image, and that means that respect and honor are due to

them as people, regardless of whether we agree with their self-perception. To see the full dignity of a transgender person means to abhor or reject any mocking humor that would demean them. It means to stand up and defend them against bullies or abuse. Dignity demands that we speak up in defense of someone's worth, even when we disagree with their way of life.[14]

Love requires empathy

Understanding the perspective of someone unlike you is absolutely vital to developing empathy and building relationships. Empathy is a prerequisite for speaking meaningfully and authoritatively into someone's life. However, empathy does not mean that you accept or affirm or encourage someone to embrace the desire to live contrary to their created gender; it does mean, however, that instead of rejecting a person outright, you take time and make the effort to listen and seek to understand.[15]

It is here that many err because, as I mentioned before, many well-meaning saints view the LGBTQ+ issue as *the* sin instead of *a* sin. I acknowledge that there is an unhealthy bias in some of our churches. However, if we are going to handle this the way Jesus would have us, we need to learn to listen. To do this, we must be willing to have a healthy, unbiased, and nonjudgmental conversation. This does not mean that we relax the principles, but if all we are thinking about is the law and principles, we are doing a disservice to those among us who are struggling with these issues.

---

[14] Andrew T. Walker, *God and the Transgender Debate: What Does the Bible Actually Say about Gender Identity?* (Turkey: The Good Book Company, 2022), 102–104.

[15] Ibid., 104–105.

Love shares truth

> Here is perhaps the most delicate aspect of loving our transgender neighbor; how can we love our transgender neighbor while not sending signals that we approve of someone living in a gender opposite of their sex, or no gender at all? The Bible's definition of love runs contrary to the Western world's definition. According to the world, loving someone means giving them license to pursue whatever they believe will bring them happiness or fulfillment. The Bible says love requires truth. Love does not mean looking someone in the eyes and affirming every desire they experience. Love means looking someone in the eyes and communicating the truth of scripture. We are to do so gently, but we are to do so nonetheless… If we accept the authority of the Bible, we must understand that affirming people in a path that is contrary to what the scripture teaches is never loving… We have to love people so much that we care about their souls more than we care about their approval.[16]

Love produces compassion

To be honest with you, while I have learned a whole lot in my research for this book, I cannot say that I fully understand the LGBTQ+ ideology, particularly being transgender.

> The Christians tendency is often to feel alarm at new ideas, especially when those ideas deny rather than support biblical truths. But compassion means we must disarm and delib-

---

[16] Ibid., 106.

erately lay down any negativity we have toward those who think or feel or live in that way—including those who experience gender dysphoria, or are seeking to become and live as the opposite gender to their birth sex, or to live with no gender at all… Compassion does not mean approval. But neither does compassion mean silence. Compassion says, "I'm so sorry you are experiencing deep inner anguish about your gender. I cannot fathom the types of struggles you experience, but I would like to listen to you and I would like to be here for you. I'm sorry for any hurt or rejection you've encountered from others. I want you to know that I'm your friend and will walk with you through the valleys of your struggles. I want you to know that I may not agree with you, but I will never look down on you. You are loved."[17]

Love has patience

While accepting the gospel means that there is a change in our lives, this change rarely happens immediately. Change and transformation take time. But all too often, as Christians and, yes, as Seventh-day Adventists, we jump on the criticism bandwagon and immediately chastise someone if they have not become what we think they should in the time we think they should. I have been as guilty of this as anyone else. At times, I am in awe of God's patience toward me. If I were God, I would have given up on me a long time ago; but God is always there, like the Father of the prodigal son, waiting for me with arms wide open. I am sure you could say the same.

A believer who experiences gender dysphoria may never be freed of their gender dyspho-

---

[17] Ibid., 108–109.

> ria. Or maybe they will. The militant transgender activist who accuses those who disagree with pro-transgender ideology of bigotry or worse may never change their mind and place themselves under Christ loving lordship. Or maybe they will. God saves the most unlikely persons... That's the beauty of Christianity; we have a patient God. All too often, God's people act as if we believe that smugness, superiority, and angry moral pronouncements are what draws people to the gospel. In God's economy, kindness, forbearance, and patience are His instruments. God is rich in "kindness and forbearance and patience"—and "God's kindness is meant to lead you to repentance" (Romans 2:4)... We must be patient as we walk alongside those experiencing the anguish of gender dysphoria. We must be patient as we engage with those angry at the Christian gospel's good news about God's design for gender. We are not here to win arguments. We are here to love people... We cannot be sure that our kindness and patience will win a hearing for the gospel. But we can always be certain that our self-righteousness and impatience will lose a hearing for the gospel.[18]

I would like to comment on Walker's statement that love requires truth, that is, the communication of truth. While I agree with Walker, one must be careful how truth is communicated. Sometimes, truth can be communicated in a way that is meant to shame someone or to feel better about oneself—as if saying, "I told you so," or "I was right." We must remember, in the context of the LGBTQ+ ideology, the issue is not who is right but what is right.

---

[18] Ibid., 109–110.

My mother always taught me that love must be more than words; it is shown through actions. Unbeknownst to her, she was proclaiming a biblical principle. Jesus said it this way, "If you love Me, keep My commandments" (John 14:15). In the Greek, the word *keep* is *téreó*, which means "you will keep."[19] In other words, "if you love me, you will perform actions that show me that love." In this case, we will obey Jesus, and, by doing this, we will be communicating our love to Him. But how do we show and communicate love to members of the LGBTQ+ community? I do not ask this question as if saying that, somehow, they are harder to love. At least for me, they are not. However, I know this is not true for some. I have had conversations with people and have even heard sermons where the language is so insulting that I have felt very uncomfortable. This is why I have a heart for those who struggle with gender identity issues. I know it may not seem that way because I am being bold and direct as to its moral implications, but in some way, I can empathize with Johnston and others who may feel uncomfortable and even insulted when they hear a preacher say, "Don't come into my church with that junk." We must do a better job communicating love to those who struggle with gender dysphoria and members of the LGBTQ+ community.

That being said, there are times when we can go the proverbial "extra mile" in showing love, and this love will not be accepted. Remember Kathy's story I shared at the beginning? We showed love to Kathy by not rejecting her, we embraced her, we greeted her and hugged her, we sat with her at potluck, and we showed an interest in her well-being. When she got sick, we visited her in the hospital. The result was that she kept coming back. Some eight years or so have passed since then, and unfortunately, today the atmosphere is very different. The ideology today is "if you do not agree with and affirm me, you really don't love me." This is what is being communicated through the media and places like YouTube. Unfortunately, it has found its way into the church.

---

[19] "5083, Téreó," Bible Hub https://biblehub.com/text/john/14-15.htm.

While Johnston does not directly say, "If you do not agree with and affirm me, you really don't love me," it is implied in her words.

> To accept Gentiles, the church had to change its beliefs; there is no other way. This is the nature of belief itself. When we believe something, we act on it. Beliefs are not mere thoughts or ideas; they inform our decisions and how we treat others… Beliefs are important because they inform our actions. Beliefs aren't neutral; they influence our decisions. It might be tempting to imagine a scenario in which someone's beliefs about someone else's sexuality wouldn't impact their decisions or behaviors. What about the grandmother who disagrees with her granddaughter's sexuality but never says anything about it and just loves her? These scenarios might be comforting but they aren't true to life. Beliefs impact the way we treat people. It could be glaring omissions in conversations. It could be outright statements of judgment. It could be a subtle separation that is felt by all. *It could be exclusion from the church.* It could be a subtle attitude of treating a gay church member as a project.[20] (emphasis supplied)

There is a lot of truth in this paragraph, but notice the subtle way she inserts, "It could be exclusion for the church." The only reason an LGBTQ+ person would be excluded (not baptized or accepted as a member) is if the church views this issue as a moral or sin problem. By the way, just because a person is not a member does not mean that they cannot come to church and worship. Kathy attended our church for close to two years. Anyway, in this case, the implication is that the exclusion from the church is due to being LGBTQ+. If they are excluded, it is because they are not affirmed. If they are not

---

[20] Johnston, 197–198.

affirmed, it is because they are not loved, no matter how much the church members believe that they are being loving. She continues,

> If beliefs are relevant to the words that we say and the actions we take, that means beliefs are relevant to how we treat others. Beliefs are relevant to our relationships. This inevitably means that *beliefs are relevant to love.* They impact our ability *to love others well.* They impact the ability of our communities to embody the loving influence of God in the world. The beliefs of some early Christians about circumcision impacted their ability to love. The requirement made them exclude Gentiles from baptism and church participation. It served as a cover for prejudice and a justification for their sense that they belonged to God in a way that Gentiles did not. *Removing the requirement of circumcision made them able to love Gentiles better...* Since our beliefs impact our ability to love, how could we separate the two? How could we ever say that we can always love someone no matter what we believe? We can't. It's not true. *Some beliefs do impact our ability to love.*[21] (emphasis supplied)

Again, there is some truth in her words, but notice the implications she makes. In the case of the Gentiles in Acts 10–11, referenced above, they were excluded from baptism and church participation, just like those of the LGBTQ+ community. It was the belief that salvation was for the Jews and that if Gentiles came into the church, they had to be circumcised. In the case of those of the LGBTQ+ community, it is the church's belief about their ideology and lifestyle. The Jewish belief about Gentiles was a cover for prejudice, so the same must apply to the church today. It was only when the early church

---

[21] Ibid., 198.

removed the requirement of circumcision that they could really love the Gentiles. The implication here is that it is only when the church removes the obstacle or changes its theology regarding the LGBTQ+ issue that "real" love will be communicated. "Some beliefs do impact our ability to love," she says, which means that the church's belief is impacting its ability to love. In other words, "if you do not agree with and affirm me, you really don't love me."

Since we have mentioned the word *affirm* several times, I believe it is important we define and compare it with love.

>Love is used to describe everything from liking something to being obsessed with an object. As Christians, the Greek word *agape* would be a better base for understanding love, since that is the type of love that Jesus modeled. Some of the definitions of agape include "a pure, willful, sacrificial love that intentionally desires another's highest good," and a "deliberate and unconditional love that is the result of choices and behaviors rather than feelings and emotions." A Christian expression of love would be choosing to act towards a person in a way that promotes their highest good, even if doing so involved sacrifice on your part. A person who was acting in love would not affirm untruths or point a person in a direction that they feel would harm them. Christians must base their assessment of what would be harmful according to what is revealed in God's Word. It is loving to be honest with someone even when they aren't going to like what you say.
>
>Affirming is a completely different and unrelated concept to love. Its meanings are listed as to "declare one's support for; uphold; defend," to "accept or confirm the validity of; ratify" and to "offer emotional support or encouragement."

> In order to affirm someone, you would need to agree with them and offer them support and encouragement in their decision. It has nothing to do with seeking their highest good but has everything to do with supportive feelings and voicing agreement.[22]

Clearly, love and affirmation are not the same thing, and while it may be hard to convince members of the LGBTQ+ community of this, it is possible to love and not affirm. Furthermore, love does not require approval. Any parent will tell you that this is true. Our children often ask us for things or want permission to go to places or do things that we as parents know are not for their welfare. Parents (for the most part) have more experience and know better. Children are not mature enough to make wise decisions, which should make us question those so-called authorities who tell us that we must accept the child's feelings on gender. Anyway, when we as parents deny our children something they want, they may say, "You don't love me." Parent, how many times have you heard that? Yet it is because of our love for them and our desire to protect them that we deny certain things.

Yet in today's crazy and backward society, we are being told, "Yep, if you don't affirm and agree with them, you don't really love them, no matter what you say or do." This is simply not true. "Love does not mean we sacrifice truth on the altar of popularity. Love does not require sacrificing conviction. In fact, love demands that we don't. But love does mean deliberately, prayerfully, and thoughtfully extending respect, empathy, compassion, and patience to everyone, equally, and indiscriminately."[23] We can truly love and not affirm. How do we do this? We will talk more about this in chapter 6.

---

[22] Marsha Inman, "How to Love LGBTQIA+ Friends and Family Yet Not Affirm Their Choices," *Living Hope Ministries*, accessed September 21, 2023, https://www.livehope.org/article/how-to-love-lgbtqia-friends-and-family-yet-not-affirm-their-choices.

[23] Walker, 112.

LGBTQ+ Is Today's Slavery

This may seem like a contradiction, but I must admit that Johnston's comparison of the crime of slavery with, as she views it, the LBGTQ+ dilemma can be somewhat convincing if the Bible did not say anything else about the issue. It is here, in my opinion, that she takes her greatest leap. She writes,

> The Bible constantly moved away from slavery and toward abolition. Our duty as Christians is to continue that trajectory by doing what was never done in the Bible, outlawing all slavery. The Bible might have never advocated such a move, but it moved in that direction, and we should continue that movement.[24]

She correctly explains,

> Ancient Israel was not moving away from slavery relative to surrounding nations. Surrounding nations often treated enslaved people like people not merely property. For instance, the ancient Code of Hammurabi (CH) is contemporary to ancient Israel and the most complete legal code outside of Israel. In CH, citizens could sell themselves as indentured servants just like in Israel, but the servitude was only three years instead of six… Some nations freed enslaved people when they conquered foreign cities, something Israel never did… Israel was better than some in some ways but worse in others. They didn't stand out. They weren't moving in an abolitionist direction. The New Testament brought no improvement to the Hebrew Bible… Slavery

---
[24] Johnston, 294.

> was even expanded from the Hebrew Bible to the New Testament... Christians enslaved one another in perpetuity. Rather than being more anti-slavery than the surrounding culture, New Testament authors went along with the majority culture... Tragically, because of perceived biblical support for slavery, any movement in the direction of abolition ended when Christianity became the official religion of Rome.[25]

She explains that, in the history of our country, many Christians supported slavery because they believed the Bible supported it. Tragically, this is true. We must also admit that nowhere in the Bible forbids slavery. There is nothing from God saying, "Thou shall not have slaves." Slavery is a historical, biblical teaching of the church. This theology was not new or unique to Western African shores or the American South. Christians didn't challenge slavery for nearly 1,800 years.

So what do we do about this? I must admit that I do not have all the answers. There are things in the Bible that I have yet to understand. The issue of slavery in the Bible, and among God's people is something that I have struggled with for a long time. All I can say is that

> Slavery is an inexcusable sin against God and against society, as well as against the slave. Yet slavery has existed in some form or other in eastern lands from time immemorial. The laws God gave Israel were designed to eliminate slavery, *in time*. Slavery violates every human right and decency.[26] (emphasis supplied)

---

[25] Ibid., 295–296.
[26] "Stealing" [Deuteronomy 24:7], *Seventh-day Adventist Bible Commentary (SDABC)*, rev. ed., ed. Francis D. Nichol (Washington, DC: Review & Herald, 1976–1980), 1:1038.

Yet it is here that things get a bit dicey with Johnston. She argues that since there are no biblical passages that condemn slavery, abolitionists obviously could not use the Bible as a source. Thus, they made their arguments "based on broad ideas of human value… Abolitionists prioritized the Golden Rule: 'Love others as you love yourself.'"[27] There is no question that as Christians, we must treat others as we wish to be treated. However, this does not mean that we should affirm others in their sinful behavior. Johnston then presents the similarities (as she sees them) between slavery and the LGBTQ+ dilemma.

1. Theology that would be good for LGBTQ+ people would challenge the institutional church just like theology that would be good for enslaved people threatened the Southern religious institutions. They would experience financial and membership losses, at least in the short term.[28]
2. Those who write theological position papers are not part of the LGBTQ community. Policy and doctrine are set by theologians who are insulated from having relationships with openly gay and transgender people, just like those who wrote pro-slavery theology.[29]
3. Theology that affirms same-gender marriage and transgender people would be a departure from historical Christianity. Theology that supports abolition was just as radical a change with respect to historic Christian teaching.[30]
4. There are no biblical examples of same-gender couples or transgender people, and there are texts that, on the surface, support a theology against same-gender couples and transgender people. There are no examples of universal abolition in the Bible. There are sufficient texts that, on the surface, affirm slavery.[31]

---

[27] Johnston, 302–303.
[28] Ibid., 306.
[29] Ibid.
[30] Ibid., 307.
[31] Ibid.

5. A small minority of LGBTQ people say a theology that does not affirm their lifestyle is good for them. The church chooses to listen to these people and ignore the majority, believing that there is a way to be loving without theological change. A small minority of enslaved and Black people said that slavery was good—and good for them. The church listened to these people and upheld the idea that they could be loving without theological change.[32]

While there is some truth to what she says about historical slavery, it is a stretch to apply it to the LGBTQ+ community. As you can see, she makes certain assumptions. For example, she believes that one of the reasons the church does not make changes in its theology about LGBTQ+ people is that in doing so, the church will lose money and members. So in her mind, the church's stance has nothing to do with the Bible but about selfish pursuits. She also assumes that those who write policies in the church regarding the LGBTQ+ issue do not have relationships with gay, lesbian, bisexual, and transgender people; how does she know that? Does she know them personally and intimately? Is it not possible for a person who disagrees with the LGBTQ+ agenda to have friends and relationships with people in that community? My wife has several friends in that community, and she does not believe that the church should affirm them, and those friends know where she stands. She just loves them, so, yes, it is possible to love without theological change, my wife has proved it, and we did as well in the church where we met Kathy.

As for not changing the church's theology because it departs from historical Christianity, her argument is weak. In fact, what history shows regarding Christianity is that it has compromised biblical truth accepting the "traditions of men" over a "this saith the Lord." We can see this clearly in the history of the Christian Church as presented by John in the letters to the "Seven Churches" in Revelation 2–3. This is why God raised a prophetic movement after the "Great Disappointment" of 1844, a movement that would call people back

---

[32] Ibid.

to the Bible. A movement is described as "keeping the commandments of God and having the testimony of Jesus" (Revelation 12:17, 14:12). The Seventh-day Adventist Church is that movement, a remnant movement. The word *remnant* is significant. It comes from the Greek *loipos*, which means "the remainder" or "what is left behind."[33] What is left behind of what? From the rest of Christianity, which has compromised. While the Seventh-day Adventist Church is not the only church opposing the affirmation of the LGBTQ+ movement (although some local congregations have compromised), we find that more and more churches are falling into line with LGBTQ+ affirmation. One has only to look at the site Gaychurch.org, where you can search for affirming churches in any area of the United States and Canada. I recently conducted a search in the Nashville area where I pastor, and thirty churches came up as affirming congregations.

Obviously, the Seventh-day Adventist Church is not the "remnant" just because it does not compromise on the LGBTQ+ issue; historically and prophetically, it is more than that (see *The Present Truth and the Three Angels' Messages*). It is the remnant because God brought it about to prepare people to meet Jesus at His soon coming. We are not to compromise our biblical theology for tradition or political correctness, no matter what pressure we receive from science, the media, political authorities, or misguided members and leaders, whether they are the minority in our church or the majority. God is the one who rules!

But Johnston says,

> The moral arguments for affirming theology are based on well-being, the Golden Rule, and human dignity. Affirming the gender of trans people is an obvious good… Affirming theology places love, compassion, and justice in the driver's seat. Love is more than how we communicate our beliefs; love is about what we believe. The fact that same-gender marriage was never mod-

---

[33] "3062. Loipos," Bible Hub https://biblehub.com/greek/3062.htm.

eled or mentioned in the Bible is less important than the Golden Rule, because the Bible was never meant to cover every possible scenario for all times and all places. It didn't cover the essential moral imperative of abolition… Only Christians who saw love, compassion, and empathy as morally strong principles would have opposed slavery 200 years ago.[34]

I am reminded of how subtle Satan was when he tempted Jesus in the desert. After Jesus quoted scripture in response to Satan's first temptation of turning stone into bread, Satan "took Him up into the holy city, set Him on the pinnacle of the temple, and said to Him, 'If You are the Son of God, throw Yourself down. For it is written: "He shall give His angels charge over you," and, "In their hands they shall bear you up, lest you dash your foot against a stone"'" (Matthew 4:5–6). Satan quoted the Bible but out of context. He did the same thing to Eve in the garden: "Did God really say…?" Notice how noble Johnston presents what she calls "affirmation theology." It is about the Golden Rule; it is about well-being and human dignity. All while saying in a very subtle way that those who do not support and "affirming theology" are not loving Christians because love is not really about what you show, it's about what you believe. Thus, if we as a church encourage, support, pray for, and simply make the LGBTQ+ people feel welcomed as they attend our services, it's really a façade because no matter what actions you take to show love, if you do not believe that LGBTQ+ people should be affirmed, you really don't love, so don't even bother. In fact, the implication is that if we as the church do not affirm LGBTQ+ people, we do not have love, compassion or empathy, no matter what our actions say.

Furthermore, notice the subtle attack on the Bible. While it is true that the Bible does not address every modern issue, there are enough principles in it that we can apply to our time and any issue we face. However, her argument seems to be that our understand-

---

[34] Johnston, 307–309.

ing of the Bible must be "repackaged" because of this new issue in society (although it isn't that new). So, I ask, do we have to correct our understanding of the Bible every time a new issue pops up in society? In a previous chapter, I mentioned the parallels between the LGBTQ+ ideology and pedophilia. Not that LGBTQ+ people abuse children, but the arguments from psychology that people are born that way are the same. I believe it is a matter of time before pedophiles will want to be affirmed and we will find people who will try to use the Bible to justify not only their behavior but will use the same arguments as to why we should accept them as normal and that the church should affirm them as well; after all, it is about human dignity, well-being, and the Golden Rule, isn't it?

The Church Is Losing Young People because It Does Not Affirm LGBTQ+ People

Johnston writes,

> We should not be ignorant of the realities of our time. One of the number one reasons people, especially young people, leave conservative Christian churches is that the church doesn't accept LGBTQ people. One of the most common criticisms of Christians is that they are anti-gay... It's difficult for people to believe in the Bible when they are taught to explain away the suffering of neighbors, friends, and family who happen to be gay, bisexual, or transgender. It's equally difficult for them to deal with the cognitive dissonance created by trying to harmonize the reality that affirming theology helps people thrive with the traditional insistence that such thriving is sinful.[35]

---

[35] Ibid., 313.

It is an unfortunate reality that our youth are leaving the church in alarming numbers. Barna Group research uncovered "six significant themes why nearly three out of every five young Christians (59%) disconnect either permanently or for an extended period of time from church life after age 15."[36] A more recent study revealed that "70% of youth stop attending church and start leaving when they graduate from high school. Nearly a decade later, about half return to church."[37] This is not just a Seventh-day Adventist problem. Six reasons are given for why the youth are leaving the church.

1. *The experience of fear-based Christianity*: Young Christians want a faith that helps them engage and navigate their world; but too often, they experience reactionary, culture war, fear-based ways of relating to the world. Young people don't see the world as a "threat" but as their home.
2. *Lack of depth and spirituality in church*: Young Christians want to be challenged, to talk about deep and vital topics, and to have a faith that is robust and rugged enough to handle life's most challenging questions. But many experience church as boring or shallow, with messages and ministries disconnected from the questions and challenges most important to them.
3. *Culture wars and the embrace of "anti-science"*: Most young Christians don't have the baggage of being at war with science. In fact, they are looking for ways to integrate and make sense of how science and religion coexist in the world as revelations of truth. Anti-science rhetoric and policies are a big turn-off to them.

---

[36] "Six Reasons Young Christians Leave Church," *Barna* (September 2011), accessed September 25, 2023, https://www.barna.com/research/six-reasons-young-christians-leave-church.

[37] Mark Yoder, "Why Youth Leave the Church: 10 Surprising Reasons Teens Disappear," *Church Leaders* (May 2023), accessed September 25, 2023, https://churchleaders.com/youth/166129-marc-solas-10-surprising-reasons-our-kids-leave-church.html.

4. *Judgmental attitudes, especially in regard to gender and sexuality*: Young Christians are looking for more faithful ways of navigating human sexuality and gender than what they've received from their parents. Purity culture, shunning LGBTQ people in ways that others are not, body shaming, and misogyny are all troubling; and churches often do not respond well to young people seeking better ways to handle the complex reality of gender and sexuality.
5. *Lack of open-mindedness*: Young people in general are growing up in more diverse communities than their parents. They're exposed to a wide variety of ethnicities, religions, and worldviews. These young Christians are looking for churches that respect differences, honor similarities, and do so without shunning or excluding people who think differently than they do. There's a value of open-mindedness and inclusion that they're looking to live into as they identify as Christian.
6. *The dismissal of serious questions and doubts with mere platitudes*: This is very similar to older generations as well: easy answers, trite platitudes, or appeals to "just listen to the authority" are not compelling to young Christians. They have a higher tolerance to hold space for doubt and questions and are looking for churches that will take them—and their doubts—seriously.[38]

Notice the fourth reason above for the youth leaving the church; it seems Johnston is correct. Of course, it is not the only reason. The youth are a special kind of people, and it takes those gifted in those areas to properly minister to them. However, notice the second and sixth. The youth do not want their questions dismissed—they want the church to address certain topics that are deep and relevant. This is why I have written this book in the way that it is written for an Adventist audience (although anybody can benefit). We need to talk

---

[38] Matt Tebbe, "Why People Leave the Church," *Gravity* (June 2022), accessed September 25, 2023, https://gravityleadership.com/why-people-leave-church.

about this issue and start having conversations without compromising. If the church compromises every time there is a "new issue" in society, the youth are going to leave as well. The youth are looking for something firm and stable, something they can count on. I believe that the LGBTQ+ issue is a problem for the youth (and even adults) because well-meaning saints are dismissive and talk down to them with a "This is a sin because I say it is" attitude, and that will not cut it. We need to sit down with them and have a respectful conversation telling them the "whys" and showing them. We need to preach about this from the pulpit and not brush it under the carpet.

However, if we as a church are going to always be worried about "Well, if we do this or say that, they are going to leave the church," we are going to have problems in other areas as well, and we will never proclaim the truth because we are worried about "numbers." I am reminded of a painful incident that took place early on in my ministry. Our church was taking a stand against one of the several apostate offshoot movements that, unfortunately, we deal with in the Adventist Church. We were having a church business meeting because there were several members of the church who were part of this one apostate movement and did not want to leave it or change their beliefs as to its misguided theology. The church board had recommended that they should be disfellowshipped. However, it is the church at business session that makes that decision. Anyway, I remember arriving at the church and getting ready when I spotted a man whom I knew was sympathetic toward those who were going to be removed from membership. This man was not a member of the church, nor did he want to be. As such, I told him he had to leave because the meeting was for church members only. He responded by saying, "I am a character witness." He, of course, was going to defend those being removed from membership. I responded by saying, "Okay, you can leave, and I will call you when it's your time to talk." After I said this, his face turned red, and he asked to speak to me in private. I honestly thought he was going to kill me; but when we were alone, through grinding teeth, he said, "This is why so many people are leaving Adventism because you are doing things like this." I responded simply by saying, "People who want to leave the church will leave regardless, but we are not looking for quantity. We are looking for quality."

I realize my response may have seemed dismissive and misguided. After all, numbers are important. Just ask any conference official. However, the quantity of members filling the pews should not be my primary concern. I pastor a church that seats close to three hundred people, but I would rather have eighty people who are totally surrendered and converted than three hundred who are nominal Christians. Quantity has its place, but I believe God is more interested in the quality. So it may be that some of our youth, and even some adults will leave the church if we do not affirm LGBTQ+ people. I believe that is a risk worth taking because the church, and even me as a pastor, is not here to make people happy but to lead people into what God wants them to be, that is, holy. Some leaders in our church will compromise on this, and it may be that the numbers in their churches will multiply. Perhaps they will receive "kudos" from those above them. But my primary concern is, "What does God think of me? Am I being faithful to Him, or am I bowing to the god of political correctness?"

I will again quote the statement made by Ellen G. White because it seems fitting:

> The greatest want of the world is the want of men—men who will not be bought or sold, men who in their inmost souls are true and honest, men who do not fear to call sin by its right name, men whose conscience is as true to duty as the needle to the pole, men who will stand for the right though the heavens fall.[39]

"Grasping at straws!" The dictionary defines this phrase as "Make a desperate attempt at saving oneself. This metaphoric expression alludes to a drowning person trying to save himself by grabbing

---

[39] Ellen G. White, "True and Honest Men," *Education*, accessed September 19, 2023, https://egwwritings.org/read?panels=p29.242&index=0.

at flimsy reeds. First recorded in 1534, the term was used figuratively by the late 1600s."[40] We have spent this chapter looking at some of the arguments made by Alicia Johnston, a former Seventh-day Adventist pastor. As I mentioned before, I learned many things from her book. It is well written, and in it, I could sense her sincerity and even her pain because of where she now finds herself. Unfortunately, she is grasping at straws, trying to find a justification when she does not have a leg to stand on. I realize she will probably say the same about me if she reads this book. I suppose we will have to agree to disagree. Still, I hope we can be friends.

---

[40] "Grasping at Straws," *Dictionary.com*, accessed September 25, 2023, https://www.dictionary.com/browse/grasp--at--straws.

CHAPTER 5

Jason Thompson
Freedom from a Secret[1]

I WAS FOURTEEN AND SAT alone in my grandparents' house with a Bible in my lap. Since my father was an Episcopal minister and I was raised in a Christian home, I was familiar with many Bible stories, but that day, I desperately needed to know what God had to say about homosexuality. It was clear from His word that God considered homosexuality a sin. This made me more confused than ever.

Not long before, I had had a dream that I was involved in homosexual behavior. I woke up scared and confused. After that, I recognized a growing strong desire to be physically close to my male peers. I felt there was something very wrong with me. I had not asked for these feelings, but as time passed, they only seemed to intensify. I didn't know where these desires were coming from, and I knew I didn't want them. And I also knew I had to keep this part of me a secret. I prayed earnestly for God to take the desires away, but unfortunately, they didn't go away. "Why doesn't He answer my prayers?" I questioned. And I wondered if God really even cared.

High school was a confusing time. Unsure of my identity, I sought out guys whom I could be emotionally close to, all the while wishing for a physical connection as well. One friend and I engaged in some sexual experimentation. The experience satisfied some curiosity that my fantasy life had created. Soon after, this friend became

---

[1] Jason Thompson, "20-freedom-from-a-secret," *Restored Hope Network*, accessed October 9, 2023, https://www.restoredhopenetwork.org/20-freedom-from-a-secret. Used with permission.

the center of my emotional world. I continued to pray, but God still did not take away my desires.

As a senior, I finally gathered up enough nerve to reach out for help. I found the number for a teen counseling helpline and called. After I nervously rattled off my story to the teen hotline worker, she coldly replied, "The guy who deals with the gays will be in on Friday." I threw the phone down in frustration, climbed on my scooter, and sped through the side streets of Southeast Portland, angry and hopeless, wanting to kill myself by slamming into a car. But God stopped me and calmed my heart.

By the fall of 1990, I had a "girlfriend" who went to my parents' church. We started to "date," and I pretended to be interested in her, but the strain of my conflicted feelings was beginning to be apparent to those who knew me. In a frightening conversation, I confided my struggle to her. Surprisingly, she had hopeful words for me. Through a recent sermon she heard, she learned about Portland Fellowship. She gave me the number, and I nervously made the phone call that would soon change my life.

Phil Hobizal, the Fellowship director, answered the phone; and after listening to me pour out my struggle, he encouraged me that he could help. Change was possible, and we arranged to meet the following week. His words were the best news I had ever heard. I didn't know if I could wait that long!

A few days later, and still riding on a wave of excitement, I told my parents about my struggle. I approached my mom with the intimidating words, "Mom, there's something I need to tell you. I struggle with homosexual desires." She stopped me and said, "Wait, let me get your father. He needs to hear this too." I tried to stop her. I didn't think I could talk to my dad about my secret. I had always felt distant from him. While I frequently shared my thoughts and feelings with my mom, I never felt like I had that freedom with my dad. Nervously, I paced the floor as she went outside and called my father in. They sat down. I told them that I struggled with homosexual desires but that I didn't want to be gay. I also told them about the hope I had learned about from the Portland Fellowship. It took only a few minutes to say, but it was a lot to drop on my parents.

I left their house feeling a freedom that I had never before experienced. The weight of the secret I had kept for years began to evaporate. I later found out that my parents were up most of that night, talking, crying, and praying. They got very little sleep, and my dad had to preach in the morning. I went to church, and before the service, Dad took me outside. He told me that he had seen many people with serious problems during his years of ministry but hadn't seen anyone deal with a problem so diligently. He told me that he had never been as proud of me as he was that day. Dad truly blessed me with his loving and supportive words. God was providing an answer.

My first year of involvement at Portland Fellowship was difficult. During their Tuesday night meetings, I learned about the roots of my homosexual desires, God's plan of forgiveness, and the freedom from homosexual struggle. But occasionally on weekends, I would drive to downtown Portland and check out what was available in the gay community, hoping someone or something could fill the still-gaping pit of emotional need.

Not only did I venture out from time to time, but pornography had a strong pull in my life, and it was a barrier to my ability to grow in what I was learning about God. It took a full year of participation with Portland Fellowship before I was even able to realize that I could not have it both ways. I could not follow God and continue to hold out hope of satisfying this homosexual urge within.

By this time, I was attending Bible college too. Phil asked me if I would consider being a small group leader, and I accepted. At school, I lived in the dorm and began to share my struggle with some of the guys in my section. It was a terrifying risk to take, and although not everyone knew quite how to handle this issue, I didn't experience rejection. One of the first guys I shared with became one of my closest friends.

God had heard me and was answering my prayers. His desire was not just to take away all my problems but to provide the Body of Christ to come alongside me to support and encourage me. It was through being open and sharing my struggle with others that I began to have my real needs fulfilled.

I continued to volunteer at Portland Fellowship and to walk in submission to God. Suddenly, I could see that the intense emotional need for male friendship was driving my desires. But slowly, through positive male friendships, my homosexual desires began to lose its power and grip. I was learning amazing lessons, and powerful healing was taking place.

One of the greatest steps I made in the change process began one night with my dad. We set up a time when just he and I could go out to dinner and talk—straight from our hearts. For the first time, my dad and I shared with each other the most personal things in our lives. I felt a new connection to him—one that began to take away some doubt and uncertainty about our relationship. In January 1993, I became part of the Fellowship staff. I wanted the opportunity to tell people that change was possible, and I particularly wanted to reach teenagers with the good news of freedom from a life dominated by sin.

I continued to mature over the next few years, working in ministry and attending classes to complete my degree in biblical studies. One day, while hanging out with some friends at the coffee shop of the college, I looked across the table and noticed a beautiful young woman. Her smile and friendly nature attracted my attention. With the encouragement of my friends, I got up the nerve to ask her out. She slowly became my first real girlfriend.

Amy knew nothing about homosexuality except that it was weird. But her love for the Lord enabled her to understand this confusing issue. Through her desire to know me better and learn what I did, she participated in the eight-month Portland Fellowship program. A year to the day from the night of our first date, I took Amy to Multnomah Falls—the spot where my dad had proposed to my mom. I dropped down on one knee and asked Amy to be my wife. She was so startled that I almost dropped her ring over the bridge! Thankfully, she said yes.

Amy and I were married on March 15, 1997, in a beautiful ceremony at Community Bible Fellowship. Our friends and loved ones were right by our sides, supporting us the whole way through. We entered marriage with an incredible honeymoon in Puerto Vallarta, Mexico.

Since then, our lives have only been blessed more by the gift of children. A great joy and sadness came with the birth and death of our first child, Abbie. She was born with a heart defect and passed away at three and a half months. God met us in our grief and reminded us of his faithfulness in our difficulties. A few years later, in 2003, we had Trevor, and in 2007 Cody was born to us. My family is not "evidence" of healing in my life but rather the blessing of the healing in my life. And I praise God for them all.

Christ is truly a God of mercy and grace. Strangely enough, I am now very grateful to have experienced homosexual struggles. When I submitted them to God, I gave Him permission to mold and shape me into the man I am today. I am thankful that He chose me to help reach out to hurting and lost people, and I am thankful that He granted me the desires of my heart. In Him, there are no secrets. He truly is a great and mighty God!

The Gospel of *Trans*formation

I remember it as if it was yesterday! My first sermon as a pastor in my newly assigned district. I was very nervous, to say the least. The title of the message was "The Perfect Will of God" based on Romans 12:1–2. It is a well-known passage: "I beseech you therefore, brethren, by the mercies of God, that you present your bodies a living sacrifice, holy, acceptable to God, which is your reasonable service. And do not be conformed to this world, but be transformed by the renewing of your mind, that you may prove what is that good and acceptable and perfect will of God." My favorite part of the sermon was the exegetical analysis of verse 2.

THE PRESENT TRUTH AND THE LGBTQ+ MOVEMENT

"And do not be conformed to the world."

In the Greek, the word *conformed* is *suschématizó*, which means to conform or fashion oneself after another pattern;[2] and *world* is *aión*, which literally means "age."[3] I prefer the word *age* because it's timeless and it can be applied to any age in which the reader lives. One of the most persistent threats to a dedicated life is conformity to the world, to fashion after its pattern. There is no greater weakness in the Christianity of our day than the fact that so many church members accept without question the dominant intellectual and social atmosphere of the age. I believe this to be a problem when it comes to the LGBTQ+ ideology and the attempts of some for it to be affirmed in the church.

What is interesting about the word *conform* is that it implies a gradual process, it does not happen instantly. Is society and, dare I say, Christians conforming to the transgender ideology? Well, if they weren't, there would be no need for this book. This conformity has been achieved through a gradual process of indoctrination. The *Washington Post* published an article back in March of 2022 where they commented on a poster of a mother bear hugging a baby bear. The colors of the baby bear are the colors of the rainbow, and the poster says, "IF YOUR PARENTS AREN'T ACCEPTING OF YOUR IDENTITY, I'M YOUR MOM NOW." I was searching for this, and I found that online stores carry shirts with this sign. The article also commented on a training session for teachers in Wisconsin,

> A recent training session for teachers on "equity, diversity and inclusion" included several references to keeping parents from being informed about their children. During the training, one of the slides said, "We understand and acknowledge that teachers are often put in terrible positions caught between parents and their stu-

---

[2] "4964, Suschématizó," Bible Hub https://biblehub.com/greek/4964.htm.
[3] "165, aión," Bible Hub https://biblehub.com/greek/165.htm.

dents. But much like we wouldn't act as stand-ins for abuse in other circumstances, we cannot let parents' rejection of their children guide teachers' reactions and actions and advocacy for our students." Teachers were told, "*Remember, parents, are not entitled to know their kids' identities. That knowledge must be earned.*"[4] (emphasis supplied)

The transgender movement has conquered American life. Activist teachers have converted classrooms into propaganda. Influencers are driving billions of social media impressions. And doctors are cutting up kids in the name of gender-affirming care.[5]

When we think of the modern transgender, Caitlyn Jenner (formerly Bruce Jenner) is unarguably the person that comes to the mind of many. When we think of how we got here regarding why the transgender movement is so popular today, we can point to the 2015 article in *Vanity Fair*.

Wearing lingerie and posing provocatively on a barstool, hands tucked behind back, Jenner copied the hyper-femininity and exaggerated sex appeal that we are used to seeing on the covers of magazines at the checkout in the grocery store. The cover was an act of self-revelation, for

---

[4] Scott Walker, "The Transgender Indoctrination in Our Nation's Schools: Parents Need to Take Back Their Children's Education—before It's Too Late," *The Washington Times* (March 2022), accessed September 26, 2023, https://www.washingtontimes.com/news/2022/mar/18/transgender-indoctrination-our-nations-schools.

[5] Christian Rufo, "How the Trans Movement Conquered American Life: The Transgender Empire," *Manhattan Institute* (July 2023), accessed September 26, 2023, https://manhattan.institute/multimedia/how-the-trans-movement-conquered-american-life-the-transgender-empire.

> Jenner's appearance signals a transition to fully identifying as and living as a woman. "Call me Caitlyn," the cover proclaimed. The picture is now world famous… The message to the world was clear; men can become women if they feel or perceive themselves to be women, and vice versa.[6]

Yet even Jenner says that "the 'indoctrination' of America's youth has led to an 'oversaturation' of the transgender community."[7] This indoctrination has led to conformity, and while it should not surprise us that secular society is conforming, it is a sad situation when Christians are doing it. As we have seen, even some Seventh-day Adventist Churches have fallen victim to "conformity." To borrow a sci-fi analogy, in *Star Trek: The Next Generation*, one of the Federation's greatest nemeses was "The Borg," and their goal is to assimilate everyone whom they encounter. When they find their victims, they say, "We are the Borg. You will be assimilated. Resistance is futile." This is the way Satan works, total assimilation. He wants to convince us that "resistance is futile." While that may work in the sci-fi world, and even in the secular world, it is not true for those who know God and maintain a biblical worldview.

"But be transformed"

The apostle Paul is saying, "Stop letting the world squeeze you into its mold," and then he gives the solution, "but be transformed." The word *transformed* in the Greek is *metamorphoó*, which is the root word for *metamorphosis*, which means "change of physical form, structure, or substance especially by supernatural means" or "a

---

[6] Andrew T. Walker, *God and the Transgender Debate: What Does the Bible Actually Say about Gender Identity* (Turkey: The Good Book Company, 2022), 21–22.
[7] Anna Skinner, "Caitlyn Jenner Says Trans Community Is 'Oversaturated,'" *Newsweek* (April 2023), accessed September 26, 2023, https://www.newsweek.com/caitlyn-jenner-trans-community-oversaturated-1795397.

striking alteration in appearance, character, or circumstances."[8] Of course, it also refers to the process by which a caterpillar becomes a beautiful butterfly. I remember hearing a humorous story that illustrates what transformation is all about.

> A family who lived in a very remote location visited the city for the first time. They registered in a hotel and were impressed by all they saw. While Mother was handling the registration, the father and his son busied themselves looking around and as they walked toward the elevator they were amazed because they had never seen one. They stared at it because they couldn't figure out what it was for. An old lady slowly made her way toward the elevator, got in, and the door closed. After about one minute, the door opened, and a beautiful woman came out. The father could not stop looking. Without moving his head, he touched his son's arm, and told him; Son, bring your mother!

Transformation implies a change into something better, something beautiful. Thus, Paul's counsel is not to let the world mold us into its pattern but to be transformed, be "metamorphoó," and allow God to change you into someone better, someone beautiful by His supernatural means.

"By the renewing of your mind"

The transformation, according to Paul, starts in the mind. This makes sense because the mind is where the battle between the desire to serve God and sin takes place. Paul described his dilemma with the

---

[8] "Metamorphosis," *Merriam-Webster.com Dictionary*, Merriam-Webster, accessed September 26, 2023, https://www.merriam-webster.com/dictionary/metamorphosis.

battle of sin in Romans 7:23: "But I see another law in my members, warring against the law of my mind, and bringing me into captivity to the law of sin which is in my members." We can relate to him, can't we? However, he described how to obtain victory: "I thank God—through Jesus Christ our Lord! So then, with the mind I myself serve the law of God, but with the flesh the law of sin" (v. 25). You see, it is only God through the Holy Spirit Who can change our minds. This is what it means to renew—it means to make new. When one is born again, there is new life; and with new life, we don't behave like we used to, we don't think like we used to, and we allow God to take over our thoughts. We must decide whether we allow the input from the world to control our thoughts or God. We must decide whether we surrender to God or to the pattern of the age we live in.

The concept of transformation is the foundation of the gospel. In fact, without it, it would not be good news. We can look forward to a complete transformation upon the Second Coming of Jesus.

> Behold, I tell you a mystery: We shall not all sleep, but *we shall all be changed*—in a moment, in the twinkling of an eye, at the last trumpet. For the trumpet will sound, and the dead will be raised incorruptible, and *we shall be changed*. For this corruptible must put on incorruption, and this mortal must put on immortality. (1 Corinthians 15:51–53, emphasis supplied)

However, the transformation starts here and now, but it will not happen unless we realize our need for change and unless our minds our renewed. If we still think the way we used to, if we think s the world does, we can never experience the complete transformation that is so necessary in the Christian walk. So how can those struggling with gender dysphoria, gender identity, or those who have transitioned into the opposite sex be transformed? Well, there is no formula that is specific to them. The solution is the same as for everyone one else, the gospel of Jesus.

The Bible teaches us that we all have a common problem, a common disease, if you will, "for all have sinned and fall short of the glory of God" (Romans 3:23). But God so loved us that He gave us a common solution:

> For when we were still without strength, in due time Christ died for the ungodly. For scarcely for a righteous man will one die; yet perhaps for a good man someone would even dare to die. But God demonstrates His own love toward us, in that while we were still sinners, Christ died for us. (Romans 5:6–8)

Jesus is the common solution to our common problem.

"But I have already accepted Jesus!" "I am an LGBTQ+ Christian who wants to be accepted and affirmed by my church." This is how I imagine LGBTQ+ activists like Alice Johnson would respond, and it is here where we come to a "hiccup." Because while acknowledging the common sin problem of humanity, they have convinced themselves that a particular behavior or lifestyle, already shown to be a sin in scripture, has been reinterpreted so as not to be a sin. But this is not everybody. That is, there are those who struggle with gender dysphoria and sexual identity that acknowledge this is not the will of God, and, if acted on, is a sin. They are crying out, "What am I going to do? Lord, how can I find freedom? How can these chains be broken?"

The Gospel of Power

When we think about the immediate benefit of the gospel, our minds go to the forgiveness of our sins. That is, Jesus died to forgive our sins. Speaking of Jesus, Paul said, "Who gave Himself for our sins, that He might deliver us from this present evil age, according to the will of our God and Father" (Galatians 1:4)? The prophet Isaiah wrote, "But He was wounded for our transgressions, He was bruised for our iniquities: The chastisement for our peace was upon Him, And by His stripes we are healed" (Isaiah 53:5). However, the gospel is not just about forgiveness. After all, if it was just about forgiveness, we would have to be asking for it for all eternity. The gospel is also power. "For I am not ashamed of the gospel of Christ, *for it is the power of God* to salvation for everyone who believes" (Romans 1:16, emphasis supplied).

Jesus sent us "The Comforter," the Holy Spirit to convict us of sin and to give us power to overcome it.

> And when He has come, He will convict the world of sin, and of righteousness, and of judgment. (John 16:8)

> But *you shall receive power when the Holy Spirit* has come upon you. (Acts 1:8, emphasis supplied)

> Therefore, brethren, we are debtors—not to the flesh, to live according to the flesh. For if you live according to the flesh you will die; *but if by the Spirit* you put to death the deeds of the body, you will live. (Romans 8:12, emphasis supplied)

The Gospel of Victory

A good friend of mine is not shy in sharing his testimony. He tells of his life of using drugs and how, at the time, he did not think he could conquer his vice. However, one day in prayer, he asked God, "Lord, take this taste away from me." I never told him, but his prayer request was something that helped me become victorious. You see, for many years in my life, I was addicted to pornography, and it was tearing my life apart. From the start, I always knew this addiction was a sin, but I thought I was strong enough to overcome it. Sure, there were seasons when I was "sober," but these did not last very long, and I would find myself right back in the gutter.

Like any addiction, there were painful struggles in those times when I was working on staying sober. Anyone who has been addicted to pornography can testify to an even physical yearning due to dopamine levels in the brain. This is what Paul talks about when he says, "But I see another law in my members, warring against the law of my mind, and bringing me into captivity to the law of sin which is in my members" (Romans 7:23). Paul spoke of a war in Ephesians 6:12: "For we do not wrestle against flesh and blood, but against principalities, against powers, against the rulers of the darkness of this age, against spiritual hosts of wickedness in the heavenly places." The struggle against sin is not an easy one. In fact, Jesus teaches that we must take bold actions when dealing with sin in our lives.

In His discourse known as the Sermon on the Mount, Jesus discusses several topics. In Matthew 5:27–29, He talks about adultery in the heart, saying,

> You have heard that it was said to those of old, "You shall not commit adultery." But I say to you that whoever looks at a woman to lust for her has already committed adultery with her in his heart. If your right eye causes you to sin, pluck it out and cast it from you; for it is more profitable for you that one of your members perish, than for your whole body to be cast into hell. And if your right hand causes you to sin, cut it off and cast it from you; for it is more profitable for you that one of your members perish, than for your whole body to be cast into hell.

Jesus repeats the same words in Matthew 18 in speaking on how to deal with sin in the church. Clearly Jesus is speaking figuratively, He does not want us to literally take our eye out. However, in these verses, He is saying that we cannot deal with sin in a "namby-pamby" way. No, one must be bold. Ellen White said it this way,

> In order for us to reach this high ideal, *that which causes the soul to stumble must be sacrificed.* It is through the will that sin retains its hold upon us. The surrender of the will is represented as plucking out the eye or cutting off the hand. Often it seems to us that to surrender the will to God is to consent to go through life maimed or crippled. But it is better, says Christ, for self to be maimed, wounded, crippled, if thus you may enter into life. That which you look upon as disaster is the door to the highest benefit.[9] (emphasis supplied)

Thus, victory over sin (no matter which sin) and transformation are possible. Sure, the heavy lifting has already been done by God, but as you can see above, the power to be bold has already been given to us. Perhaps the reason certain "authorities" in science and medicine and some in the LGBTQ+ community do not believe that a person can overcome their gender confusion or unnatural sexual orientation is that they don't believe in God. I am reminded of the story of the healing of the lame man in Acts 3. This man lay daily at the gate of the temple and asked for alms. Everyone, including the religious leaders, knew this man was a cripple. Peter and John did not have any money to give them, but "in the name of Jesus Christ of Nazareth, rise up and walk." And he took him by the right hand and lifted him up, and immediately his feet and ankle bones received strength. So he, leaping up, stood and walked and entered the temple with them—walking, leaping, and praising God" (vv. 6–8). Yet even after the miracle, the religious leaders did not believe.

---

[9] Ellen G. White, *Thoughts from the Mount of Blessing*, page 61, accessed October 3, 2023, https://egwwritings.org/read?panels=p150.322&index=0.

The same thing happened in the story of the healing of the blind man in John 9. The blind man in the story was well known by the community, including the Pharisees. Jesus healed the man and the latter declared, "One thing I know: that though I was blind, now I see" (v. 25). Yet even though they knew he had been born blind and that now he could see, the Pharisees did not want to believe in the power of Jesus.

> The Pharisees saw the man born blind, heard his testimony, heard about his past and how it was completely different from the present one, and refused to believe the miracle because of Who the miracle pointed to. They were skeptical of the miracle because they didn't have a real faith in the God who'd done it.[10]

I suppose that not having faith in God is to be expected from our modern science and medicine, but not LGBTQ+ people who identify as Christians. God can and is willing to do what may appear impossible for us. This is why the apostle Paul, in speaking to the church at Corinth, could say,

> Do you not know that the unrighteous will not inherit the kingdom of God? Do not be deceived. Neither fornicators, nor idolaters, nor adulterers, nor homosexuals, nor sodomites, nor thieves, nor covetous, nor drunkards, nor revilers, nor extortioners will inherit the kingdom of God. *And such were some of you.* But you were washed, but you were sanctified, but you were justified in the name of the Lord Jesus and by the Spirit of our God. (1 Corinthians 6:9–11, emphasis supplied)

---

[10] Jackie Hill Perry, *Gay Girl, Good God* (Nashville, TN; B&H Publishing Group, 2018), 116.

Paul was able to testify to the transformation that some in the church of Corinth had experienced. Some had been adulterers, but not anymore. Some had been involved in sexual immorality, but not anymore. Some had been addicted to alcohol, but not anymore. And yes, some had been guilty of engaging in what today would be called LGBTQ+ ideology and lifestyle, but not anymore. Why? Because they had realized that they were engaging in a sinful lifestyle that did not coincide with Christianity and "because the expectation of Scripture is that anyone who comes to Christ experiences continual transformation as they surrender each area of life to Him."[11] They had to make a choice: Would they follow Christ, or would they continue to give in to the desires of the flesh, even those that could be argued they were born with? Clearly, they chose Christ and relied on the power of the Holy Spirit, this is why they no longer engaged in the behavior and lifestyle that Paul mentioned.

Christians should not continue to live as the world does:

> This I say, therefore, and testify in the Lord, that *you should no longer walk as the rest of the Gentiles walk*, in the futility of their mind, having their understanding darkened, being alienated from the life of God, because of *the ignorance* that is in them, because of *the blindness* of their heart; who, being past feeling, have given themselves over to lewdness, to work all uncleanness with greediness. (Ephesians 4:17–19, emphasis supplied)
>
> If then you were raised with Christ, seek those things which are above, where Christ is, sitting at the right hand of God. *Set your mind on things above, not on things on the earth.* For you died, and your life is hidden with Christ in God. When Christ who is our life appears, then you

---

[11] Linda A. Seiler, Ph.D., *Transformation: A Former Transgender Responds to LGBTQ* (Grand Rapids, MI: Credo House Publishers, 2023), 127.

also will appear with Him in glory. Therefore, *put to death your members which are on the earth*: fornication, uncleanness, passion, evil desire, and covetousness, which is idolatry. Because of these things the wrath of God is coming upon the sons of disobedience, in which you yourselves once walked when you lived in them. (Colossians 3:1–7, emphasis supplied)

We could go on and on about the fact that Christians should not think or behave like the world and that if those who have a secular or even sinful lifestyle accept Jesus and become part of His church, there should be a change or transformation. This, indeed, applies to those who struggle with gender identity confusion and LGBTQ+ ideology and lifestyle. Is transformation possible? Yes, and the testimonies that I have shared thus far prove it. But what does transformation look like? Will those transformed ever struggle with temptation? Before answering these questions, I would like to share just a few more stories of transformation.

Jackie Hill Perry

Today Jackie Hill Perry is an author, poet, bible teacher, and hip-hop artist. She is also a former lesbian. In her book (already quoted) *Gay Girl, Good God*, she describes her journey. In the introduction of her book, she says,

> There are many who, while reading, won't understand gayness as something possible of being in the past tense. It is either who you are, or what you have never been. To this, I disagree. The only constant in this world is God. Gayness, on the other hand, can be an immovable identity only when the heart is unwilling to bow.[12]

---

[12] Perry, 12.

I have already shared her view as to the reason she became a lesbian (see chapter 1), but she also talks about the process of her transformation.

One night while watching TV, and while involved in a romantic relationship with a woman, she heard God speak to her, saying, "She will be the death of you!" She realized He was warning her and that she needed to make a choice, either God or her girlfriend and that lifestyle. At first, this seemed difficult because in her mind "choosing God was the same as choosing heterosexuality."[13] While what God was calling her to do was a struggle, God was clearly working in her through the Holy Spirit to give her clarity. She narrates,

> She (her girlfriend) was an answered prayer that God forbid me to speak. I loved her, but according to God, our love was no different than death. Why would God want to keep me from this, I thought again—wasn't He love? Shouldn't He understand it best? Especially the ways in which it made all of His creatures feel a little more like Him every time they were in it. On the other hand, if He was love, the embodiment of it without the slightest wrinkle in His robe, what love is when devils cannot interfere—then all other loves must've been a lesser love at best. Could it be that God would not have me going about the rest of my life believing that these lesser forms of "love" were the real thing?
>
> Perhaps this love He, filled to the brim with, was pouring over into His dealings with me. And perhaps this love was compelling Him, on the basis of grace—an undeserved love—to help me see that every person, place, or thing that I loved more than Him could not keep its promise to love me eternally. Nor was my heart created

---

[13] Ibid., 58.

for them to hold. But they would instead do to me what all sin does, separate me from God, and thus true love, forever. It would be the death of me.[14]

From that day on, things were not the same, as she says, "I arrived at work the next day, a new creature."[15] However, as those of us who have received the gift of salvation through Jesus can testify, being a new creature does not mean that all a sudden we have it all figured out and that we no longer struggle with temptation and sin. The apostle Paul said it best in Romans 7:

> Has then what is good become death to me? Certainly not! But sin, that it might appear sin, was producing death in me through what is good, so that sin through the commandment might become exceedingly sinful. For we know that the law is spiritual, but I am carnal, sold under sin. For what I am doing, I do not understand. For what I will to do, that I do not practice; but what I hate, that I do. If, then, I do what I will not to do, I agree with the law that *it is* good. But now, *it is* no longer I who do it, but sin that dwells in me. For I know that in me (that is, in my flesh) nothing good dwells; for to will is present with me, but *how* to perform what is good I do not find. For the good that I will *to do,* I do not do; but the evil I will not *to do,* that I practice. Now if I do what I will not *to do,* it is no longer I who do it, but sin that dwells in me. (vv. 13–20)

While Perry felt that a change had taken place and others saw a change in her, the complete transformation did not happen imme-

---

[14] Ibid., 60–61.
[15] Ibid., 66.

diately. She continues to narrate the story of her journey that eventually led her to meet the man who would become her husband and father of her daughter. After living her life as a lesbian and now a loving wife and mother, she concludes,

> It is through faith in Him, initiated by His pursuit of me, that I, a gay girl, now new creature, was made right with God. Given sight, able to recognize my hands and how they'd been calloused by sin, and how Jesus had come to cleanse me of them all. Now seeing, I worship. One thing is sure, if ever I am asked, how am I able to see now, after being blind for so long, I will simply say, "I was blind, a good God came, and now, I see."[16]

Linda A. Seiler

Dr. Linda Seiler serves as the executive director of ReStory Ministries, which equips churches to address LGBTQ issues. She is also a former transgender. While I have already shared her point of view as to why she struggled with her gender (see chapter 1), in her book *Transformation: A Former Transgender Responds to LGBTQ*, she tells us the story of her journey. "I have zero childhood memories of being content in a female body… Somehow, I just knew I was born in the wrong body and that I wouldn't be complete unless I had male anatomy."[17] This happened in the 1970s when nobody was really talking about gender dysphoria and being transgender was the "cool thing." She continues,

> When I was about nine years old, I heard about "sex change operations," and I decided that was the answer to my dilemma. I charted

---

[16] Ibid., 117.
[17] Seiler, 9.

> out my plan: As soon as I was old enough and had enough money, I would change my name to David (which is what my parents would have named me if I had been a boy), get a sex change, and live happily ever after.[18]

Had this happened today, the school nurse may have given her gender hormones and puberty blockers (without the knowledge or consent of her parents) to get her ready for the SRS (sex reassignment surgery).

While the desires she experienced as a little girl were not sexual in nature, "when the adolescent hormones kicked in, the desire for emotional and physical connection became confused with my normal sex drive."[19] Although she felt she was born in the wrong body, Seiler was ashamed of her feelings. In her junior year of high school, she attended an evangelistic outreach and accepted Jesus as her Savior. She was hoping that this would change the feelings inside of her, but she was disappointed. Over the next few years, she got involved in ministry activities and even received counseling.

> I thirsted so deeply for female nurture that I seemed to get worse (i.e., acting out sexually with another woman) before I got better. I was disillusioned when I realized my fantasy of being a man who slept with women would never fill the deep ache in my soul. I broke off that relationship, repented before my pastor, and received his help to focus on the Lord and get connected to accountability… Through a counselor I came to realize that my sexual addictions were merely fruit from a deeper root. The evil one had taken advantage of wounds of rejection to lure me into believing lies about my sexuality. The path of

---
[18] Ibid.,10.
[19] Ibid., 11.

resolving the pain in my heart was to renounce the lies, receive the truth, and find comfort in my heavenly Father instead of in the arms of another woman.[20]

While she still struggled for some time, with the help of caring individuals and a connection to God through prayer, she could say,

> Each day that I walk with Jesus I walk further away from my past and step into a greater wholeness as the unique woman God created me to be... The transformation I've experienced doesn't erase the history of my vulnerabilities. There are times I still hunger for maternal love, and God has graciously provided spiritual moms... Healing from sexual brokenness is rarely instantaneous—it's more like peeling back the layers of an onion, one at a time. But if we are determined to hold fast to the truth of God's word, lean on God's family, and allow His healing touch into the deepest wounds of our heart, we can experience the transformation that Jesus died to give us.[21]

Rosaria Butterfield

Rosaria Butterfield, a former tenured professor of English and women's studies at Syracuse University, converted to Christ in 1999 in what she describes as a train wreck. Her memoir *The Secret Thoughts of an Unlikely Convert* chronicles that difficult journey. Rosaria is married to Kent, a Reformed Presbyterian pastor in North Carolina, and is a homeschooling mother, author, and speaker.

---

[20] Ibid., 14–20.
[21] Ibid., 24–25.

Raised and educated in liberal Catholic settings, Rosaria fell in love with the world of words. In her late twenties, allured by feminist philosophy and LGBTQ+ advocacy, she adopted a lesbian identity. Rosaria earned her Ph.D. from Ohio State University, then served in the English department and women's studies program at Syracuse University from 1992 to 2002. Her primary academic field was critical theory, specializing in queer theory. Her historical focus was nineteenth-century literature, informed by Freud, Marx, and Darwin. She advised the LGBTQ+ student group, wrote Syracuse University's policy for same-sex couples, and actively lobbied for LGBTQ+ aims alongside her lesbian partner.

In 1997, while Rosaria was researching the Religious Right "and their politics of hatred against people like me," she wrote an article against the Promise Keepers. A response to that article triggered a meeting with Ken Smith, who became a resource on the Religious Right and their Bible, a confidant, and a friend. In 1999, after repeatedly reading the Bible in large chunks for her research, Rosaria converted to Christianity, leaving academia and her lesbian lifestyle behind. Today, she is a wife, a mother, and an acclaimed speaker. Her first book, *The Secret Thoughts of an Unlikely Convert*, details her conversion and the cataclysmic fallout—in which she lost "everything but the dog" yet gained eternal life in Christ.[22]

The Process of Transformation

The stories I have shared so far reveal that the first step in transformation and victory over sin is acknowledging that we are sinners in need of a Savior. God made it clear that their lifestyle and desires were contrary to His will and were sinful. As I have already mentioned in this book, gender dysphoria, confusion over sexual orientation, or really anything related to LGBTQ+ identity is a moral issue. It is sinful and a result of the fall. One cannot "break free from the

---

[22] Rosaria Butterfield Biography, accessed October 10, 2023, https://rosariabutterfield.com/biography.

effects of the fall by following the course of the fall in your own life and decisions."[23] Yet there is hope.

The apostle Paul says, "Therefore, if anyone is in Christ, he is a new creation; old things have passed away; behold, all things have become new" (2 Corinthians 5:17).

> To be a new creation in Christ is to experience the promise of what fully awaits those who place their trust in him—to be able to anticipate the certainty of a coming day when the disorder of creation is put back together, and when this dysphoria of any kind is replaced by euphoria of every kind. To be a new creation is to know why the world is the way it is, why our bodies are the way they are, and why our minds think as they do. It is to be equipped with the power of God's Holy Spirit to live in relationship with God. A new creation in Christ recognizes that even in broken minds living in broken bodies living in a broken world, there is a definitive and clear "very good" blueprint of creation. And new creation has ceased to belong to this "old," fallen world, even as they live in it, for they are walking toward the full newness of a renewed, re-perfected world.[24]

While I have no doubt that God can transform a person caught up in a sinful lifestyle in an instant, He often does everything in His timetable. Transformation follows a process because God wants us to learn patience and trust in Him. Thus, transformation can be painful. Earlier, I quoted Romans 12:2: "And do not be conformed to this world, but *be transformed* by the renewing of your mind" (emphasis supplied). The word *transformed* in the Greek is *metamor-*

---

[23] Walker, 88.
[24] Ibid., 89.

phoó, which is the root word for *metamorphosis*, which is the process through which a caterpillar becomes a butterfly. Have you ever thought about what happens to the caterpillar during this process of transformation?

The caterpillar, or what is more scientifically termed a larva, stuffs itself with leaves, growing plumper and longer through a series of molts in which it sheds its skin. One day, the caterpillar stops eating, hangs upside down from a twig or leaf and spins itself into a silky cocoon or molts into a shiny chrysalis… First, the caterpillar digests itself, releasing enzymes to dissolve all of its tissues. If you were to cut open a cocoon or chrysalis at just the right time, caterpillar soup would ooze out. But the contents of the pupa are not entirely an amorphous mess. Certain highly organized groups of cells known as imaginal discs survive the digestive process. Before hatching, when a caterpillar is still developing inside its egg, it grows an imaginal disc for each of the adult body parts it will need as a mature butterfly or moth… Once a caterpillar has disintegrated all of its tissues except for the imaginal discs, those discs use the protein-rich soup all around them to fuel the rapid cell division required to form the wings, antennae, legs, eyes, genitals and all the other features of an adult butterfly or moth. The imaginal disc for a fruit fly's wing, for example, might begin with only 50 cells and increase to more than 50,000 cells by the end of metamorphosis… Getting a look at this metamorphosis as it happens is difficult; disturbing a caterpillar inside its cocoon or chrysalis risks botching the transformation.[25]

This sounds like a painful and grueling process, yet the result is a beautiful new creature. A wonderful example of the miracle of creation by an omnipotent God Who transforms those who are "in Christ" into a new creation. You see, the transformation of those struggling with LGBTQ+ identity is a miracle that God does. The problem many have is that they think they must do the transformation by their own might, and since they lack the power within themselves, they fail. Once they have experienced failure after failure, they give up. In the case of those in the LGBTQ+ community, they end up convincing themselves that transformation is impossible and rationalize that maybe they cannot change because God made them that way, and since it was His will for them, He must approve it. Trust me, this does not just happen with those in the LGBTQ+ community who advocate for affirmation. It is the same story in the struggle with any sin. I know what I am talking about because I have been there.

During the time I struggled with pornography, I failed many times in trying to conquer my addiction all by myself. I didn't want to bother God with this because it was my problem. So I fell on my face time after time after time. It wasn't until I finally said, "God, I cannot do this. I need you to take control over this," that I finally found victory. I imagine God answering me, "Well, it's about time. I was waiting for you to come to your senses and let me fight your battle." Yet in fighting our battles, God doesn't defeat the enemy all at once. I am reminded of the children of Israel after they finally made it to the Promised Land. "Now Joshua was old, advanced in years. And the Lord said to him: 'You are old, advanced in years, and *there*

---

[25] Ferris Jabr, "How Does a Caterpillar Turn into a Butterfly?" *Scientific American* (August 2012), accessed October 10, 2023, https://www.scientificamerican.com/article/caterpillar-butterfly-metamorphosis-explainer/#:~:text=The%20caterpillar%2C%20or%20what%20is,molts%20into%20a%20shiny%20chrysalis.

remains very much land yet to be possessed'" (Joshua 13:1, emphasis supplied).

> The plan was for the tribes, after they were established in their inheritance, to extend their own territories. Many battles remained yet to be fought in order to complete the possession, but God's blessing in the past was an assurance for the future. So it is in the spiritual warfare. The work of overcoming the defects of character is progressive. The dispossessing of enemies from the heart is a continuous struggle. Conflict after conflict must be waged against hereditary and cultivated tendencies toward evil.[26]

Since transformation is a process, from her experience, Dr. Linda A. Seiler describes key components of transformation that are worth mentioning.

Keys to Transformation

1. *Transformation happens through intimacy with Christ.* The key to transformation is first and foremost intimacy with Jesus. I cannot stress that enough. My goal was not to be free as much as it was to be His—whether or not my desires ever changed. Transformation came as a byproduct of intimacy with Jesus. As I surrendered everything and sought Him with all my heart, He began to expose the lies I believed and the wound of rejection that had become lodged in my soul… As the Lord showed me the reasons for my disordered desires, He gave me hope and expec-

---

[26] "There remaineth" [Joshua 13:1], *Seventh-day Adventist Bible Commentary (SDABC)*, rev. ed., ed. Francis D. Nichol (Washington, DC: Review & Herald, 1976–1980), 2:240.

tation for resolution... Knowing *why* helps, but knowing *Him* is what heals.[27]

As a pastor, I spend a lot of time teaching my church how to stay connected with Jesus. The most powerful and effective way is through the study of His word and prayer. This must happen every day. In some cases, adding fasting to prayer helps in difficult situations (see Matthew 17:21).

2. *Transformation does not happen by force.* If a person struggling with LGBTQ+ identity isn't motivated to seek intimacy with Jesus and to surrender every area of their life to His Lordship, change is unlikely to happen. In the same way that you can't force the gospel on someone who doesn't want it, you can't force transformation on someone who isn't seeking transformation... Only someone who is seeking Jesus for the sake of Jesus will be able to persevere through the ongoing journey of transformation.[28]

3. *Transformation happens through holistic surrender.* Some try to make a deal with God by saying that they will give up homoerotic behavior *if God takes their attractions away.* Thus, they hold their morality for ransom and dictate to God their terms of surrender. But the attitude of the overcomer must be that they will follow God whether or not their desires ever change—because their goal is not just a change in attractions but to know Jesus and become as surrendered to Him as possible.[29]

It is important to clarify this by saying that we must believe that God will do the transformation. It is His will that we are transformed by His power: "Now this is the confidence that we have in Him, that if we ask anything according to His will, He hears us" (1 John 5:14). However, we must adopt the same attitude that Daniel's three friends

---

[27] Seiler, 141.
[28] Ibid., 144–145.
[29] Ibid., 145.

had when confronted with the command to bow down and worship the image of gold:

> Shadrach, Meshach, and Abed-Nego answered and said to the king, "O Nebuchadnezzar, we have no need to answer you in this matter. If that is the case, our God whom we serve is able to deliver us from the burning fiery furnace, and He will deliver us from your hand, O king. But if not, let it be known to you, O king, that we do not serve your gods, nor will we worship the gold image which you have set up." (Daniel 3:16–18)

Those who struggle with LGBTQ+ identity, like any of us who struggle with sin, can believe God can give us victory; but we must first acknowledge our sin.

Adopting a gay/trans identity is a form of unbelief, turning disordered desires into an idol that has the power to dictate an overcomer's identity and determine their destiny. If the overcomer believes they were born that way and cannot change, they will bear the fruit of that unbelief. Surrendering to Christ's Lordship means the overcomer repents for wrong beliefs and surrenders to what God's Word says rather than following their subjective feelings or cultural trends. Without first surrendering to Christ in the areas of behavior, beliefs, and identity, an eventual change in desires is unlikely.[30]

4. *Transformation happens over time.* The overcomer needs to understand transformation as a lifelong journey, not a one-

---

[30] Ibid., 148.

time event. I was hoping for the latter and that God would instantly "cure" me of my sexual brokenness in response to an altar call: I'd get slain in the spirit, fall on the floor sexually broken, and rise anew, content in a female body and attracted to men. If only transformation were that easy. But that's not generally how progressive sanctification happens. Disordered sexual desires don't develop overnight, and they typically don't resolve overnight. Sanctification is a lifelong journey that involves continual growth and transformation as we repent of sin, draw near to God, and become conformed to the image of Christ… Some go back to the old life or concede to an unscriptural "gay Christian" identity because they didn't see the amount of change they had hoped for in a certain period of time, revealing that they had made change itself—not the Lord—their primary goal.[31]

Of the process of sanctification, Ellen White says, "There is no such thing as instantaneous sanctification. True sanctification is a daily work, continuing as long as life shall last."[32]

5. *Transformation happens one layer at a time.* The Lord knows what we can bear and will not overwhelm us in the process. He determines how many layers of the onion need to come off and when. Sometimes, He peels back a few layers at once. Sometimes, He waits months or even years before we are ready to face another layer. He's not slow in keeping His promise to transform us—although sometimes He doesn't move as quickly as we think He should.[33] Earlier, I mentioned the experience of the Israelites after they crossed into the Promised Land. They still had much land to conquer, but God did not have them conquer all

---

[31] Ibid., 148–149.
[32] Ellen G. White, "Substituting feeling for reason," *The Sanctified Life* page 10, accessed October 10, 2023, https://egwwritings.org/read?panels=p138.35&index=0
[33] Seiler, 149–150.

at once because they still had things to learn. Although Dr. Seiler was transformed from her transgender lifestyle, the process took eleven years: "In the end, I discovered that my greatest problem wasn't sexual at all. It was my sinful responses to wounds of rejection that lay at the root of my disordered desires."[34]

6. *Transformation happens at the root.* There are often developmental deficiencies and accompanying wounds in the soul that contribute to sexual brokenness. The most common developmental influences include gender nonconformity, childhood sexual abuse, or adverse family dynamics. When puberty hits, unmet needs for same-sex attachment can become sexualized, manifesting as attractions to the same sex. If we focus only on changing the outward sexual behavior but fail to address the emotional-relational deficits that fuel the attractions, the overcomer may eventually return to old coping mechanisms, as the emotional thirst in their soul combined with their God-given bodily sex drive remains difficult to resist.[35]

In other words, there are reasons for LGBTQ+ identity. This is why those who struggle with this should not make premature decisions and act on their desires without first seeking answers. This will not happen in one or two days; it will take time to explore what is hidden beneath. Anyone who has had to seek help from mental health professionals can testify to how eye-opening and liberating it can be to find out what is at the root. I remember that, as a young married couple, my wife and I (against my initial desires) sought help from a marriage counselor. The man was a psychologist, and during our meetings, he helped me discover why I acted a certain way with my wife. It was very helpful.

---

[34] Ibid., 151.
[35] Ibid., 152.

Unfortunately, today mental health professionals, as already pointed out in this book, are quick to jump the gun. Instead of seeking a psychological reason for those struggling with LGBTQ+ identity issues, they simply say it's normal, and in the case of those struggling with gender dysphoria, they prescribe hormones to get them prepared for sex reassignment surgery (SRS). If the root of the cause is never resolved, happiness will never come, no matter how many hormones and surgeries a person goes through.

7. *Transformation happens when we understand temptation.* The tendency for the overcomer is to become fearful of same-sex attractions and run away from them. While I don't encourage meditating on tempting desires, I do encourage overcomers to become curious about their patterns of temptation, as many times those patterns can function as proverbial breadcrumbs that lead us to root lies and wounds in the soul that God wants to heal.[36]

Temptation is not a sin. After all, Jesus Himself was tempted by the devil. "For we do not have a High Priest who cannot sympathize with our weaknesses, but was *in all points tempted as we are, yet without sin*" (Hebrews 4:15, emphasis supplied). This passage is key. Sin does not come from the temptation; it's what we do about the temptation that can lead us to commit the sinful act.

Let no one say when he is tempted, "I am tempted by God"; for God cannot be tempted by evil, nor does He Himself tempt anyone. But each one is tempted when he is drawn away by his own desires and enticed. Then, when desire has conceived, it gives birth to sin; and sin, when it is full-grown, brings forth death. (James 1:13–15)

---

[36] Ibid., 153.

This is where many of us struggle. During the time of my struggle with pornography, I remember that all I did was meditate on that; I often fantasized about it. In doing this, obviously, I could not be victorious over my sin. This is why we ought not to meditate on sinful desires. However, just because a person is tempted does not mean that God is not doing His part in the work of transformation. "Progressive sanctification doesn't eliminate temptation… The goal of the Christian life is not to experience freedom from temptation but to know Jesus and become like Him."[37]

It is here where many struggling with LGBTQ+ identity fall. Many acknowledge that they have a sin issue, and they decide to submit to God and follow His plan of transformation. However, since they still deal with same-sex temptation or still feel that they are in the wrong body and want to act on it, they give up because in their minds God should take away the temptation if He wants to transform them. While God has the power to do anything He wants, He usually doesn't work that way with sin. God does call us to repentance, and He promises He will forgive our sins (see Acts 2:38, 1 John 1:9), but He also gives us the power to overcome. Paul declared, "For I am not ashamed of the gospel of Christ, for *it is the power of God* to salvation for everyone who believes" (Romans 1:16, emphasis supplied).

In 1 Corinthians 6, after reminding his readers that the unrighteous will not inherit the kingdom of God and highlighting a few examples of unrighteous behavior, including homosexuality, Paul says, "And such were some of you. But you were washed, but you were sanctified, but you were justified in the name of the Lord Jesus and by the Spirit of our God" (v. 11). Jesus gave us the Holy Spirit, Who empowers us to walk in His ways: "At the cost of infinite sacrifice and suffering, Christ has provided for us every essential to success in the Christian warfare. The Holy Spirit brings power that enables man to overcome."[38] Thus, the Holy Spirit is the active agent in our process

---

[37] Ibid., 133–134.
[38] Ellen G. White, "Christ's Representative," *Our High Calling*, page 152, accessed October 10, 2023, https://egwwritings.org/read?panels=p81.1050&index=0.

of transformation, and if we let Him work in us, we will find that eventually those things that used to tempt us have lost their power.

> As we grow in intimacy with Christ and are conformed to His image, we discover over time that although we may on occasion experience a former temptation, the old life doesn't have hold on us like it used to.[39]

> When he died, he died once to *break the power of sin*. But now that he lives, he lives for the glory of God. So you also should *consider yourselves to be dead to the power of sin* and alive to God through Christ Jesus…For *sin shall not have dominion over you*, for you are not under law but under grace. (Romans 6:10–11, 14 NLT, emphasis supplied)

Be Imitators of God

When we speak about transformation, our desire should be to be more like Jesus. That is what Christianity is all about. In Paul's letter to the Ephesians, he declared, "Therefore be imitators of God as dear children. And walk in love, as Christ also has loved us and given Himself for us, an offering and a sacrifice to God for a sweet-smelling aroma" (Ephesians 5:1–2). Wow, that is a tall glass to drink, but Paul tells us that the way to imitate God is through walking in love as Christ loved us. We ought to love as Christ loves. LGBTQ+ activists will argue that based on this we ought to love them, which means affirming a sinful behavior. Yet in the following verses, Paul tells us

---

[39] Seiler, 134.

that, although we must love like Jesus did, there is still no room for those who willingly walk in sin.

> But fornication and all uncleanness or covetousness, let it not even be named among you, as is fitting for saints; neither filthiness, nor foolish talking, nor coarse jesting, which are not fitting, but rather giving of thanks. For this you know, that no fornicator, unclean person, nor covetous man, who is an idolater, has any inheritance in the kingdom of Christ and God. Let no one deceive you with empty words, for because of these things the wrath of God comes upon the sons of disobedience. Therefore do not be partakers with them. (Ephesians 5:3–7)

The Greek word for *fornication* is *porneia*, which means sexual immorality.[40] I say this with all due respect, but LGBTQ+ ideology and lifestyle will lead to sexual immorality, which, according to Paul, is inconsistent with being imitators of God.

> One of the most difficult challenges facing Paul was the need for a total reformation in sexual attitudes and actions among the Gentile populations he preached to. His converts came out of a world with a corrupt sexual ethic. Yet a reformation in sexual ethics was one of the greatest transformations accomplished by the early church.[41]

Today, we also need a reformation of sexual ethics. We ought not to be deceived by a world that is proclaiming empty words. People

---

[40] "4202, porneia," Bible Hub, https://biblehub.com/greek/4202.htm
[41] George R. Knight, *Exploring Galatians and Ephesians: A Devotional Commentary* (Nampa, ID: Pacific Press Publishing Association, 2005), 269.

who identify as LGBTQ+ and live this lifestyle are victims of Satan who has "deceived them into thinking that their disordered sexual desires or gender insecurity dictate their identity and determine their destiny."[42] The solution is "The Gospel of Transformation."

---

[42] Seiler, 238.

CHAPTER 6

Pastor, What Do We Do? We Have a Transgender in the Church!

WHILE THE TITLE OF THIS chapter may appear a bit comical, it is a reality. As I mentioned in chapter 4 with the story of "Kathy," the conference administrators did not know how to handle this situation, saying, "Nelson, in my day, we never had to face situations like this." While this is true at the local church level, it is also true in the homes of our church members. Parents are asking for prayer because their child is experiencing confusion as to their sexual or gender identity. Furthermore, as I mentioned before when I quoted Alicia Johnston, there are people sitting on church pews Sabbath after Sabbath who are experiencing gender dysphoria or are already part of the LGBTQ+ community and have not yet come out because they are afraid of the repercussions. At some point, however, they will come out. What do we do when the long-time female church member is absent for a few weeks but comes back dressed like a man and insists that you call her by a male name? What will we do when Mom asks the church to call her son by his now female name because her child believes he was born in the wrong body? What do we do about the couple who, after many years of marriage, divorce because one spouse realizes they are attracted to the same sex? For the sake of setting the stage, allow me to share a few stories from the book *Understanding Gender Dysphoria* by Mark A. Yarhouse.[1] I would like you to imagine this is happening in your church.

---

[1] Mark A. Yarhouse, *Understanding Gender Dysphoria: Navigating Transgender Issues in a Changing Culture*, (Downers Grove, IL: IVP Academic, 2015), 64–65.

Ted is a thirty-nine-year-old biological male who has been growing out his hair and wearing light makeup for the past eighteen years. He finds that these rather simple steps help him manage his experience of gender dysphoria. He essentially doesn't mind that people relate to him as male despite thinking of himself as essentially more gender fluid than anything else.

Sherrie is a thirty-nine-year-old biological female who has been cross dressing for four years. She likes to dress in masculine, or at least androgynous, attire, and is told by others that she has a more masculine appearance and plays into various male stereotypes. She says she is most comfortable in this presentation.

Bev is a seventeen-year-old biological female who has experienced gender incongruence for as long as she can remember. She's always been more interested in things the boys did growing up, and she has had no interest whatsoever in playing with girls. She enjoys rough-and-tumble play and identifies with many interests of the boys around her. She believes God made a mistake. She says she is a boy.

Mike is a fifty-six-year-old male who has been married for thirty-three years. He and his wife have two grown children together. He believes himself to be neither male nor female. He tends not to use a gender pronoun in describing himself to others; certainly not in how he thinks of himself. He and his wife love each other and are committed to staying together, as difficult and challenging as this experience has been.

Tom is a forty-four-year-old biological male who recently completed a transition with the aid of his therapist, hormonal treatment, and sex-reassignment surgery. He uses the name Terrie, which he has always seen himself to be. He was married for twenty years, but he and his wife were unable to continue on after he finalized his plan to transition. Although she loves her husband, she has said she cannot be in what amounts to a same gender relationship.

I have learned through conversations with fellow church members and by browsing through social media that people in the church would handle these scenarios in different ways, and they are not shy in telling the pastor how it should be taken care of. And, while our church has come out with statements about the LGBTQ+ movement, there really isn't a standard in the Seventh-day Adventist Church on how to handle this dilemma. I suppose a good reason for this is that, for the most part (although this is rapidly changing), leaders view the sin of homosexuality and everything covered by "LGBTQ+" as any other sin, and the solution to sin is Jesus. Yet people have questions, like the church member who inspired me to write this book. Although the message of the three angels is important and part of the end-time message to be communicated to the world, "What do I tell my child when they come home and ask me questions about what it means to be transgender or gay, etc.?" Furthermore, we need to be thinking about those in our churches who are struggling with these issues. How do we minister to them?

It is my hope that you will find help in this chapter. However, I know that I cannot expect everyone to agree on what I recommend, and that's okay. If all I accomplish is to get people talking to each other about these issues and being willing to talk to those who are struggling with these issues in a redemptive way, we are making progress because, make no mistake, progress is needed in the way the church relates to members of the LGBTQ+ community and how leaders address this from the pulpit, with the church board, and in business meetings.

Common Responses from Church Members and Leaders

As I mentioned above, when it comes to having members of the LGBTQ+ community in Seventh-day Adventist churches, there are a variety of responses. A sad reality, in my opinion, about Adventism is that, like in politics, you will find those who are very liberal, some are more moderate, and some are ultraconservative. As such, people have different perspectives on how to address different issues that arise in the church. For example, there used to be a time when you could tell who an Adventist was simply by looking at them. The way they dressed, adorned themselves, and behaved was different. This isn't the case anymore, as people have adopted a more "flexible" view of adornment and dress, and unfortunately, many are not addressing these issues from the pulpit as we used to not so long ago. Perhaps some have convinced themselves that these issues are not all that important, and some leaders do not want to die on those mountains.

I believe the same is happening with LGBTQ+ ideology. Yet we have no shortage of opinions as to what leaders should or should not do from those who sit in the pews Sabbath after Sabbath. Dr. Linda A. Seiler shares five approaches people take in responding to the LGBTQ+ ideology that I have also noticed by talking to church members and listening to sermons and teachings from church leaders online.

Condemnation[2]

People who are under this umbrella believe that those who struggle with gender dysphoria or are in any way part of the LGBTQ+ community are beyond redemption. That is, there is no way these people can be saved and that we as a church should have nothing to do with them. Furthermore, we should not even allow them in our churches. One example of this is the Westboro Baptist Church. If you were to search for this church online, you would be directed

---

[2] Linda A. Seiler, Ph.D., *Transformation: A Former Transgender Responds to LGBTQ* (Grand Rapids, MI: Credo House Publishers, 2023), 193.

to Godhatesfags.com.³ I am sure you have seen videos and pictures of people marching around with signs saying this very thing, "God Hates Fags." While I am not aware of any local SDA Church actively proclaiming that God hates those of the LGBTQ+ community, there are people in our local churches who feel this way, even if they do not proclaim it publicly. I believe this is due to seeing homosexuality as *the* sin and not *a* sin. The same applies to any behavior or lifestyle under the LGBTQ+ umbrella.

It is the opinion of this writer that it is a mistake to respond this way to those of the LGBTQ+ community. I do not believe that this sin should be placed in a different category from others as if saying, "God can forgive and cleanse us from all sin with the exception of this one…" When the apostle John says, "If we confess our sins, He is faithful and just to forgive us our sins and to cleanse us from all unrighteousness" (1 John 1:9), he is referring to any sin, no matter how big and filthy we may see it. God's mercy and grace are bigger than our sins. I think that while the Westboro Baptist Church and others like them have good intentions, they unwittingly are giving Christianity a black eye. Their approach has convinced many LGBTQ+ people that all Christians feel this way, which is not true.

Every person struggles with sin; and I, for one, am very thankful that God has been patient, merciful, and gracious with me. That is the kind of God we serve, and it is the One we should be proclaiming, not a God who has given up on certain people who, in our opinion, are unredeemable. There is no such thing as a sin that, having been repented of and confessed, God cannot forgive.

Affirmation[4]

To affirm can mean to declare something to be valid.[5] Thus, those who believe in affirming LGBTQ+ ideology and lifestyle want

---

[3] *Westboro Baptist Church*, accessed October 16, 2023, https://www.godhatesfags.com.
[4] Seiler, 195.
[5] "Affirm," *Merriam-Webster.com Dictionary*, Merriam-Webster, accessed October 16, 2023, https://www.merriam-webster.com/dictionary/affirm.

the church to declare it as valid and correct. This is the view of Alicia Johnston, whom I have quoted extensively in this book. Obviously, this approach is the opposite of condemnation.

> Affirmation proponents endorse the modern construct of gender identity, gender expression, biological sex, and sexual orientation, insisting that a person can fall anywhere on each of those spectrums based on inborn determinates. Because they believe people are born gay/trans and cannot change, affirmation proponents consider it cruel to suggest that transformation is possible… Affirmation proponents elevate the second-greatest commandment (to love our neighbor) over the first and greatest commandment (to love God, including His word).[6]

While the Seventh-day Adventist Church does not support affirming the LGBTQ+ ideology and lifestyle, there are local congregations that have described themselves as safe places where LGBTQ+ people can worship without being "judged," as they put it. Thus, there are churches that—in an effort to appear more "loving," as opposed to the church at large—have compromised and have become affirming churches. One only has to go to the SDA Kinship International website to find an "affirming church." Yes, sadly, this is the world we are living in.

I will say it again: to affirm is to compromise. Mohler said it this way:

> To accommodate to the moral revolution and affirm its morality is to look at what the Bible calls sin and call it something else… Moreover, it would mean declaring to our friends and neighbors that their sin is not actually sin.

---

[6] Seiler, 195–195.

It would mean disregarding their need for a Savior… Rejecting or reducing the sinfulness of sin slanders the cross of the Lord Jesus Christ. According to Scripture, Christ died for our sins. To take what scripture declares as sin—sin for which Christ died—and to downplay the severity insults the cross of Christ and misleads sinners about their needs for the salvation only available in Christ's atonement. When it is demanded that Christians respond with compassion at the expense of truth, we understand that any compassion severed from truth is false compassion and a lie against the truth.[7]

Friends, this is a threat to the gospel and a work of Satan. Even now, SDA Kinship International is carrying out their own version of evangelism by putting out a book titled *UnClobber*, which is supposed to "shine new light on the texts that are typically used by people to condemn LGBTQ people. Kinship is currently sponsoring an outreach project to send 2,500 copies to SDA pastors and church leaders to help improve the conversation around LGBTQ issues in SDA communities."[8]

LGBTQ+ activists in the Seventh-day Adventist Church will not rest until the church at large changes their view on LGBTQ+ ideology and affirms their lifestyle. This should not surprise us, which is why the Bible counsels us to "be sober, be vigilant; because your adversary the devil walks about like a roaring lion, seeking whom he may devour" (1 Peter 5:8). Satan is working overtime because "he knows that he has a short time" (Revelation 12:12). While God is in control, and we should never forget this, let us pray and be diligent. May we never compromise the gospel of Jesus Christ.

---

[7] R. Albert Mohler Jr., *We Cannot Be Silent: Speaking Truth to a Culture Redefining Sex, Marriage, and the Very Meaning of Right and Wrong*, (Nashville, TN: Nelson Books, 2015), 138–139.

[8] "UnClobber," *Seventh-day Adventist Church Kinship International*, accessed October 16, 2023, https://sdakinship.org/en.

Accommodation[9]

It could be argued that this approach is a compromise between condemnation and affirmation. They understand that the LGBTQ+ lifestyle, meaning having same-sex relationships and/or living as a transgender is a sin. As such, they have decided to live as "celibate gay Christians." Many in the church will see this as a "happy medium" that would make everyone happy. After all, "the sin is in the action, not the belief." While this approach seems inviting, it falls short because it ignores God's power of transformation. In fact, "accommodation proponents refer to transformation as 'conversion therapy' which has been vilified by the media and LGBTQ+ activists. To borrow a contemporary term, most of the rhetoric being promulgated today is 'fake news.'" Here is an example:

> So-called "conversion therapy," sometimes known as "reparative therapy," is a range of dangerous and discredited practices that falsely claim to change a person's sexual orientation or gender identity or expression. Such practices have been rejected by every mainstream medical and mental health organization for decades, but due to continuing discrimination and societal bias against LGBTQ people, some practitioners continue to conduct conversion therapy. Minors are especially vulnerable, and conversion therapy can lead to depression, anxiety, drug use, homelessness, and suicide.[10]

---

[9] Seiler, 197.
[10] "The Lies and Dangers of Efforts to Change Sexual Orientation or Gender Identity," *Human Rights Campaign*, accessed October 16, 2023, https://www.hrc.org/resources/the-lies-and-dangers-of-reparative-therapy?utm_medium=ads&utm_source=GoogleSearch&utm_content=ConversionTherapy-General&utm_campaign=GoogleGrant&utm_source=GS&utm_medium=AD&utm_campaign=BPI-HRC-Grant&utm_content=627545435750&utm_term=conversion%20therapy&gclid=CjwKCAjwvrOpBhBdEiwAR58-3Hajqxn

Thus, any attempt to teach and preach about God's power of transformation is either ignored, ridiculed, or vilified. At the very least, God can transform other sins, but He stops short of LGBTQ+ issues.

Another challenge with this approach is that one can be gay as long as you are not a practicing one. Here again is the issue of being called a "celibate gay Christian." But we need to think carefully about this. As I shared in the previous chapter, for many years, I struggled with pornography, yet God has given me victory. Now a sin like pornography is a sin of the mind. Thus, some will argue that the only sinful action that may be accompanied by pornography is masturbation. Yet from personal experience, I can testify that the sin of pornography does not stay in the mind; if one continues to "caress" this sin, it will eventually lead to other sinful actions.

The pitfall of this approach is that it makes a distinction between desire and behavior; and this, in the mind of some LGBTQ+ activists, creates a loophole. Here is an example:

> Accepting that people don't choose and can't change their sexual orientation is progress. The distinction between orientation and behavior creates space for LGBTQ Christians. It acknowledges the reality that should be obvious by now: there is a burden that comes with hiding fundamental aspects of our human experience. Distinguishing between desires and behaviors could alleviate the need to hide or pretend to be straight. If the church could come to the point of not discriminating against people who are gay but committed to celibacy, it would be good for LGBTQ Adventists.[11]

JOl2X8Imp4OdXsW0cDFnC7Tky8qGF2TfewByO7RgOkm893hoC_hIQAvD_BwE.

[11] Alicia Johnston, *The Bible and LGBTQ Adventists: A Theological Conversation about Same-Sex Mariage, Gender, and Identity,* (Affirmative Collective, 2022), 283.

Sin starts in the mind, which is why Paul invites his readers to be transformed by the "renewing of your mind" (Romans 12:2). Homosexual desires are sinful just as much as heterosexual ones if they do not conform to the will of God. If I am constantly thinking about having a sexual relationship with a woman who is not my wife but do not act on it, the desire is as sinful as the action. "You have heard that it was said to those of old, 'You shall not commit adultery.' But I say to you that whoever looks at a woman to lust for her has already committed adultery with her in his heart" (Matthew 5:27–28). Sinful desires and sinful actions cannot be separated.

I feel that those who refer to themselves as "celibate gay Christians" are using an oxymoron because they identify themselves with the sin they are trying to avoid. It would be like me saying that I am a "celibate pornography-addicted Christian." While it is true that the lifestyle of the LGBTQ+ community (same-sex relationships, transitioning to the opposite sex, etc.) is sinful and while transformation may not happen instantaneously, to continue to identify oneself with the sin is counterproductive. God wants to change us entirely: "Then I will give them one heart, and I will put a new spirit within them, and take the stony heart out of their flesh, and give them a heart of flesh" (Ezekiel 11:19). "Therefore, if anyone is in Christ, he is a new creation; old things have passed away; behold, all things have become new" (2 Corinthians 5:17). To identify oneself with the sin one is struggling with is to deny the new birth, "knowing this, that our old man was crucified with Him, that the body of sin might be done away with, that we should no longer be slaves of sin. For he who has died has been freed from sin" (Romans 6:6–7).

"A 'celibate gay Christian' identity fixates on fallen desires, keeping the believer enslaved to sinful impulses with no hope for change. It is essentially a mindset of unbelief that cuts against any expectation of transformation."[12] All this being said, I believe there is some room for the accommodation approach, and I will tell you why later.

---

[12] Seiler, 200.

Mortification

In my view, this approach is similar to accommodation.

> It renounces the gay identity and urges believers to mortify (or kill) sin, including homoerotic desires and behaviors… Mortification proponents emphasize repentance, which includes renouncing a gay identity and dying to sinful impulses by replacing those desires with spiritual disciplines (Bible reading, prayer, scripture memorization, devotional reading, etc.). They don't anticipate a change in their attractions, but rather a change in behavior and identity that may or may not result in a change or attractions. Their main emphasis is faithfulness to the Lord despite one's attractions.[13]

It would seem that this is a works-oriented approach, that is, "as long as I do certain good things, I am covered because those good things will outweigh my sinful desires." While practicing spiritual disciplines is an important part of being a disciple, they are only a way of bringing us closer to Jesus, to abide in Him, to keep our connection, if you will; and it is that connection that will give us spiritual victory.

One key factor in victory over the LGBTQ+ lifestyle is finding the root cause of those desires. These causes can include childhood sexual abuse, teasing because one is different, a negative environment in the family dynamic, etc.

> Overall, the mortification approach is biblically sound, encouraging believers to renounce a gay identity and repent from homoerotic behavior. However, it stops short of the trans-

---

[13] Ibid., 206–207.

formation approach in that it does not take into consideration sinful reactions to developmental influences that may underline same sex attraction compulsions.[14]

Transformation

This approach is similar to mortification in that it renounces sinful behaviors, but it does not ignore the root causes of same-sex attraction including the fact that it all can be traced to the fall. Transformation is the goal of the gospel, when "this corruptible must put on incorruption, and this mortal must put on immortality" (1 Corinthians 15:53). But we do not have to wait for the sound of the heavenly trumpet on resurrection morning; we can start living the transformed life in the here and now: "Therefore we were buried with Him through baptism into death, that just as Christ was raised from the dead by the glory of the Father, even so *we also should walk in newness of life*" (Romans 6:4, emphasis supplied). Like the butterfly after the process of metamorphosis, we are no longer the same person we were. We are better, different, and beautiful because the one who has accomplished the transformation is none other than our Creator. While it is true that the term *transformation* has gotten a bad reputation in LGBTQ+ circles, as Christians, we should not shy away from proclaiming this as the goal for anyone struggling with sin, no matter which sin. However, some saints may struggle with transformation because they feel that it must be instantaneous. While I acknowledge that God can change us instantly and at times He has, sometimes this takes time. So what shall we do while we wait? I would like to propose another approach that will help church members and leaders deal with the LGBTQ+ dilemma.

---

[14] Ibid., 213.

Transaccomodation

As the word implies, this approach combines accommodation and transformation. Again, the goal of the gospel is that of complete transformation. Thus, this should be our goal when dealing with members who are struggling with LGBTQ+ issues. However, since there are misunderstandings about transformation (instant transformation vs. time released), we must accommodate to the process.

As already pointed out, some think transformation means a person reaches the point where all temptation disappears, but this may not be realistic. Again, God has given me victory, and certainly, the temptations related to pornography have lost their power, but they have not completely disappeared. In a world where "sex sells," we find that companies use sex to sell anything and everything. Thus, those who struggle with sexual temptations are bombarded left and right. Because of this, I have to keep my guard up, and I would imagine that those who struggle with gender/sexual orientation confusion are in the same boat.

Transformation takes time, and we must be patient just as God is patient. When I think about how patient God has been with me, I am filled with awe. During the time of my addiction to pornography, I fell many times. I would get up and fall again, and this was the cycle for many years. If I were God, I would have given up on myself a long time ago. But God never gave up and has not given up on me yet. You might be able to testify to the same thing. Thus, our approach to dealing with LGBTQ+ people in our churches should reflect how God has dealt with us.

In the accommodation approach, while encouraging people not to act on their sinful desires, the label "gay Christian" is kept because transformation is not believed to be possible. In this transaccomodation approach, total transformation is believed to be possible and expected, whether instantly or in God's timing. In the meantime, our duty as believers and members of a Christian family is to accommodate God's timing by building relationships with church members who are part of the LGBTQ+ movement. We should be intentional in opening the lines of communication so that we can get to know them better and perhaps even learn about the possible root causes for their confusion. We need to love and respect them and be honest enough to tell them that, while we do not agree with their ideology and lifestyle, we are here for them, we want to be friends, we are available if they need us, and we welcome them in our church.

Welcome Them to Our Church?

Being a welcoming church does not automatically mean an affirming church, just like being an affirming church does not necessarily mean it is a welcoming one. I have already shared my experience with Kathy in a church I pastored several years ago. The reason she stayed was we were a welcoming church, but we did not affirm her, and she knew it. This is key: as church members and leaders, we need to clearly communicate what we believe scripture teaches about the LGBTQ+ ideology and lifestyle. Being unclear on this can create confusion and hurt people. Alicia Johnston gives an example of a gay friend who attended a church that never spoke about issues of sexual orientation. She faithfully attended the church every week. At one point, she became interested in participating in the music program and was rejected and told, "We can't have someone who is openly gay leading worship."[15] She had been attending that church for two years, and nobody had ever approached her to talk about this, even when she was openly gay.

It seems clear that nobody had visited her to befriend her and that the subject was not brought up from the pulpit. Needless to say, she was hurt and was the victim of what Johnston calls a "bait and switch."[16] She adds,

> Too often, those who advocate waiting to talk about sexuality and focusing on building a relationship believe its kindness. But it's not kind-

---

[15] Johnston, 214.
[16] Ibid.

ness to withhold this information. Something is wrong with theology that must hide. Something is wrong when Christians think they must hide the truth in order to love. It's much more loving to be up front.[17]

    I totally agree with Johnston. Yes, we must be willing to develop relationships with those of the LGBTQ+ community who are either guests or members but not at the expense of being honest with them. While the church at large has made it clear where it stands on LGBTQ+ issues, as we have seen, there are local congregations that have compromised. Thus, you may find a situation where a gay or transgender person has attended an affirming church and then visits or moves to your area. They start coming to your church assuming that it is also an affirming church, only to be disappointed. The disappointment, however, may not come until sometime later, as in the case of Johnston's friend. This should never happen.

    As a pastor, I make it a point to talk to guests. I ask them if they are just visiting the area for the weekend or if they have recently moved to the area. If they have moved to the area, I immediately ask them for their information, and I tell them that I would like to visit with them. It is on these visits that one learns about them and their families. I realize, however, that this is easier for a pastor like me who only leads one church. It is trickier for a pastor who leads three or four congregations. This is why we must train our elders and leaders to do the same thing. At the very least, as was the case in the church that Kathy visited, the elders get the information and pass it on to the pastor.

    If you find a situation where the guest identifies as gay or transgender, do not judge the person. Be aware of your reaction, as it might say that you are judging even if you don't speak. In a situation like this, if they are Seventh-day Adventists, during a visit, which I would try to arrange, I would remind them of where the church stands on the issue and tell them that our local congregation believes

---

[17] Ibid., 215.

the same way. If the person is not a Seventh-day Adventist, I would ask them, "What do you know about the Seventh-day Adventist Church?" Their response will help me determine what to say next. At some point, however, I will bring up the issue of where the church stands. At the same time, I would make it clear that we welcome them to attend our church and worship with us. This is exactly what my head elder and I did on our visit with Kathy. In some cases, the person will disagree and may even feel disrespected and ask us to leave. The person may not come back to our church; this is a real possibility. But we should not shy away from being honest because we fear that in doing so the person may not come back. We must remember that our goal is to please God, not men.

In Kathy's case, she kept coming back. During this time, we visited her several times because she wanted to dialogue with us. The reason, of course, was that she was hoping to change our minds and was wanting us to give her a platform to "educate our church." We politely declined and explained that our beliefs were based on scripture and that, as such, we could not give her a platform or an opportunity to participate in any position or ministry. Yet she kept coming back. Love is more powerful than compromise.

So, yes, we can welcome people who identify as LGBTQ+, they can worship with us, and we can befriend them, even invite them over to our home for a meal. This does not mean we are compromising or welcoming sin our church. After all, we are all sinners who come short of the glory of God. We should treat others as we wish to be treated.

> The current discussion about homosexuality poses a great challenge to the church. At the same time, it is a moment of great opportunity. The current debate offers us an opportunity to think through the Christian sexual ethic clearly and carefully. More importantly, it calls us back once again to God's bountiful grace. The divine call to live out our sexuality in ways that bring honor to God is a difficult challenge, especially

in our permissive society. Yet the resources of the Holy Spirit are greater than the obstacles that would thwart us. And because the challenge is one we all face, whether "straight" or "gay," we face it best together. For the sake of the gospel in the world, therefore, we need to assist each other and rely on each other, so that by the power of the Spirit working through us, we might live in true biblical chastity to the glory of God. In the end, this is what it means to be welcoming, yet not…affirming community.[18]

But someone will ask, "What if the individual is already a member of our congregation?" or "What if Susan (a fictitious character), who has been a member of our church for ten years, suddenly comes to our church the following Sabbath dressed as a man insisting that she be called Sam?" or "What if George (another fictitious character), who is an elder in the church, leaves his wife and moves in with a man because he realized that he was gay?" These are difficult situations, but they are realistic. As a pastor, I cringe at the prospect of handling situations like these, but they must be handled. Fortunately, Jesus has given us instructions on how to handle sin in the church.

Matthew 18 starts with a question the disciples ask Jesus, "Who then is greatest in the kingdom of heaven" (v. 1)? Jesus answers by giving an object illustration, "Then Jesus called a little child to Him, set him in the midst of them, and said, 'Assuredly, I say to you, unless you are converted and become as little children, you will by no means enter the kingdom of heaven'" (vv. 2–3). He then goes on to talk about the judgment of a person who causes one of these "little ones" to sin, "It would be better for him if a millstone were hung around his neck, and he were drowned in the depth of the sea" (v. 6). In

---

[18] Stanley J. Grenz, *Welcoming but not Affirming: An Evangelical Response to Homosexuality* (Louisville, KY: Westminster John Knox Press, 1998), 157.

verses 15–20, Jesus seems to take a different direction and addresses how to handle sin in the church. There are three steps:

1. "Moreover if your brother sins against you, go and tell him his fault between you and him alone. If he hears you, you have gained your brother" (v. 15). In this passage the issue is clearly between two people who have a "beef" with each other. However, the principle is the same for how to handle sin in general. Thus, if a member of the church suddenly comes out as gay or transgender, the leaders must talk with this person. If the situation is, like in verse 15, that one individual finds out about the issue and nobody else in the church knows about it, that individual must care enough for the person coming out to address the sin with the intention of convicting the individual to repent, confess, and take whatever steps are needed to correct the situation. However, LGBTQ+ issues are very complex, since there are root causes for the sinful desires and actions. Thus, one cannot expect that the situation will be resolved at this stage. That is not to say God cannot resolve the issue instantly, but as I have already said, often the transformation takes time. Still, the goal is for the individual to acknowledge the sin and take corrective steps to be at peace with God and have sins forgiven. If the situation is not resolved (by repentance and confession), then a second step must be taken.

2. "But if he will not hear, take with you one or two more, that 'by the mouth of two or three witnesses every word may be established'" (v. 16). More than one person is involved with this step. Of course, it is possible and maybe even necessary for more than one person to be involved in step one because often the issue of being gay or transgender is known by at least several people in the church. Still, we must take the second step; perhaps in this step church leaders may be part of the visiting team, which can include the pastor. The goal is the same, that the individual in question

repents, confesses, and takes the necessary steps to be at peace with God and anybody hurt because of the situation. Here again, the conversation may reveal some, if not, all the root causes for the desire and/or behavior that need to be addressed to facilitate the process of transformation. If this step is not successful, the third step must be taken.

3. "And if he refuses to hear them, tell it to the church. But if he refuses even to hear the church, let him be to you like a heathen and a tax collector" (v. 17). In the context of the Seventh-day Adventist Church, this would mean addressing the issue with the church board who will make recommendations to the church at large.

In situations like this, when we have reached the third step, the church has two ways in which disciplinary measures can be taken:

1. by a vote of censure and
2. by a vote to remove from membership.

In cases where the offense is not considered by the church to be so serious as to warrant the extreme course of removing membership, the church may express its disapproval by a vote of censuring your brother. Censure has two purposes: (1) to enable the church to express its disapproval of a grievous offense that has brought disgrace upon the cause of God and (2) the right to impress offending members with a need for a change of life and reformation of conduct and to give them a period of grace and probation during which to make those changes… Members under censure have no right to participate by voice or by vote in the affairs of the church or lead church activities, such as teaching a Sabbath school class. They are not deprived, however, of the privilege of sharing the blessings of Sabbath school, church worship, or communion… Removing individuals from membership in the church, the body of Christ, is the ultimate discipline that the church can administer.[19]

It is important to point out that it is only the church at large in business session that can vote a censure or removal from membership and only after the steps in Matthew 18 have been followed. In some cases, depending on the situation, the vote might be to remove from membership. These steps, like those of Matthew 18:15–17, are redemptive in nature. The goal is restoration, and even though a person has been removed from membership, it does not mean that the person is forgotten and lost without hope, no. Jesus said, "Let him be to you like a heathen and a tax collector" (Matthew 18:17). What should be done with the heathen and tax collectors (those living in sin and rejected by society)? We preach the gospel to them so that they may repent of their sins and accept Jesus as Savior.

Taking the steps above can be very difficult, especially if we have a relationship with the individual involved. It is very painful, but it must be done because open sin does not only affect the individual committing it; if not addressed, it will affect the church as well. In speaking of the story of Achan found in Joshua 7, Ellen White writes,

> There are many who do not have the discretion of Joshua and who have no special duty to search out wrongs and to deal promptly with the sins existing among them. Let not such hinder those who have the burden of this work upon them; let them not stand in the way of those who have this duty to do. Some make it a point to question and doubt and find fault because others do the work that God has not laid upon them. These stand directly in the way to hinder those upon whom God has laid the burden of reproving and correcting prevailing sins in order that

---

[19] General Conference of Seventh-day Adventists, *Seventh-day Adventist Church Manual* (Silver Spring, MD: General Conference of Seventh-day Adventists, 2022), 68–69.

His frown may be turned away from His people. Should a case like Achan's be among us, there are many who would accuse those who might act the part of Joshua in searching out the wrong, of having a wicked, fault-finding spirit. God is not to be trifled with and His warnings disregarded with impunity by a perverse people... Those who work in the fear of God to rid the church of hindrances and to correct grievous wrongs, that the people of God may see the necessity of abhorring sin and may prosper in purity, and that the name of God may be glorified, will ever meet with resisting influences from the unconsecrated.[20]

The Seventh-day Adventist Church and Homosexuality

The Seventh-day Adventist Church voted its statement on homosexuality during the Annual Council of the General Conference Executive Committee on Sunday, October 3, 1999. While it can be found online, it seems appropriate to quote it so as to help guide us in how to handle these issues in the church.

The Seventh-day Adventist Church recognizes that every human being is valuable in the sight of God, and we seek to minister to all men and women in the spirit of Jesus. We also believe that by God's grace and through the encouragement of the community of faith, an individual may live in harmony with the principles of God's Word.

> Seventh-day Adventists believe that sexual intimacy belongs only within the marital relationship of a man and a woman. This was the design established by God at creation. The Scriptures declare: "For this reason a man will leave his father and mother and be united to

---
[20] Ibid., 64–65.

his wife, and they will become one flesh" (Gen 2:24, NIV). Throughout Scripture this heterosexual pattern is affirmed. The Bible makes no accommodation for homosexual activity or relationships. Sexual acts outside the circle of a heterosexual marriage are forbidden (Lev 18:5–23, 26; Lev 20:7–21; Rom 1:24–27; 1 Cor 6:9–11). Jesus Christ reaffirmed the divine creation intent: "'Haven't you read,' he replied, 'that at the beginning the Creator "made them male and female," and said, "For this reason a man will leave his father and mother and be united to his wife, and the two will become one flesh?" So they are no longer two, but one'" (Matt 19:5, NIV). For these reasons Seventh-day Adventists are opposed to homosexual practices and relationships.

Jesus affirmed the dignity of all human beings and reached out compassionately to persons and families suffering the consequences of sin. He offered caring ministry and words of solace to struggling people, while differentiating His love for sinners from His clear teaching about sinful practices. As His disciples, Seventh-day Adventists endeavor to follow the Lord's instruction and example, living a life of Christ-like compassion and faithfulness.[21]

---

[21] "Homosexuality," *Seventh-day Adventist Church* (2012), accessed October 17, 2023, https://www.adventist.org/official-statements/homosexuality.

The Seventh-day Adventist Church and the Transgender Movement

Since the transgender movement is a more recent development, the church also issued a statement that will help leaders handle these issues at the local level.

As the transgender phenomenon must be evaluated by Scripture, the following biblical principles and teachings may help the community of faith relate to people affected by gender dysphoria in a biblical and Christ-like way:

1. God created humanity as two persons who are respectively identified as male and female in terms of gender. The Bible inextricably ties gender to biological sex (Gen 1:27; 2:22–24) and does not make a distinction between the two. The Word of God affirms complementarity as well as clear distinctions between male and female in creation. The Genesis creation account is foundational to all questions of human sexuality.
2. From a biblical perspective, the human being is a psychosomatic unity. For example, Scripture repeatedly calls the entire human being a soul (Gen. 2:7; Jer. 13:17; 52:28–30; Ezek. 18:4; Acts 2:41; 1 Cor. 15:45), a body (Eph. 5:28; Rom. 12:1–2; Rev. 18:13), flesh (1 Pet. 1:24), and spirit (2 Tim. 4:22; 1 John 4:1–3). Thus, the Bible does not endorse dualism in the sense of a separation between one's body and one's sense of sexuality. In addition, an immortal part of humans is not envisioned in Scripture because God alone possesses immortality (1 Tim. 6:14–16) and

will bestow it on those who believe in Him at the first resurrection (1 Cor. 15:51–54). Thus, a human being is also meant to be an undivided sexual entity, and sexual identity cannot be independent from one's body. According to Scripture, our gender identity, as designed by God, is determined by our biological sex at birth (Gen. 1:27; 5:1–2; Ps. 139:13–14; Mark 10:6).

3. Scripture acknowledges, however, that due to the Fall (Gen. 3:6–19) the whole human being—that is, our mental, physical, and spiritual faculties—are affected by sin (Jer. 17:9; Rom. 3:9; 7:14–23; 8:20–23; Gal. 5:17) and need to be renewed by God (Rom. 12:2). Our emotions, feelings, and perceptions are not fully reliable indicators of God's designs, ideals, and truth (Prov. 14:12; 16:25). We need guidance from God through Scripture to determine what is in our best interest and live according to His will (2 Tim. 3:16).

4. The fact that some individuals claim a gender identity incompatible with their biological sex reveals a serious dichotomy. This brokenness or distress, whether felt or not, is an expression of the damaging effects of sin on humans and may have a variety of causes. Although gender dysphoria is not intrinsically sinful, it may result in sinful choices. It is another indicator that, on a personal level, humans are involved in the great controversy.

5. As long as transgender people are committed to ordering their lives according to the biblical teachings on sexuality and marriage, they can be members of the Seventh-day Adventist Church. The Bible clearly

and consistently identifies any sexual activity outside of heterosexual marriage as sin (Matt. 5:28, 31–32; 1 Tim. 1:8–11; Heb. 13:4). Alternative sexual lifestyles are sinful distortions of God's good gift of sexuality (Rom. 1:21–28; 1 Cor. 6:9–10).

6. Because the Bible regards humans as wholistic entities and does not differentiate between biological sex and gender identity, the Church strongly cautions transgender people against sex reassignment surgery and against marriage if they have undergone such a procedure. From the biblical wholistic viewpoint of human nature, a full transition from one gender to another and the attainment of an integrated sexual identity cannot be expected in the case of sex reassignment surgery.

7. The Bible commands followers of Christ to love everyone. Created in the image of God, they must be treated with dignity and respect. This includes transgender people. Acts of ridicule, abuse, or bullying towards transgender people are incompatible with the biblical commandment, "You shall love your neighbor as yourself" (Mark 12:31).

8. The Church as the community of Jesus Christ is meant to be a refuge and place of hope, care, and understanding to all who are perplexed, suffering, struggling, and lonely, for "a bruised reed He will not break, and smoking flax He will not quench" (Matt. 12:20). All people are invited to attend the Seventh-day Adventist Church and enjoy the fellowship of its believers. Those who are members can fully participate in church life

as long as they embrace the message, mission, and values of the Church.

9. The Bible proclaims the good news that sexual sins committed by heterosexuals, homosexuals, transgender people, or others can be forgiven, and lives can be transformed through faith in Jesus Christ (1 Cor. 6:9–11).

10. Those who experience incongruity between their biological sex and gender identity are encouraged to follow biblical principles in dealing with their distress. They are invited to reflect on God's original plan of purity and sexual fidelity. Belonging to God, all are called to honor Him with their bodies and their lifestyle choices (1 Cor. 6:19). With all believers, transgender people are encouraged to wait on God and are offered the fullness of divine compassion, peace, and grace in anticipation of Christ's soon return when all true followers of Christ will be completely restored to God's ideal.[22]

Clearly, the above statements do not cover every possible scenario we might encounter in the church regarding LGBTQ+ issues, but they are helpful. I would like to comment on statement 5 because it is probably the one that some of our members and critics will argue about. "As long as transgender people are committed to ordering their lives according to the biblical teachings on sexuality and marriage, they can be members of the Seventh-day Adventist Church." I can hear someone ask, "How can we accept a transgender person as a member of the church?" Clearly, being members implies that they can participate in every area of the church according to their gifts.

---

[22] "Statement on Transgenderism," *Seventh-day Adventist Church* (2017), accessed October 17, 2023, https://www.adventist.org/official-statements/statement-on-transgenderism.

As mentioned earlier in the chapter, when an individual realizes that their desires are sinful and want to live according to God's will, they should no longer identify themselves by the sin they are repenting of. However, a person who is gay does not always have something physical that identifies them as gay. But what if the individual who comes to Christ in repentance is a transgender who has already transitioned to the opposite sex? These are complex issues because, as we have mentioned in earlier chapters, a person who has transitioned has received a series of hormone treatments and, in some cases, has undergone sex reassignment surgery. This is not something that can be corrected in a day; and yet if they have repented and confessed, the Bible tells us that they are forgiven and are a new creation (1 John 1:9, 2 Corinthians 5:17). It is here that we must apply wisdom and act redemptively.

Andrew T. Walker asks, "What would it look like for someone to experience gender dysphoria and follow Jesus? What would it look like for someone who has had hormones and undergone gender transitioning surgery to follow Jesus?"[23] He then presents a fictitious character named Alex. Alex is a transgender woman (a biological male who has transitioned into a woman) who has come to accept Jesus as Savior and Lord. As such, she has repented of her sins, including the sin of transitioning into a female. He asks,

- Must "she" revert to a "he"? Should Alex ask people to speak to and about Alex as a "he"? And if so, does this have to begin immediately?
- Does Alex stop the hormones?
- Does Alex have surgery to reverse the appearance of being a female?
- Must Alex no longer have feelings of gender dysphoria?[24]

---

[23] Andrew T. Walker, *God and the Transgender Debate: What Does the Bible Actually Say about Gender Identity?* (Turkey: The Good Book Company, 2022), 115.

[24] Ibid., 123.

While there are church members who would be quick to share their opinions as to how leaders should answer these questions, the truth is that there are not easy questions to answer. While sin is a black-or-white issue, I have found that in dealing with people and some of the issues we are seeing today, like the issue of transgenderism, there are some gray areas. I am not compromising with sin by saying this, I am, however, acknowledging that there are issues that are not easy to handle when one is trying to act redemptively and is seeking to treat others as one wants to be treated. Walker suggests,

> The first step in discipleship for Alex is to come to grips with the call of discipleship: to obey Jesus—even when it runs contrary to strong inner desires. With Alex, we must patiently, compassionately, and lovingly plead for him to see his created anatomical biology as the God-given evidence of who he is. He is Alexander.[25]

The question is, How soon should these actions take place?

> It is arbitrary to suggest that someone in Alexander's position needs to be restored to full masculine appearance and self-identity from day one. What matters is whether there are intentional efforts to work toward reversing the effects of taking on a transgender identity. Alex "becoming" (or, rather, reverting to living as) a man instantaneously is less important than seeing himself as a new creation in Christ instantaneously. So, in Alexander's particular situation, this is going to mean, over time, returning to his original name. Hormonal therapy should begin to decrease to the point of stopping. But then there is the question of whether someone who

---

[25] Ibid., 124.

has had gender-reassignment surgery should undergo additional surgery to revert.[26]

There is going to be plenty of disagreement in the church regarding how soon these changes must take place and, in particular, whether the individual (Alex) should even undergo surgery to revert. Will it even be possible? If possible, can Alex afford it? If Alex cannot afford it, should the church help financially to pay for the surgery? These are questions that the average church member does not have to think about, even when giving their opinions; but leaders must, and the truth is, there are no easy answers.

So let us say "Alex" is coming to our church and has accepted Jesus, has repented of "his" sins, and wants to live "his" life according to how God created "him." Alex has received Bible studies, agrees with all the baptismal vows, and has expressed the desire to be baptized. Yet he has not yet reverted, and medically speaking, he cannot stop the hormone treatment abruptly. Should he be baptized? Absolutely! As such, he would be a member in good standing and can participate in church activities and ministries, as statement 5 under the church's transgender response suggests. I realize some are going to disagree with this, but it is what acting redemptively looks like, and it is how people wish to be treated.

Let me address one of the questions asked by Walker, "Must Alex no longer have feelings of gender dysphoria?" Some in the church will say, "Absolutely!" "After all, this is just a term that was invented to make people feel comfortable in their sin," a church member once told me. While I believe (as I have shared already in this book) that the current struggles people have with gender are the result of the fall, there are complexities with gender dysphoria that I do not fully understand. I will go as far as to say that I do not believe that everyone chooses to have gender dysphoria. As we have seen, there are root causes to the issues surrounding LGBTQ+ desires. Furthermore, many become convinced that they have gender dysphoria because that is what everyone is talking about. It is "the popular thing today."

---

[26] Ibid., 125.

Yet there are those who are truly struggling with these feelings. Are we to suggest that the moment we accept Christ these struggles will disappear? In some cases, yes; in some cases, it is a struggle, as Paul suggests in Romans 7.

I have heard testimonies of smokers, for example, that the moment they accepted the gift of salvation and realized that smoking is not part of God's will for humanity, they quit and never had cravings again. The same is true with some alcoholics, others who are addicted to pornography, etc. However, we know this is not true for everyone. Why doesn't God completely transform all people instantly and take away their sinful desires and temptations the moment they accept Christ, I don't know. But we must remember that once we accept God's gift of salvation, He takes us through a process of sanctification, and "there is no such thing as instantaneous sanctification. True sanctification is a daily work, continuing as long as life shall last."[27] So, while the end goal is that the feelings of gender dysphoria disappear in the new believer, there is work to be done. Speaking about the "new man," the apostle Paul writes, "That you put off, concerning your former conduct, the old man which grows corrupt according to the deceitful lusts" (Ephesians 4:22). Part of the work the individual must do is to realize that these sinful desires are part of Satan's deceptions. But to see a change in desires, one must address the root causes. As members of the church family, we need to help individuals in this process.

Paul continues by saying, "And be renewed in the spirit of your mind, and that you put on the new man which was created according to God, in true righteousness and holiness" (vv. 23–24). The word *renewed* in the Greek is *ananeoó*,[28] a derivative of the word *ana* (as a preposition denotes upward)[29] and *neos* (new).[30] Thus, it could be

---

[27] Ellen G. White, "Substituting Feeling for Reason," *The Sanctified Life*, page 10, accessed October 10, 2023), https://egwwritings.org/read?panels=p138.35&index=0.
[28] "365, ananeoó," Bible Hub https://biblehub.com/greek/365.htm.
[29] "303, ana," Bible Hub https://biblehub.com/greek/303.htm.
[30] "3501b, neos," Bible Hub https://biblehub.com/greek/3501b.htm.

said that "renewed" is a continuous upward movement to be made new, not a one-time event.

> They need to be "continually renewed" in the spirit of their mind (verse 23). Salvation is a process. It may have begun with conversion, with a putting on and a putting off, but day by day throughout our lives the Holy Spirit works to convict us of sin, lead us to righteousness (see John 16:8–11), and provide our minds with ever fuller knowledge of Christ and His will for us. Our minds are being "continually renewed" as the new identity that we have already put on continually deepens and develops.[31]

What does this mean for Alex? If Alex has accepted Jesus and in so doing has repented of his sins, including transitioning to the opposite sex, and desires to walk with Jesus, we must accept Alex's word and baptize him. As such, he is a member in good standing who can participate in the church, even though initially he may still struggle with gender dysphoria. God is working in him, just like He is still working in all of us, "being confident of this very thing, that He who has begun a good work in you will complete it until the day of Jesus Christ" (Philippians 1:6).

Cities of Refuge

It has been said that the church is a hospital for sinners. We all have the "sin disease." As such, the church should be the safest place

---

[31] George R. Knight, *Exploring Galatians and Ephesians: A Devotional Commentary*, (Nampa; ID: Pacific Press Publishing Association, 2005), 256.

one can go to seek healing. Therefore, the church should be a city of refuge.

> In the early history of the world, provision was made for the punishment of the murderer. "Whoso sheddeth man's blood, by man shall his blood be shed," was the decree of Jehovah. The one nearest of kin to the murdered man, usually executed the murderer; but lest in the excitement of the occasion undue haste should be exercised and individuals be slain who did not deserve death, God made provision that the murderer might flee and lay hold upon his altar. None could be taken from the altar without an examination, and if it was found that the murderer had presumptuously planned to kill the man, then he was taken from the altar and slain; otherwise, his life was spared. After the children of Israel entered the promised land, six cities were set apart as cities of refuge. These were conveniently located three on each side of the river Jordan. The roads leading to these cities were always to be kept in good repair, so that the one fleeing before the avenger of blood might not be hindered in his flight. The cities were on elevated ground and could be seen at a distance.[32]

As you read the above quote, you may be thinking that the context for the cities of refuge is a bit different from equating the church

---

[32] Stephen Haskell, *The Cross and Its Shadow* (Jasper, OR: Adventist Pioneer Library, 2017), 235.

with the cities of refuge, and you would be correct. However, notice what else Haskell says:

> Every time an Israelite looked upon one of the cities of refuge, God designed he should be reminded of Christ, the "tower of the flock, the stronghold of the daughter of Zion," to whom every sin-burdened soul could flee for shelter. Satan, the accuser, is upon the track of everyone; he as "a roaring lion, walketh about, seeking whom he may devour." But the person who forsakes sin and seeks righteousness stands securely sheltered by the atoning blood of Christ.[33]

I am reminded of the time I was confronted with the sin of my addiction to pornography and how it had hurt my wife. I felt lost and hopeless, on the verge of losing everything and everyone I valued. Yet God spoke to me at church on Sabbath morning through the words of the pastor speaking that day. His words assured me I was forgiven and accepted. I found hope and refuge at church. This should be true for everyone and in every case, no matter what sin.

I believe this is true in most churches, but as I have already alluded to, some of the saints are especially hard on the LGBTQ+ community because they see it as *the* sin, and not *a* sin. It is clear that some of those who struggle with gender dysphoria and/or are part of the LGBTQ+ movement do not feel welcomed in some of our churches. Part of this has to do with the fact that as a church we will not compromise with sin. Being this the case, if the church does not affirm the LGBTQ+ ideology, then its members will not feel welcomed and accepted no matter what we do. However, the church needs to be the place where a person struggling with sin can be honest and find help in order to gain victory over their sin. Thus, the concept of the cities of refuge has implications for the church today.

---

[33] Ibid., 236.

Since Jesus is our refuge and since we as the church are supposed to be the body of Christ, it only follows that the church should be a place of refuge. Jesus welcomed all kinds of people. Many of these people put their trust in Christ even though the world had cast them aside. The demon possessed, the physically disfigured, tax-collectors, lepers, prostitutes, children, even religious hypocrites. *Jesus never condoned the sinful behaviors of these people, but He still reached out to them in love.* I believe this is what Jesus wants the church to do as well. He told us to love one another as He has loved us. The church should be a place where class distinctions are gone. It should be a place where people can find grace no matter what lurked in their past.[34] (emphasis supplied)

What Do We Tell Our Children?

As I mentioned in the introduction, the idea for this book came about after a conversation with a church member during the 2023 KYTN Camp meeting. "What do I tell my children when they come home asking questions about sexual/gender identity?" This is a good and relevant question because it is what many parents are facing these days, especially those who have their kids in public schools. There are various opinions about this, but a good source is *Focus on the Family*. Below are some insights from one of their publications.

---

[34] Alan Hamilton-Messer, "The Church: Place of Refuge or Judgement," accessed November 9, 2023, https://www.academia.edu/7165359/The_Church_Place_of_Refuge_or_Judgement.

When Transgender Issues Enter Your Child's School[35]

Scenario: Your eight-year-old child comes home and says, "Did you know there aren't just men and women? We learned today that there are lots of genders—and people can change genders. Our teacher read us a book about a boy who changes into a girl."

Responding to your child

Ask questions: "What did you think about that lesson?" "How do you feel about the lesson?" (Boys may have a harder time with "feeling" questions.) "How did the other children in your class respond?" "Did you and your friends talk about this afterward?" This isn't an inquisition, but it is an opportunity to find out what happened in the classroom and how it affected your child. Keep your tone conversational and friendly. If you are angry and upset, assure your child that you're not upset with them. Explain that you're unhappy with the school giving these kinds of lessons. Your child may sense your feelings anyway, so it's better to be honest and upfront about it.

Affirm your child: Thank your child for coming and talking to you: "I'm so glad you came and told me what happened in class today. I'm proud of you, and I always want you to be able to talk with me when you're upset or concerned about something."

Teach the truth: "Yes, some people do feel confused about being a boy or a girl. We know that in the beginning, God made a man and a woman, Adam and Eve. He made humans male and female—and both are good. When Adam and Eve sinned, all kinds of confusion and pain entered the world. But this doesn't change God's design, and He wants us to live in the truth of how He created us." You don't have to explain everything at once, but keep this an ongoing conversation, a dialogue with your son or daughter. Affirm and bless your child as a boy or girl—made in God's image. Teach children that

---

[35] Jeff Johnston, "When Transgender Issues Enter Your World: How Christians Can Respond with Compassion, Courage and Truth," *Focus on the Family*, accessed November 9, 2023, https://www.focusonthefamily.com/get-help/when-gender-issues-enter-your-world.

biology and social research confirm what Scripture says—women and men really are different.

Practical Issues

So far, we have addressed how to handle this difficult issue at the church level and how to respond to our children when they have questions prompted by what they may hear in school or other avenues. It is easy to provide counsel as to what others should do when confronted with LGBTQ+ ideology. I would imagine it is totally different when one must handle this directly because it takes place in our own families. So what do you do when your son tells you he feels he was born with the wrong body and insists you now call him by a female name? How should we react when this is our spouse, brother, daughter, especially in a culture that says, "If you disagree with me, you hate me"? Dr. Linda A. Seiler explains,

> Nothing could be further from the truth. Loving someone doesn't mean you agree with everything they think, say, and do. Imagine if we applied that standard to God. It would be impossible for Him to love us because many things we think, say, and do are far from agreement with His standards. To love someone means to value them as a person, whether we agree with them on everything or not.[36]

---

[36] Seiler, 237.

She then shares six tips to engage with LGBTQ+ identified friends and loved ones.

1. *Focus on connecting them to Christ, not on changing their views about sexuality.*[37]

   If you persuade them to adopt a biblical position on sexuality, but they never come to know Jesus, it profits nothing. When they come to know Jesus, the Holy Spirit will begin to deal with their beliefs.

2. *Build relationships and ask lots of questions.*[38]

   Invest in LGBTQ+ identified friends and loved ones just as you would anyone else who doesn't know Jesus. Ask them questions about their life to get to know them better. For example, "Tell me your story." Take a genuine interest in hearing how they arrived at embracing an LGBTQ+ identity... Listen to their heart, empathize with their struggles, and love them the same way Jesus has loved you and me in our brokenness.

3. *Avoid gay-bashing jokes and trite phrases.*[39]

   There's no context where gay/trans-bashing jokes are ever appropriate.

4. *When appropriate, apologize for the way Jesus has been misrepresented.*[40]

   There are Christians out there who respond with compassion and represent Jesus well. But some Christians have failed

---

[37] Ibid., 239.
[38] Ibid., 242.
[39] Ibid., 243.
[40] Ibid., 244–245

in that regard, and we need to recognize the hurt they have caused. If, in the course of conversation, we discover that our friend or loved one has been hurt by those who misrepresented Jesus, we should listen intently and empathize with them as they express the pain they have experienced. We should apologize for how Jesus has been grossly misrepresented to them, and let them know we are not coming in that spirit... At the same time, we should not apologize for the gospel or for God's design for sexuality. We can't apologize for the truth—only for the way my friend or loved one may have been treated in a hurtful manner by those who misrepresented the heart of Christ.

5. *When disagreement arises, talk about ideas, and avoid personal attacks.*[41]

If you sense the tension rising one option to avoid personal attacks is to move the conversation away from the heated topic of LGBTQ+ and use a less-triggering comparison. For example, Seiler says, "I was once asked to speak in an auditorium full of people who were likely to oppose my perspective, so I asked the Holy Spirit what I should do first to disarm the opposition in the room and gain a hearing. I sensed the Lord directed me to start with cupcakes. To ease the tension, I introduced myself as a lover of chocolate and asked if there were any fellow chocolate lovers present. Then I asked, if we were to have chocolate or vanilla cupcakes

---

[41] Ibid., 245–246.

for lunch, who would choose vanilla over chocolate every time. Several hands went up, but not as many as for chocolate. I then asked one of the vanilla lovers whether we could be friends, even though they always choose vanilla, and I always choose chocolate. Is it possible to agree to disagree agreeably about our flavor choices? Of course, it is." If you keep the conversation grounded in the realm of ideas, while still affirming your love for the person, it diminishes the potential to interpret your disagreement as a personal attack.

6. *Don't force change on those who don't want it.*[42]
There will always be people who choose to embrace an LGBTQ+ identity and don't want to hear the message of transformation. Pray for them asking the Holy Spirit to open their eyes to God's truth and bring healing to their wounded hearts. Ask the Lord to grant you His compassion to see them through His eyes so they know you love them for who they are, whether or not they ever change.

What about Pronouns?

As I write this chapter, "at least nine states this year have passed laws regarding how pronouns are handled in school. Florida's law explicitly prohibits teachers and students from discussing their preferred pronouns. Kentucky has a law saying teachers can't be required

---

[42] Ibid., 247–248.

to use pronouns for students that differ from their sex."[43] Yet many employers insist that their employees use gender-neutral pronouns. The list of these gender-neutral pronouns is long and confusing, but if the powers that be get their way, it may become the law of the land that these be used.

> Some think that as a personal courtesy, you should refer to a transgender person by their preferred pronoun as a way to extend courtesy in hopes of developing a relationship in which biblical truth can eventually be shared. Others think that it is wrong to inject further confusion into a person's situation by referring to them with a pronoun that is not aligned with their biological sex. Some Christians argue that referring to a person by their preferred pronoun furthers the deception and delusion within a person's mind.[44]

Clearly, there are disagreements about this, and I am not sure if this would be considered making a mountain out of a molehill. However, if you struggle with this, a solution would be to try to avoid pronouns altogether. This would take some getting used to, and you may need to train yourself, but it is an approach many are taking, as I have found out by talking to some of my church members who have been mandated by their employers to use gender-neutral pronouns. So how does this work? Here is an example: instead of having to refer to a biological man as a she or her, use their name, even if that name does not match their gender. "Calling a person by their legal name or preferred name is more acceptable because names are not objectively

---

[43] Adeel Hassan, "States Passed a Record Number of Transgender Laws. Here's What They Say," *The New York Times* (June 2023), accessed November 9, 2023, https://www.nytimes.com/2023/06/27/us/transgender-laws-states.html#:~:text=At%20least%20nine%20states%20this,that%20differ%20from%20their%20sex.

[44] Walker, 164.

gendered but change from culture to culture."[45] This is the avenue I took with Kathy, whom I referred to earlier.

However, this can be adjusted based on the relationship you have with the transgender individual. If the person is a stranger, it would be inappropriate to be dogmatic and tell them, "Your name is not Susan. It is Stan." By doing this, you are sure to offend the individual. But what if the subject is a family member or perhaps a fellow church member? Since you have a relationship with this person, you may be in a better position to say, "I will not address you in any way contrary to God's design." The same may apply to a fellow church member if you have already developed a close relationship with them. That being said, I would not be dogmatic about this, follow your conscious.

As I end this chapter, I acknowledge that I may not have addressed everybody's concerns and that there may be disagreements on some of the things I have addressed. I suppose this is perfectly natural when addressing a subject as sensitive as this one. I hope, however, that while I have taken a firm approach against LGBTQ+ ideology for the sin that it is, at the same time I hope to have shown mercy and grace just as God has shown me mercy and grace. When it's all said and done, that is what this should be about. Jesus never compromised with sin. He was firm and bold yet merciful and gracious. It is my hope and prayer that we would reflect Him.

---

[45] Ibid., 165.

CONCLUSION

Be on Guard!

Scripture provides us with various passages that admonish us to be on guard. As part of the description of the Great Controversy, the apostle John writes, "Now salvation, and strength, and the kingdom of our God, and the power of His Christ have come, for the accuser of our brethren, who accused them before our God day and night, has been cast down" (Revelation 12:10). Peter said it this way, "Be sober, be vigilant; because your adversary the devil walks about like a roaring lion, seeking whom he may devour" (1 Peter 5:8). And Paul tells us to "put on the whole armor of God, that you may be able to stand against the wiles of the devil. For we do not wrestle against flesh and blood, but against principalities, against powers, against the rulers of the darkness of this age, against spiritual hosts of wickedness in the heavenly places" (Ephesians 6:11–12).

In many ways, Adventists are isolationists. We do not want to attend certain functions, associate with certain people, etc. We have good reasons for this. After all, we want to be the holy people God wants us to be. Because of this, we have the mistaken idea that some of the things we see in secular society will not affect the church. We hear about sinful behaviors in other churches and believe "that will never happen in the Adventist Church." Well, we are wrong. As we have seen, there are people in our churches who identify as LGBTQ+. They may have already come out, or in some cases, they may be struggling with their gender identity or sexual orientation and have not told anybody. This is our reality!

In my opinion, one way for us to be on guard is to educate ourselves on these issues. This is why I have written this book. I believe, as LGBTQ+ activists do, that we need to start a conversation. We need to be willing to listen. We need to stop being judgmental and be loving Christians. But make no mistake, we need to know what the Bible says about this issue, and we must stand our ground and be faithful to God no matter how powerful and convincing some of the arguments of LGBTQ+ activists may appear to be. I realize this is easy for me to say because, thank God, nobody in my family, to my knowledge, struggles with these issues or has identified as transgender. I know that those who are suddenly faced with this in their families may change their minds as to where they stand. As a church, however, we must never compromise with sin.

While I have covered a lot in this book, the basic premise is that by compromising on this issue, we weaken and hinder our witness and message. The Present Truth Message as proclaimed in the Three Angels' Messages of Revelation 14 is too important, for it is a message of preparation, a message that will help us be on guard against the deceptions of Satan. Make no mistake, the reason the issues surrounding the LGBTQ+ movement have become so prominent in our day is that "the devil has come down to you, having great wrath, because he knows that he has a short time" (Revelation 12:12).

In *The Present Truth and the Three Angels' Messages*, I mentioned, and I have alluded to this in an earlier chapter, the unwritten rule that "for every truth that God has, Satan has a counterfeit." For a counterfeit to work, it must be almost identical to the real thing. It is the belief of this writer that the arguments being presented by LGBTQ+ activists, especially those in the Adventist Church, are Satan's counterfeit. LGBTQ+ ideology—in the context of how it is being presented by some Christians in an effort to convince the church to affirm their behavior—is a counterfeit of creation, for it adds to the creation story some "maybes" that totally change the intention of the writer of Genesis and the clarity of the creation account. Since this ideology counterfeits creation, it also has an impact on the Sabbath and sets the stage to justify the Sabbath away.

LGBTQ+ ideology also counterfeits love as presented in scripture, for it teaches that unless one agrees with them and affirms them, then love is not authentic. However, as we have seen, true love does not brush sin under the carpet. LGBTQ+ ideology also counterfeits the concept of grace, for one can go around sinning (by engaging in the LGBTQ+ lifestyle) and believe that God accepts this because He is gracious. Ultimately, this ideology impacts our trust in the Word of God because it seeks to explain things according to science and so-called medical evidence. However, as we have seen in the last few years, science is untrustworthy because it changes constantly. In fact, that is one of its foundations, for "the body of scientific knowledge is continually evolving."[1] However, "the grass withers, the flower fades, But the word of our God stands forever" (Isaiah 40:8). The Bible does not need to be adjusted to match the changes in society and its values. It is society that must adjust to a "Thus saith the Lord" even when this goes against our grain because we recognize that God knows better than us.

It is my hope that reading this book may provide you with tools and ideas as to how to handle the issue of LGBTQ+ ideology in our families and in our churches. It is also my hope that it would encourage you to build relationships and have nonjudgmental conversations with people who identify as LGBTQ+, some of whom are already visiting our churches and, in some cases, may even be members. More importantly, that it has also convinced you, if you had not yet been convinced, that the church must *never affirm this ideology*. To do this would be to compromise with Satan and to accept his counterfeit. Be on guard—the time is short: "And do this, knowing the time, that now it is high time to awake out of sleep; for now our salvation is nearer than when we first believed" (Romans 13:11).

---

[1] Tania Lombrozo, "What Makes Science Science?" *NPR* (January 2017), accessed November 9, 2023, https://www.npr.org/sections/13.7/2017/01/30/512402110/what-makes-science-science#:~:text=First%2C%20the%20body%20of%20scientific,just%20growing%2C%20it's%20also%20changing.

ABOUT THE AUTHOR

Nelson Mercado has been a student of Bible Prophecy for over thirty years. He is passionate about evangelism and the proclamation of the gospel and has conducted evangelistic meetings in Nashville (Tennessee), Chattanooga (Tennessee), Louisville (Kentucky), Moldova, Guatemala, Cuba, Colombia, and Peru. He has also served as a mentor for evangelistic preachers in the Dominican Republic.

He has a bachelor's degree in theology and a master's in evangelism and missions, both from Southern Adventist University. He is the pastor of the Nashville First SDA Church and lives in LaVergne, Tennessee, with his wife, Lucy, and children Jean-Luc and Ariana.

Printed in the USA
CPSIA information can be obtained
at www.ICGtesting.com
CBHW031918221024
16238CB00011B/128